BIG DADDY

The publisher gratefully acknowledges the generous contribution to this book provided by the Humanities Endowment Fund of the University of California Press Foundation.

BIG DADDY
JESSE UNRUH
AND THE ART OF POWER POLITICS

BILL BOYARSKY

UNIVERSITY OF CALIFORNIA PRESS   BERKELEY   LOS ANGELES   LONDON

University of California Press, one of the most distinguished university presses in the United States, enriches
lives around the world by advancing scholarship in the humanities, social sciences, and natural sciences. Its activities
are supported by the UC Press Foundation and by philan-
thropic contributions from individuals and institutions.
For more information, visit www.ucpress.edu.

University of California Press
Berkeley and Los Angeles, California

University of California Press, Ltd.
London, England

Library of Congress Cataloging-in-Publication Data

Boyarsky, Bill.
    Big Daddy : Jesse Unruh and the art of power politics /
Bill Boyarsky.
        p.   cm.
    Includes bibliographical references and index.
    ISBN: 978-0-520-21967-0 (cloth : alk. paper)
    1. Unruh, Jesse, 1922–1987.   2. Politicians—Califor-
nia—Biography.   3. Legislators—California—Biography.
4. California. Legislature. Assembly—Speakers—Biography.   5. California—Politics and government—1945–.
6. California—Social conditions—20th century.   7.
Unruh, Jesse, 1922–1987—Influence.   8. United States—
Politics and government—1945–1989.   9. Center parties—United States—Case studies.   10. United States—
Social conditions—1945–.   I. Title.
F866.4.U57B695   2008
328.794092—dc22   2007012133

Manufactured in the United States of America
15   14   13   12   11   10   09   08
10   9   8   7   6   5   4   3   2   1

This book is printed on New Leaf EcoBook 50, a 100% re-
cycled fiber of which 50% is de-inked postconsumer
waste, processed chlorine-free. EcoBook 50 is acid free and
meets the minimum requirements of ANSI/ASTM D5634–01
(Permanence of Paper). ∞

This book is dedicated to the women in my life:
Nancy, Robin, Jennifer, Anabelle, and Lila

CONTENTS

ACKNOWLEDGMENTS

One night my wife, Nancy, and I were out with our friends Douglas Jeffe and his spouse, Sherry Bebitch Jeffe. They told us of the intricate and dramatic battle being waged over the estate of the late Jesse M. Unruh, for whom they had both worked, and whose career I had covered. Unruh had died in 1987, but the fight continued for years. When we got home, Nancy told me that I had to write the story for my newspaper, the *Los Angeles Times.* Later, she insisted his life would make a compelling book.

I said Unruh was too regional, had been dead for years, and that few people remembered him anymore. But then I read John Jacobs's magnificent biography of the late congressman Phillip Burton, *A Rage for Justice,* published by the University of California Press (1995). Burton was another once-famous California politician memory of whom was fading away into oblivion. I called John and asked him if he thought the University of California Press would be interested in a book on Unruh. Yes, he said with enthusiasm, and he steered me to his editor, Naomi Schneider, the press's executive editor. She was enthusiastic too, and she became my editor.

By then I had moved from covering state political news for the *Los Angeles Times* to directing local government and political coverage. But my editor, Bill Rood, was willing to let me work on the Unruh story full-time. Eventually, with the great help of Unruh's daughter Linda, I untangled the mess and wrote the story for the *Times,* which grew into this book.

Sitting down to acknowledge those who had helped me, my thoughts turned especially to Nancy, who is an extremely talented editor, writer, and communications expert, as she demonstrated in her eighteen years as a communications director for Arco. She was my line editor for this book, which means what it says, going over every damn line, word by word, and reorganizing when my narrative was confusing. We were in Sacramento during the Unruh years, and she knew him and had sharp insights into his character.

Doug and Sherry Jeffe, who were close to Unruh, shared their memories, and Sherry, a senior scholar at the University of Southern California's School of Policy, Planning and Development, also read the manuscript and made excellent suggestions.

John Jacobs died in 2000. A year later, after I retired from the *Times,* I was honored to be named the first John Jacobs Fellow at the Institute of Governmental Studies at the University of California at Berkeley. I taught a course in urban column writing at the Graduate School of Journalism, researched this book, and hung out at IGS, using the library and observing a scholarly way of life that was much different from working on the newspaper. My only regret was that my parents, both Berkeley grads, weren't alive to see me teach there.

I was helped by conversations both with Bruce Cain, the director of IGS and a scholar of California politics and the legislature, and with the late Nelson Polsby, Heller Professor of Political Science at the University of California, Berkeley, and a notable raconteur and wit, who was director of IGS from 1988 to 1999. They had a view of politics and the legislative process that got me thinking in new ways and made this a better book than it would have been without their help. I'll always remember Nelson's kindness in inviting me to tea with his graduate students, unfailingly a stimulating event. Orville Schell, the dean of the Graduate School of Journalism, was supportive of me and my class, as was Susan Rasky, an expert teacher of political journalism and sophisticated observer of Sacramento and electoral politics, who offered good ideas based on her extensive experience. Other faculty members helped me with my class and my thinking and made me feel part of a community.

Thanks also to Professor Ann Crigler, chair of the University of Southern California's political science department and former director of USC's Jesse M. Unruh Institute of Politics. She read the manuscript and made the important suggestion that I broaden my examination of womanizing by Sacramento politicians by framing it in the context of how women in politics, and life, were treated in those days.

Linda Unruh provided me with insights, information, and photographs, and her mother, Virginia, shared memories of Unruh family life. Paul Unruh, Jesse's cousin, grew up with Unruh on the farm the family sharecropped in Texas and has amazingly detailed memories of those difficult days. Unruh's widow, Chris Unruh, shared the story of their life together.

I spent many hours with Unruh's friends and associates. Sometimes reliving those days was painful for them, but mostly they enjoyed it. They gave me a lot of information—much more, in some cases, than they had when I was a reporter. Among them were Frank Burns, Carmen Warschaw, Bob Wells, Grover McKean, Marvin Holen, Bee Lavery, Jaci DeFord, Joe Cerrell, Jerry Waldie, Phil Schott, Art Bolton, and Larry Fisher. Thanks, too, to Harry Farrell, Los Angeles County supervisor Yvonne Burke, Robert Hertzberg, the late Manning Post, Robert T. Monagan, Judge Richard Mosk, Tom McDonald, John Quimby, and Hank Lacayo.

And thanks to the librarians at the UCLA Special Collections Library, the State Archives in Sacramento, the Bancroft Library and the Institute of Governmental Relations Library at the University of California, Berkeley, and the Southern California Library for Social Studies and Research in Los Angeles. Thanks also to the staff of the Los Angeles County Human Relations Commission who led me to files in a back room that told much of the story of the civil rights movement in the segregated Los Angeles of the 1940s, 1950s, and early 1960s.

Thanks, too, for advice and recollections from my friend George Skelton of the *Los Angeles Times,* who was a fierce competitor when we covered Jesse Unruh years ago—I for the Associated Press, he for UPI.

Prologue

IN A TIME WHEN Americans are being pummeled by ideologues of the Left and Right, much can be learned from the life of Jesse Marvin Unruh, a politician who believed that, as Bismarck said, politics is the art of the possible. As speaker of the California State Assembly and later state treasurer, Unruh was one of the most influential of the centrist pragmatists who dominated American politics in the post–World War II era, exemplified also by Harry S. Truman, Dwight D. Eisenhower, and John F. Kennedy. Such political leaders set the national tone through the transition to a peacetime economy, the Cold War, the civil rights movement, and the other momentous developments of the mid to late twentieth century. Their practical philosophy and accomplishments gave birth, moreover, to a later generation of pragmatists, most notably Bill Clinton.

I thought of Unruh's place in American political history as I pondered a question that had nagged at me since I began this project: Would readers care about the life story of a long-dead California politician, remembered now only by family, surviving friends, and a few dedicated admirers?

The lessons of Unruh's life and career are important—not just to Californians—because he represents an era when government worked more effectively perhaps than it does now. Along with Governors Earl Warren and Edmund G. "Pat" Brown Sr., Unruh was one of those responsible for California's remarkable period of growth after World War II. Warren and Brown built public works—schools, highways, and prisons; Unruh, however, built institutions—a professional legislature, a better system for financing schools and making them more accountable, and a shareholders' rights movement that still influences Wall Street today.

He was also a great character, a combination of intelligence, political power, idealism, wit, anger, and cynicism. His behavior encompassed woman-chasing vulgarity and charm, intellectual acuity, and drunken excess, all wrapped up in one huge package. He was the first famous person I covered as a young reporter, and I followed him off and on for years afterward, reporting on most of the events that defined his remarkable career. He had been a participant in much of the history of post–World War II America, and I had been a witness.

I met him at the beginning of 1961, when he was on the way to becoming state assembly speaker and my AP bureau chief, Morrie Landsberg, assigned me to cover it. I knew little about the workings of the California State Capitol in Sacramento and not much more about politics. I had majored in political science at Berkeley, concentrating on international relations. As a journalist, I had reported on crime and other general subjects, not politics. I took the assignment in Sacramento because my wife, Nancy, and I wanted to move away from our hometown, Oakland, and lead a life that we hoped would be more interesting and exciting. Once I began to cover the assembly, I saw that political reporting was what I wanted to do with my journalistic career.

I found my new job intimidating. The senior reporters at the Capitol, who were also the top political reporters in the state, were older, and they seemed to know more than they wrote or even talked about. They were confidants of most of the legislative leaders. They exuded gravitas, and I was awed that I, a young former crime reporter from Oakland, was covering stories with them.

But I soon realized that my inexperience and my status as the most junior member of the AP staff made no difference to Jesse Unruh. He didn't trust any reporter, young or old, and treated me no better and no worse than he did the veterans. To him, all reporters were worthless. As a result, I was the equal of anybody in dealing with him, the most important person on my beat. Moreover, I had a mentor. Landsberg told me to work closely with Tom Arden, the *Sacramento Bee* reporter in the assembly. One of our jobs was to sort the carbon copies of bill summaries that were given to the press when the legislation was introduced, making them available to the other reporters. During a portion of the assembly session, we stood side by side putting the summaries in the boxes assigned each news outlet. Some might have considered this drudgery. I found it higher education. As we sorted, Tom gave me the inside story of what was happening behind the scenes: the dirt, gossip, and hidden motivations that the elite reporters kept to themselves. Tom knew more than they did. That's how I learned about the assembly.

The work was intensely fast-paced and demanding. When there was big news, I ran from the assembly chamber to the AP office across the hall, wrote the story on a typewriter, and gave it to an editor, who would then hand it to a teletype operator, who punched it into a teletype machine and sent it on a wire to newspapers and broadcast stations. When I was slow, there was hell to pay. "Take a ten [a break] Roger, we'll send it out by carrier pigeon," Landsberg once yelled to the teletype operator. Such journalism didn't allow much room for complexity or subtlety. Yet our small bureau dealt with complexity better than most of the other news outlets, even those whose reporters had more time to write their stories. Our boss had a vision of a better journalism that put him ahead of his time. But even we—young, educated, motivated journalists—could not capture the full picture, with its many shadings.

Unruh benefited from this kind of journalism, as did many other skirt-chasing politicians, most famously JFK. Unruh and his crew raced through bars and bedrooms unconcerned that their activities would ever be revealed, except perhaps as the subject of insider gossip. What happened in Sacramento stayed in Sacramento. Unruh would have been destroyed in the twenty-first-century world of mass communications, with its 24-hour news channels, instant Internet communications, obsession with celebrity, and contempt for privacy. In his day, Unruh was a celebrity, a big man in media-hot Los Angeles. His private life would have been rich fare for the scandal-hungry media machine.

But the simpler nature of news coverage then and the demands of daily journalism prevented most of us from capturing the intricacies of Unruh's personality and political philosophy. In a way, this hurt him, because neither his talent for behind-the-scenes maneuvers nor the deals he struck for the benefit of the less fortunate were ever spelled out to the public. He felt that reporters were too superficial or stupid to understand what he was doing, and so he never bothered to explain. And if he had, would we have had the time or patience to listen?

Take his drive for power and domination, reflected in the name "Big Daddy." We journalists believed a story that went back to the early twentieth century and Governor Hiram Johnson, the Progressive who chased the Southern Pacific Railroad out of power in state politics and initiated decades of nonpartisan "good government." The myth of nonpartisan good government was as deeply ingrained in the California political psyche as any story from the Bible. No matter that Johnson had been an ill-tempered, small-minded racist whose reforms had the unintended result of creating a Capitol dominated by secretive corporate lobbyists. Unruh, brazenly gathering power in his own hands, offered another, more complex narrative, unfamiliar to us, but understood by the late Texas columnist Molly Ivins. Writing about a man who was much like Unruh, President Lyndon B. Johnson, she observed: "In order to get anything done, first you have to get the power; if you don't get the power, you can't help people. But getting power is usually ugly. The way one judges politicians, in my opinion, is by what they do when they have power: help people or screw people."[1]

Unruh accumulated power to help people. He flourished at a time when most people believed in government. Political leaders compromised and made deals as they steered a course between extremes. Unruh did this in a state that, then as now, mirrored the complex political, demographic, economic, and cultural currents that ran through the United States.

Media analysts, political consultants, and academics like to divide the nation into red for conservative Republican and blue for liberal Democratic, following the pattern of television election-night charts. The red-blue division is overly simplistic. Better than most, Unruh understood that the electorate could not be easily divided into clear-cut patterns. He knew that the majority of Californians preferred the broad road between the extremes. That remains true today. There is a red California flourishing in the interior, reaching from the agricultural Imperial Valley, through the farms and residential subdivisions of the Central Valley, to the mountains and forests at the Oregon border. It tends to vote Republican. There is a more populous blue California occupying the coast. But not all these coast-dwelling Californians are liberals, and neither is the state, despite its reputation as the "Left Coast." Nor are those in the center of California all conservatives.

Voter registration figures tell the story. In 1994, just 10.4 percent of voters registered as independents or "declined to state." The number has increased in every state election, reaching 18.5 percent in 2006. In the same period, the number of registered Democrats and Republicans declined.[2] Given the strong probability that the majority of Republicans and Democrats are not extreme left-wingers or right-wingers, California remains as centrist as it was in Unruh's day, as does the nation as a whole.

Throughout the postwar years, Unruh sought to follow a moderate road. He navigated it through conflict over issues that remain central to the nation, such as war, race, public school education, economic disparity, and care for the mentally ill. He understood that World War II and the postwar period had produced a growing middle class that viewed life and politics differently from the way the stricken victims of the Great Depression had. As David M. Kennedy notes in his history of America in the Depression and World War II, *Freedom from Fear,* the middle class more than doubled in the quarter of a century after the war. Postwar America was fueled by consumer hunger and the need for the long-delayed building of schools, housing, highways, civilian aircraft, sewers, and everything else that had been left undone during the Depression and the war.[3] These Americans, Unruh knew, were neither left- nor right-wing radicals. He understood them because he was one of them.

During the Cold War, he shared their opposition to Communism, both at home and abroad, a stand that alienated him from the party's left wing. As the civil rights movement took hold in America, he was the author of a strong law against discrimination. But, aware of the potential for a backlash among the white middle class, he hesitated to go further. He supported the Vietnam War at first but began to have doubts about it when he witnessed thousands of middle-class Los Angeles residents join in a protest against President Johnson. His journey from support to skepticism to opposition paralleled the thinking of many Americans.

Yet protest against the government was foreign to Unruh, whose life had been changed for the better by public schools and the GI Bill. As a result, he dedicated himself to strengthening old institutions and building new ones, all with the goal of giving people the tools with which to improve their lives and their government.

The idea seems quaint in today's polarized society. Each day, I follow the political blogs of the Left and Right. It is a depressing but enlightening exercise. They remind me of my youth when I covered the meetings of strongly ideological political groups such as the liberal California Democratic Council and the right-wing United Republicans of California. They've got the same sort of self-righteousness and uncompromising ferocity toward those who disagree.

Unruh had a much clearer understanding of how to bring about change. By studying his life and the story of the institutions he built, we can learn something about why government worked so well in his era, when it served both the poor and the middle class through institutions carefully built by a California government that confronted issues remarkably similar to those Americans face today.

ONE

The Death of a Boss

THE LAST DAYS OF Jesse Marvin Unruh were a fitting end to the life of a great American political boss: drinks, stories, and friends and family mourning, not only for the boss but for themselves. He was dying of prostate cancer, having refused to permit his prostate to be surgically removed. Unruh spoke to several people about this decision, including family and friends.[1]

A radical prostatectomy might have saved him but he dreaded that it would leave him impotent, taking him out of a game that was very important to him, the game of sex, played over and over again, with many, many women. Impotence in sex, politics, or anything else was unacceptable to this domineering man, who had raised himself from Texas sharecropper poverty to becoming, at the height of his power, the single most influential politician in California, first as an assemblyman, then as state assembly speaker, and finally as state treasurer. Unruh was one of those rare elected officials whose power reached far beyond the offices he held. Other state assemblymen, assembly speakers, and state treasurers have served and been quickly forgotten. Unruh took these jobs in new directions, and during his lifetime and long afterward, he exemplified the word *politician* in its finest sense.

Unruh was much more than a California politician. He was part of a line of postwar Democratic political leaders, beginning with Harry Truman, who espoused the center of American liberalism. It was a position that would be made untenable in the 1960s by conflict over race and the Vietnam War. Unruh's effort to keep California Democrats on this centrist path anticipated and encapsulated the struggles that were to tear the Democratic Party apart.

Unruh embodied much of what was accomplished in postwar California. In his prime, California was already the most important state in the union, exceeding the wealth and influence of most nations. Its impact on national policy and politics was huge, and Jesse Unruh was part of it every step of the way as a lawmaker, policy maker, and political prophet. Unruh foresaw the challenges and problems of the postwar era, and proposed and enacted solutions that were accepted both in his own state and in the other places where he had influence, on Wall Street and in Washington, D.C. In doing so, he made his way between the extremes of a volatile California. If his path had been followed by his party in later years, it might have saved the Democrats from their estrangement from working-class America.

In his years in power, from the late 1950s to his death in 1987, Unruh was a pragmatic visionary, focused on individuals like himself, who had struggled from poverty to the middle class. He retained a sense of what he had in common with middle-class and working-class Americans. He looked at such people weathering economic, social, and cultural hardships and wondered what government could do to protect their financial and civil rights. He also worried about their right to a decent education that would help propel them upward, just as his own path up had been cleared by public schools and the GI Bill.

He did this in an era of California's great projects, while the state was busy constructing a system to deliver water from the wet north to the semi-arid south, building university campuses and freeways, replacing wartime portable classrooms in the public schools with well-designed buildings on large campuses. Unruh supported them all. But, having been raised in extreme poverty, his vision was focused more on the human condition than on concrete and bricks. Let others preside at groundbreakings and dedications. He cared most about what went on inside the classroom.

Concern for the little guy—and his own indignation over high interest on an appliance he'd purchased for his own young family—inspired him to secure passage of a state law protecting consumers who bought on the installment plan.[2] His outrage when an African American girl was denied admittance to a Los Angeles private school—along with his experiences in the Jim Crow South, the segregated Navy, and his racially troubled legislative district—impelled him to write and secure passage of a civil rights bill that, strengthened over the years, remains the state's strongest such law.[3]

Knowing that a legislature intellectually and financially subservient to lobbyists and state bureaucrats could not prescribe for the new postwar California, Unruh persuaded the voters to approve a full-time legislature with a large staff of its own experts, a pattern adopted around the nation. Eventually, it became clear the new system was flawed, although not as badly as the old one. Full-time status and higher pay did not make the lazy more productive or the greedy more honest. But in their early years, Unruh's innovations turned the assembly into a creative body that originated policies preparing California for the changes in economic and social conditions of the 1960s and 1970s.

Unruh's state assembly team of legislators and consultants initiated a vast change in the treatment of the retarded and mentally ill, improving their care, as well as giving them civil rights. The warehousing of children was ended, as was the practice of shipping the mentally ill to state hospitals after only perfunctory hearings. Sharing Unruh's belief that civil rights laws alone were not enough to overcome generations of discrimination and segregation, assembly consultants developed a policy of tutoring and aid that, if enacted, would have made college much more available for the needy of all races, accomplishing the purposes of affirmative action without falling into the bottomless pit of racial politics.

Against the opposition of school administrators and teachers, Unruh and his team pushed through testing and other accountability measures that forced the schools to prove they were doing the job required of them. Before anyone else in power saw the danger, his assembly committees warned that California's deteriorating public education system and dependence on the aerospace industry would leave the state ill-equipped to compete in the increasingly complex technological society that was then only dimly viewed by futurists. In part because of Unruh's farsightedness, these warnings were heeded, helping set the stage for developments such as the technological explosion of Silicon Valley.[4]

Unruh reached into the streets of South Central Los Angeles and, for the first time, brought substantial numbers of African Americans into power in the California legislature and Democratic Party. "Jesse genuinely believed that South Central Los Angeles ought to elect black officials," said Leon Ralph, an African American who represented one of the assembly districts Unruh created in a reapportionment that increased chances of minority representation. "He genuinely believed that and put his money and power where he spoke."[5]

But it was not all high idealism. Unruh skillfully used money to assure he would become and remain boss. Where once businesses and their lobbyists gave directly to legislative candidates, Unruh figured out a system in which the money would come to him, and he would pass it on to candidates who supported him. It was a brilliant invention, a breakthrough, and the forerunner of the corrupt or corruptible methods of campaign contributions that came to dominate politics in the following decades.

Now he was on a hospital bed on the second floor of the three-story home he and his wife Chris had built near Santa Monica Bay. They had been lovers for ten years and had recently married. She was a bright, attractive presence at social events, a former nightclub singer whose upbeat personality contrasted sharply with Unruh's dark moods and inveterate and often brutal sarcasm. "To me, Jesse Unruh was bigger than life. And I loved him with a passion," she told me. "When I met him, I thought this guy is something! He can't just belong to me, he belongs to everybody. But I thought Jesse really needed a main person in his life, and I think I was that."[6]

Chris was Unruh's second wife. Virginia Lemon, a college physical education teacher whom Unruh met while serving at a Navy base during World War II, was his first. After the war, Virginia steered him to college, helped launch his political career, and bore him five children. Their marriage began to crumble when Unruh, on his way to becoming a big shot, took up with other women in Sacramento; but it survived, painfully, for almost twenty more years.

Other women were a constant with Unruh. He was always on the prowl, and as his power grew, the chase became easy. He mixed long and short-term relationships. In the short term, his criterion was availability. "He'd fuck a filing cabinet," said one friend. "As long as it was a girl filing cabinet," another friend said.[7] But other relationships were long term and deep, and his partners in them spoke of him with admiration and affection long afterward.

From the front, Chris and Jesse Unruh's house near Santa Monica Bay resembled a stucco fortress, with small, high windows. It sat on a street with one three-story residence after another, almost as tightly packed as row houses. As with all the houses, the rear, facing the bay two blocks away, was where the designers and builders had put their best effort. It was finished in brown shingles, evoking an image of the New England shore. The second floor was the heart of the house, a place for parties, with a large living room and dining room separated by a bar. Two sliding doors opened onto a terrace, recessed into the house to give guests more space and to shield them from neighbors just a few feet away.

When he was healthy, Unruh could sit on the terrace and look down at a murky stream called the Grand Canal. The canal actually was neither grand nor a canal. Rather, it was a relic of a failed dream, part of a plan conceived by an early twentieth-century real estate promoter, Abbott Kinney, who tried to build his own Venice on the Pacific shore. Canals extended from a large plaza—his version of St. Mark's—with bungalows lining either side of them. Unfortunately, the tides of Santa Monica Bay weren't strong enough to circulate water through the canals, and they stagnated. Kinney's bungalows went unsold, and, after a few years, oil was discovered. Venice became a polluted tangle of tall oil-drilling towers in a time when oil was king in Los Angeles.[8]

But with the ocean so near, the dream would not die. After the oil was exhausted, enterprising Californians saw how to profit from the seaside desolation the Southern California way, as Kinney had hoped to, through real estate. With local government financing the work, and real estate developers profiting, construction crews dredged and dug the world's largest man-made marina. Restaurants, apartment buildings, and houses, some built by developers and others by individuals such as the Unruhs, rose over the years from the old oil fields, an evocation of the postwar California conviction that nature can always be overcome with enough government funds, private investment, creative engineering, and the drive to make a profit. It was a belief so common, so deeply ingrained, that it became the engine that drove post–World War II expansion and shaped the philosophy of Unruh and his generation of political leaders.

Unruh's bed when he lay dying was in the living room, adjacent to the bar and dining room. Friends had drinks from the bar. The large dining area and kitchen adjoining the living room left plenty of space for the continuous farewell. "We had something that must have been like an Oriental potentate dying," said a friend. "People all over the house. The death of an emperor." When the pain wasn't overwhelming, Unruh got up from bed and joined Chris and guests in the dining room. But more frequently, he lay in bed, injecting morphine with a pumping device. He had lost weight, and his face muscles had grown slack. At the foot of the bed was a television set with a VCR, and Unruh watched old movies. "He was in terrible shape," said his friend Frank Burns. "It got to the point where the morphine pump was going pretty constantly."[9]

Weakened, drugged, often unable to speak, Unruh still had a powerful quality that made him larger than life. Even dying, he retained the ability to dominate the lives of those around him. His sharp eyes had once seemed capable of boring into a person's inner depths, finding the most carefully concealed weaknesses. His voice was deep, with a hint of impoverished rural Texas, often warm and friendly, just as often fierce. Even though he had set one follower against another, they all loved him. He could make you feel like his closest friend, his most trusted adviser—or the dumbest person in the world. He had huge strengths, which propelled him to power, and huge weaknesses, which prevented him from making it to the top. Our political figures are now plastic, fashioned for television. The life we see in public may have little relationship to what happens in private. But Unruh was not a hypocrite. He lived his life fully, without apologies. His story is more like a novel than a humdrum political biography.

In the last years before his death, Unruh often reflected on his life. He had learned he had prostate cancer in 1984. His friend Larry Margolis was present when Unruh received the diagnosis. Unruh was state treasurer and Margolis was one of his top assistants, and they were in Manhattan at the Fraunces Tavern Restaurant awaiting the arrival of their luncheon companion. "Unruh called back [to California] to get the results of the prostate test he had had a couple of weeks before and learned that it was malignant. He got the news while we were standing there waiting for our guests to arrive for lunch. It was pretty much a downhill spin from that point on. At that point he was told it was a very slow growing malignancy and the most responsive to treatment. But it wasn't."[10]

"We all knew, those of us who were real close to him, that the only decision you had to make in those days . . . was you either had an operation or you didn't," said his friend Carmen Warschaw, who, with her husband, Lou, had been with him from the beginning of his political career. "Of course, the main thing was that supposedly you could never have an erection again." Unruh chose X-ray treatment. "To him, sex was his ultimate goal, because he was not attractive physically," she said. "And although he had power in the legislature, I think he felt this was his big attraction. And because he was raised in . . . poverty, [he felt] that you never really achieved anything unless you had sexual prowess. That's part of my interpretation of the way he lived, and that was part of the reason I think he had those women, because he did not feel he was accomplishing this at home . . . and this was to show his power."

Later in 1984, after his decision was made, the Warschaws invited the Unruhs for a cruise through the Greek islands and up the Italian coast. Their yacht was named *The Dragon Lady*, the nickname given Carmen by her opponents in the many Democratic Party fights she waged as an Unruh ally—against the party's liberal wing, against the Democratic governor, Edmund G. "Pat" Brown Sr., as well as against foes by then gone from the memories of all but a few like Carmen and Unruh, neither of whom ever forgot or forgave a double cross. She wore the name "Dragon Lady" with such pride that she affixed it to the family yacht.

Although his death was more than two years away, Unruh knew he had made a fatal decision. He played cards, ate the meals prepared by the Warschaws' excellent chef, read, and spent much of his time on deck in a swimsuit watching the scenery. They all went ashore to visit Delphi. Unruh, then state treasurer, amused himself and the others by posing in front of the ruins of the Athenian Treasury, orating while his picture was taken. Mostly, "he was very quiet during the trip, and he would cry at intervals, he even would cry when Chris was around," Carmen said. "He would sit there and there were just tears. And you'd say, 'What's the matter, Jess?' and he'd say, 'I'm just thinking about, I don't have long to live, have I been able to do everything I should?' . . . He would start to think about his future and he just felt there was none," she said. At times, he "was so melancholy. I remember we would sit up with him, especially Lou. They would sit on the back deck and talk about it. And he would cry very easily, really weep that he made that choice. [But] he still felt it was the right one to make." Chris "was so sweet to him and kind to him and would ask him if there was anything she could do for him. She would kiss him. She would sit on his lap. She would tell him how much she loved him. She'd tell him how wonderful he was."[11]

In 1986, Unruh was elected to a fourth term as state treasurer, but his illness worsened. By early 1987, he was on heavy pain medication, and soon he was bedridden. Toward the end, a hospice nurse, a specialist in ministering to the dying, was with him. She talked to him and helped him confront the final stage of his illness.

But neither she nor his friends could give him a peaceful death. The turmoil of his personal life followed him to the grave. Although Unruh had been on the public payroll for more than thirty years, he had accumulated an estate estimated at more than $1 million in property, stocks, and cash, and a separate fund containing at least $1.3 million in unused campaign contributions. In his will, he had provided for a young woman with whom he'd lived for a time in a house he owned in Sacramento. From all accounts, it was a warm relationship, not as tempestuous or unsettled as some of those in his past. A friend remembered going on picnics with her, Unruh, and her young child. "She was very nice to Jess," Burns recalled. "This was a very rough time for Jess. It was when he was coming to grips with the fact that he was going to die, that there was nothing that could be done. And he and Chris weren't getting along."[12] But as the cancer spread to his bones Unruh left Sacramento, reluctant to burden the single mother with the task of caring for a dying man. He returned to Los Angeles to marry Chris. Chris Unruh was in the will, along with the young woman in Sacramento and

Unruh's grown children: Bruce, Bradley, Randall, Robert, and Linda. He had divorced their mother, Virginia, in 1975.

As death neared, Unruh, often groggy from painkillers, tried to sort out his obligations. He changed his bequests seven times in nine days. The last and final version of the will is in a weak, barely legible handwriting. Chris's share was increased, his children's reduced. And, just before he died, the young woman was dropped from his will.[13] "I told him it was chaos," a friend said. "I told him it would result in the chaos that happened. He didn't care. He felt that who wins, wins. It was vintage Jesse Unruh."[14]

His public persona was captured by his nickname, "Big Daddy," after the domineering father in the Tennessee Williams play *Cat on a Hot Tin Roof.* It added to the widespread impression that he was a ruthless political boss. He loathed the reputation, the nickname, and being fat. Chris said: "Someone would come up and pat him and say, 'Oh, you're gaining some weight there.' That would drive him up the wall. 'I know I'm heavy [he'd say]. I don't need some asshole to come up and pat me on the belly.' And he also had a very difficult time when people called him Big Daddy. He hated that."[15]

His friend Ann Walsh recalled that, after a fund-raising dinner, she and Unruh "went into the bar and they had a band, and (I asked) 'Do you want to dance?'" He refused. A couple of years before, she recalled, "he had been photographed dancing with a woman, looking like a dancing bear, and it so hurt his pride that he never was going to allow himself to be put into that position again."[16]

People continued to call Unruh "Big Daddy" even after he lost almost 100 pounds. For the name had perfectly fitted his pre-diet five-foot-ten, 280-pound-plus body, which he draped in expensive suits tailored to disguise his huge physique. He had thick lips and a bulldog face, with jowls that hung around his shirt collar until a surgeon trimmed them.

Whatever his weight, he had an insatiable hunger for alcohol, food, and women. When drunk, he was angry and belligerent. He left one woman for another or, more typically, saw more than one at the same time. But he was honest about this and, several of them recall, treated women with consideration and affection. Ann Walsh was a political consultant and organizer in San Diego when she met Unruh. "I'm not embarrassed to say this because I'm an old broad now, but I was one of the multitude of women he slept with," she said.[17] "I was so intrigued with him because under this big hulking man was a very gentle spirit. He talked about his parents. And one of the things that motivated him to push legislation . . . that would help elderly people was the poverty Jess's parents lived in. You know there is . . . Jess who was the kingmaker, and then there was the other side of Jess who wanted to fight injustice, and that so impressed me. He was just very, very sensitive about his parents."

Jaci DeFord, Unruh's lover and friend for twenty years, said:

> There was something about him. I think it was a charisma. He had an enormous charisma, and again, I think it was this ability he had to zero in, and [it] probably happened with all of his friends. I don't think it just happened with women; this incredible ability that when he was talking to you . . . you were the most important person in his world at the moment. The saddest thing when he did run for governor was that talking to a crowd of people you never got that incredible feeling that you got when it was one on one . . . when he was talking to a crowd, it was never the same thing.[18]

He had the gift of knowing instinctively what someone wanted, or needed. When John Quimby was a beginning assemblyman, he saw this side of Unruh, who was then speaker. He was in a hotel bar with Unruh. "I was just depressed," Quimby said. "My wife and I were having a lot of money troubles. We were paid . . . $600 a month and my wife was a legal secretary making about that amount. We were strapped. We had five kids and all the expenses thereto . . . I wasn't complaining, but I was really concerned about my wife and my financial ability to continue. Jess picked up on this somehow. He just intuitively picked up on it. The guy knew things about you on a personal basis. He said to me, 'John, what's happening?' I said 'Jess, same old stuff, the wife and the kids and money.' He said, 'I want to give you some help.'"

Unruh's legislative salary was no more than Quimby's, and he also had five children. But this was an era when cash was king in politics; little was in writing, and paper bags were as common as checkbooks for delivering contributions. Unruh, by then a master collector of campaign money, pulled out fifteen one hundred dollar bills on the spot and gave them to Quimby, "Cash money," said Quimby. "I just can't tell you what that meant. He said just: 'Take this and use it for the best advantage.' Never mentioned it again. . . . I am not saying he [just] gave people money. He gave people what they needed that he could come up with even if it was a hug or a kind word or a phone call. . . . I think that was his secret."[19]

His loyal lieutenant during his years of legislative power, Larry Margolis, explained that Unruh was so close to [his fellow assembly members] and so involved on all levels. I just don't mean on legislation. I mean on their personal lives, on their districts, on their philosophies and politics and their love affairs and everything. He just knew every detail there was to know. . . . A lot of people misunderstood what he was about because they believed he must have this mysterious hold on [people] . . . to get what he wanted them to do. And that it must be nefarious because it didn't meet the eye. Yet what they were failing to understand was that he knew this fellow's problems better than this fellow knew them, and the guy trusted him because of that.[20]

These were political skills, some natural, some learned. But there was more to this gifted and complex political leader, and it was revealed in a personal history he shared with many of his fellow Californians.

Unruh was part of the huge migration from the Southwest to California in the 1930s and early 1940s, which infused the state with the same energy the immigrants had expended from dawn to dusk on their failing Texas, Oklahoma, Arkansas, and Missouri farms. Unruh was as poor as any of them while growing up on his parents' sharecropper farm 200 miles south of the Dust Bowl. And he was part of the generation of World War II veterans that emerged from wartime service with a spirit and determination that energized the state.

California after World War II was a place of frenetic motion. Magazines like *Look* sent writers there to discover the secret of its energy, to ponder what it meant for the rest of the country. Elementary and high schools were built in the new suburbs extending far outward from San Francisco and Los Angeles. Fields and redwood forests gave way to new public university campuses. Their graduates provided the intelligence and imagination that turned the wartime aircraft industry into something much bigger, aerospace, and eventually something bigger even than that arose, the computer industry. Dams created huge reservoirs, storing water to be carried to farms and cities in aqueducts defying the limits nature had placed on development on Southern California's semiarid coastal plain and in the great interior valley and desert, where agriculture had once been either limited or impossible. Distant rural areas were linked with cities by new freeways, which often destroyed old neighborhoods, encouraging sprawling growth but permitting fast transportation of crops and manufactured goods throughout the country and state, including the harbors that were the gateway to Asia.

As the vets crowded into universities and colleges, moved into mass-produced subdivisions, and went to work, they demanded more schools for their children, better highways, new dams and water aqueducts, more parks, and, with a sophistication born of education and maturity, a decent state system of care for the mentally ill and retarded. Tax collections from wartime plants and shipyards and their workers had filled a state treasury badly depleted by the Depression. California had the money to build and a population with the will to do it. Unruh took his place as a leader of the generation determined to see that government would assure an education for the young from kindergarten through college and provide security for the old.

It is striking how much of what is good about California—the parks, the universities, the highway system, much of the water importation and distribution system—dates from those days. California at the start of the twenty-first century is the California Unruh and the others of his generation had built half a century earlier. They were a generation of hope and optimism, men and women who had survived the Depression and the war and emerged into the bright dawn of seemingly endless possibilities.

In Unruh's day, the state—and national—consensus embraced common goals. It was a broad consensus, reaching across party lines and led by two postwar governors, Republican Earl Warren and Democrat Edmund G. Brown Sr., and by Unruh. Blacks and Latinos had to fight for a piece of the power, but even as they battled, there was agreement on where they were headed. When the relative unity collapsed in the political and social revolution of the mid 1960s, the broad center vanished amid attacks from the Right and the Left. The center of the Democratic Party was particularly hard hit, its heart and soul cut apart by the competing claims of different interest groups. Unruh saw the deleterious impact these attacks could have on a state and nation that had in the past basically been wedded to middle-of-the-road politics. He believed that the Democratic Party as an institution should continue along this moderate path.

There have been enormous changes since Unruh's death. Leaders without a common goal struggle to appease rival interests. For example, the new symbol of California is not a university but a prison, a monument to interest groups that have exploited the public's fear of crime. Drive through rural California, and you are likely to see one, constructed by a new generation of governors and legislators afraid their constituents will vote them out of office whenever a murder or robbery is reported on the television news. Legislators, their terms now limited by the state's constitution, merely pass through the Capitol on their way to other public offices or other careers.

How did we get from there to here? Where did California go wrong? By looking at those bright days through the life and career of Jesse M. Unruh, we can chart the peaks and valleys. The past can't be recaptured. The experiences that shaped Unruh are history. Yet the promise of California, with its natural and human resources, remains, just as it did when Unruh was beginning his career.

TWO

The Road to California

JESSE UNRUH WAS BORN IN Newton, Kansas, about twenty miles north of Wichita, on September 30, 1922, but spent the formative years of his adolescence in Texas. His climb from poverty to economic security left him with a seething populism and a resentment of the rich. These were feelings shared by other members of the impoverished generation of immigrants from the Southwest who were known as Okies no matter where they originated. The stories of Unruh and the others—their troubles and how they persevered—help explain the political and social currents that shaped California during and after World War II and shook it so thoroughly in the 1960s.

In the worst of the Depression, Unruh's family was living on a worthless Texas sharecropper cotton farm, located on sandy land on the fringe of the Dust Bowl and the once fertile Great Plains, almost 200 miles from Dallas. Dust storms, drought, mechanization, reckless land management, and bank foreclosures drove the southwesterners from the land, trapping them in a downward spiral that began years before the stock market crash of 1929. The only hope came from the reassuring voice of Franklin D. Roosevelt on the radio and from the famous highway of emigration—U.S. Route 66, the road to California.

So painful to him, so humiliating was his poverty that Unruh rarely spoke of those days in later years. Even some close friends remained ignorant of his bad times. Other politicians flaunt their early hardships for the voters. Unruh walled them off. He scorned political public relations, although he envied the politicians who were good at it. In a way, his attitude was admirable, but it was unfortunate in an era where politics was shaped by marketing techniques. If he had been able to tell his story, it would have explained much about him and might have made him a more sympathetic figure.

His first wife, Virginia, knew. "They were the lowest of the low in the community," is how she described Unruh's family.[1] His nephew, Paul Unruh, who grew up with him, remembered the poverty. Paul was raised by Unruh's parents and Jess Unruh, at 12, became Paul's big brother. The impact of those days remained with both of them: "We were talking one time about some of his frustration that people who were enormously wealthy could buy their way into something and convince people to do something that, no matter how just the cause or how much he worked on it or what effort he put into it, someone without money had no way of convincing people, had no way of proving his point. . . . I think that started when we were small. He saw the advantages that the other people around there had."[2]

With prospects so dim at home, the young Jess Unruh headed west to join a brother, a sister, and a brother-in-law who had already gone to California. That was the way it worked in the Great Depression. Relatives, sick of the farm, went west, clearing the way for the rest of the family. It was one of the great migrations of American history, particularly for the Texans, Oklahomans, Arkansans, and Missourians immortalized by John Steinbeck's novel *The Grapes of Wrath;* in the songs of Woody Guthrie; and by the photographs of Dorothea Lange. The words and the images evoke an America where poverty reached deep into the heart of the working class in a nation that had lost its bearings and hopes. There had been other depressions, or crashes, as they were sometimes called, but this was the first in the age of mass media, when newsreels, mass-circulation magazines, and movies provided graphic images more powerful than most newspaper accounts. Even those not affected personally—by a father unemployed, an aunt, uncle, and cousin moving in—were touched by the images and knew they were living in a time of national tragedy.

The southwesterners moved west on two paths. Some, seeking the familiarity of farmwork, turned north after crossing into California on U.S. Route 66 and drove to the misery of the factory farms of the San Joaquin Valley. These farmworker migrants became a symbol of the Depression, as vivid as the photographs of the men selling apples on the streets of New York. The majority, including the Unruhs, had a different vision, however. They continued west on 66 and settled in cities and suburbs mostly in and around Los Angeles. These Los Angeles–bound emigrants, who constituted the largest number of newcomers, were less well known than the San Joaquin Valley farmworkers but just as important to the future of California.

Unruh moved in with his oldest brother, Ervin, in the town of Hawthorne, where aircraft plants were rising on the flatlands southeast of Los Angeles. By the time Unruh arrived, the Depression was fading as the nation prepared for war. The nature of California was changing, too. The population centers—metropolitan Los Angeles, the San Francisco Bay Area, and San Diego—were becoming industrialized. A strong working-class, blue-collar way of life was taking hold.

Ervin was the first of the Unruhs in California. "He was a wanderer," said Paul Unruh. "In the Depression, he left home and worked in Kansas and different states, riding the rails, hitching rides on the freight trains, and eventually for some reason he ended up in California." Settled, working in an aircraft plant eight hours a day and at a bakery another four, he persuaded his sister, Mildred, and her husband, Webb Johnson, to join him. Webb Johnson, in turn, wrote to Jesse Unruh. Unruh moved in with Ervin, who had a chicken shed on his property. Unruh cleaned the shed, turned it into a bedroom, and got a job at the Douglas Aircraft plant in Santa Monica, a few miles to the north.

World War II had started, and with it gas rationing. Unruh borrowed his brother's small old Willys automobile and loaded it with fellow Douglas workers, all of whom were as big as he was. He thought he could use the money contributed by his fellow workers to fix up the car, and he had heard he could get extra ration coupons for driving people to work. But at least one of the old tires blew out every few days, partly because of the weight of the passengers. Paul recalls Ervin saying, "No wonder the goddamn tires were flat. Jess was about 200 pounds, and he had three other bruisers in the car, all of them bigger than him. With good tires it would have been quite a load."[3]

Jammed in the Willys for the 20-mile drive north to the Douglas plant, Unruh and the others were part of a growing number of workers building the planes, ships, trucks, tanks, and other military goods that flowed out of Southern California. With the arrival of this large workforce, unions grew stronger. The power of the old union-busting Los Angeles industrialists faded in the face of a national wartime manufacturing effort greater than anything the United States had experienced before. New Deal labor laws protected workers. As the unions gained in power, the long dormant Democratic Party began to revive.[4]

The southwesterners were an important part of the change. They had a common heritage, family ties, and youth. They comprised a population bulge that would influence the state for many years. Ninety-five percent of them were white. A total of 60 percent were under thirty-five. The migrants were better educated than those who stayed behind. And, contrary to the popular image of large extended families crowding into old cars or trucks, the more common immigrant family consisted of a husband, a wife, and children.

Unruh's life, and that of the other southwesterners who migrated to Southern California, was much different from that of emigrants to the San Joaquin Valley farm country. In the valley, immigrants lived in farm labor camps or subdivisions of frame houses scornfully called "Little Oklahomas" by old valley residents. Life, although still difficult, was easier in the metropolitan areas. Granted, the Dust Bowl immigrants were put off by a society where neighbors, then as now, might not know each other. The "Okie" taunt was heard as much in city schools as it was in the farm towns of the Central Valley. But they had a chance to earn good wages. The perpetual debt of the dead-end sharecropper economy was behind them.

The southwestern immigrants tended to flock together in distinct communities. Hawthorne, where the Unruhs settled, was a working-class town, named after the writer Nathaniel Hawthorne, who might not have blended in. It was built on land about fifteen miles from downtown Los Angeles that had formerly been dairy and vegetable farms.[5] Unruh's brother-in-law, Webb, worked on a dairy farm, as did Unruh's father when he came to California a few years later.

So many southwesterners settled in another southeast Los Angeles County community, Bell Gardens, that it was known as "Billy Goat Acres."[6] A real estate advertisement for houses defined the growing residential area:

> $20 DOWN AND $10 A MONTH. Good schools, churches, race restricted. Transportation. Outside city limits. Rich sandy loam soil. Deep wells; fine water at $1.25 a month. Ideal climate. Sunshine, fresh air, room for children to grow; Give their eager hands something to do and make fine citizens of them.[7]

The words of the advertisement reflect many of the values described by the historian James Gregory as "Plain Folks Americanism": a combination of rural and blue-collar southwestern and southern values, shaped by fundamentalist Protestant religion, racial segregation, populist politics, country-and-western music, and the experience of surviving difficult times in distinct communities.

Religion was a powerful bond, cementing belief and cultural values half a century before the national political emergence of the religious Right. From congregations large and small, scattered through Hawthorne, South Gate, Huntington Park, and other enclaves, the plain folks flocked to the fringe of downtown Los Angeles. It was 1949, and a young Southern Baptist evangelist, Billy Graham, was conducting a Christ for Greater Los Angeles crusade in a large tent named the Canvas Cathedral. Fundamentalism in cultural and political values had long been a powerful strain in the South and Midwest. The westward movement of the southwesterners had strengthened these potent forces in California.

Graham captured the religious yearnings of the plain folks, and he understood their tastes. There was no better place for him to begin his crusade than in postwar Los Angeles. Nowhere else in America could he find such a large potential audience amid such a collection of mass media, including two newspapers owned by William Randolph Hearst. Hearst knew his readers and he gave the crusade blanket coverage.

Graham also knew his audience. He put country music and fundamentalist religion together perfectly when he presented a popular, brawling, hard-drinking country singer, Stewart Hamblen, who announced in the Canvas Cathedral that he had accepted Jesus Christ as his savior. He gave up drinking, wrote a hit, "It Is No Secret What God Can Do," and with his wife, Suzie, hosted the *Cowboy Church of the Air* on a Los Angeles radio station.[8] Such stars, along with daily favorable newspaper stories, made the crusade a success and launched Graham's long reign as America's most famous evangelist.

The southwestern heritage wasn't all Christ and country music. As the real estate advertisement for homes in southeastern Los Angeles County makes clear, with its reference to "race restricted," racism was another value inherited from the Southwest. It was ingrained in southern and border-state populism. "If we are looking . . . for central tendencies, it would have to be said that racism remained the subculture's dominant voice," Gregory observes.[9]

When Katherine Archibald, a graduate student at Berkeley, took a job at the Moore Drydock Co. in Oakland during World War II, she found that the southwesterners ranked low in the shipyard hierarchy, and were the object of considerable scorn. These immigrants, in turn, joined in against African Americans, who were subjected to merciless prejudice and job discrimination. Archibald illustrates her point with an anecdote. In talking to a woman shipyard worker from Oklahoma who was loudly and frequently

anti-black, Archibald mentioned that blacks were also subjected to prejudice. The woman took this as an insult, burst into tears, and said, "But I'm
no nigger, I'm not black." She complained to her friends, who turned on
Archibald and scrawled "Nigger lover" on her desk.[10]

Jess Unruh didn't share such bigotry. He was of the southwesterners, but
not quite like them. His unique perspective allowed him to understand the
southwesterners and sympathize with them while being a strong and effective foe of racism.

Living in Kansas, before the family moved to Texas, Unruh had exploded
when a group of boys taunted a black friend and threw his hat into a privy.
Paul Unruh, his nephew, said, "Jess became unglued and got mad and beat
up a couple of them for it. Even in Kansas, the way people were then you
were not supposed to take the part of black people. But he did, and he was
that way about everything. If it presented a challenge, he took it. . . . In
Texas he learned to keep his mouth shut because it got him in so much
trouble. But he hated the way [black] people were treated."[11]

The Unruhs did not share the fundamental Christian beliefs of many of
their neighbors. The family, while not religious, was descended from religious dissenters who had suffered hundreds of years of persecution for their
beliefs. These forebears were Mennonites, a stubborn and rebellious people,
whose tendencies were evident in future Unruh generations. Although
Unruh's father, Isaac, broke away from the more religious side of the family, he had grown up in the church and spent much of his childhood in en-
forced listening to Mennonite preaching. He could neither read nor write,
but as an adult still remembered portions of the Bible. He knew his scrip-
tures, and he loved to argue about passages with his friends.

Even if the Unruhs had wanted to be observant, there were few Mennonites in Texas with whom to form a congregation. Their minority status
in the intolerant 1920s and 1930s was another reason—along with their extreme poverty—that the Unruhs would have been considered outsiders and
outcasts. Such was the condition of life for the Mennonites.[12]

As Mennonites, the Unruhs were descended from Dutch Anabaptists
who broke with the Roman Catholic Church during the Reformation under
the leadership of Menno Simons (1496–1561), a former Catholic priest. They
rejected the papacy and priesthood, believing that Christ, rather than any
priestly intermediary, was the head of the church. They refused military service or oaths of allegiance to a nation. They opposed infant baptism, insisting that the rite be administered only to adults who consciously accepted

Christ. Many lives were lost as believers struggled to uphold their religion against the power of the Roman Catholic Church and its royal allies, who saw their regimes threatened by such a determined minority.

Confronted with such powerful enemies of their faith, some of these believers, the Amish, who broke away from the Mennonites, but shared doctrinal beliefs, immigrated to America before the American Revolution.[13] The Unruhs and the other Mennonites left Holland and moved to a more hospitable Germany. There, under kings such as the religiously tolerant Frederick the Great,[14] the Mennonites practiced their religion and were exempted from military service. But they were taxed to support the state military academy, an obligation that was increased by Frederick William II, who also took away many of the Mennonites' freedoms. Catherine II of Russia, wanting the industrious Mennonites to help fill her vast land, invited them to settle in territory she had recently taken from Turkey, providing land, financial aid, free transportation, limited self-government, use of the royal forest, and exemption from military service. Among the earliest immigrants were the Unruhs, who settled as farmers in southern Russia, along the Dnieper River.

Catherine's promises were distant history by the early 1870s, when Czar Alexander II took away the Mennonites' privileges. Even though they were pacifists, the Mennonites did not accept their fate passively. Rather, when persecution threatened, they moved. A twelve-man Mennonite expedition immediately crossed the Atlantic to look for a new home. Among the places they chose to settle was Kansas, a choice made easier by the encouragement of railroads offering low prices for their vast holdings of government-granted fertile land. The Santa Fe Railroad sent an agent, C. B. Schmidt, to Russia with promises of reduced railroad rates, barracks to accommodate the Mennonites while they built homes, and a Red Star steamer to bring their farm implements and household goods to America.

The Mennonites made their way to seaports, often traveling at night and hiding in the woods or in brush to avoid hostile residents. Jesse Unruh's grandfather Peter Unruh, the son of a cobbler, his wife, Anna, and their son Heinrich, the first of fourteen children, boarded the SS *City of Montreal* in Liverpool. It arrived in New York on November 27, 1874. In an old family photo, Peter looks a bit like a thinner version of Jesse Unruh, unsmiling, as was the custom for photographs of that era.

The Unruhs lived in Ohio for a year and a half before joining sixty-five Mennonite families who had settled on the Kansas prairie north of the town of Newton, where the first wave of immigrants had built one-story houses,

20 by 40 feet, before the winter snow. The delay in Ohio was costly to the Unruhs. The first arrivals bought land from the railroad for between $3.50 and $5 an acre. The late-arriving Unruhs had to pay $6.45 an acre for the 40 acres they bought from the Santa Fe. Bad luck or bad choices dogged the family. Peter Unruh paid $850 for an 80-acre farm in Kansas in 1906, but it was too small, and the family remained mired in poverty.

Many other Mennonites prospered. They had brought with them a winter wheat, hard Turkey red, well suited for Kansas, and within twenty years, it had become the main wheat crop in Kansas, Oklahoma, and Nebraska. Many were well off when they arrived, and virtually all were literate. That, in itself, was an advantage in towns like Newton, filled with outlaws, cowboys, railroad construction workers, prostitutes, and gamblers.[15]

But prosperity and their invaluable contribution to Kansas agriculture weren't enough to protect the rural Mennonite communities from the intolerance and anti-German hysteria that swept through the country during World War I. The immigrants from Russia, including the Unruhs, were the largest group of Mennonites. Since they were theoretically committed to following the precepts of their religion and not being swallowed by the culture of their new country, many had retained their German language and spoke it in church and at home. So when some of these German-speaking pacifists refused to buy Liberty bonds, they were tarred and feathered by xenophobic neighbors. The *Newton Kansan-Republican* editorialized against "the viciousness that exists in the encouragement of the German language as a means of communication in America."[16] Although no Mennonites died in the violence, the historian James C. Juhnke writes, "it must be said that violent Kansans who took the law into their own hands effectively terrorized the Mennonite community into unwilling participation in the war effort."[17]

Jesse Unruh's father, Isaac Unruh, Peter's son, moved from one failure to another, finally landing in Texas in 1930, where he grew wheat but couldn't sell it. He traded the wheat farm for a cotton farm farther south in Texas and failed again, finally becoming a sharecropper.[18] As the Depression deepened, Isaac, called "Ike," was always in debt and had to work as a day laborer on neighboring farms and even, to his disgust, for the New Deal WPA, the Works Progress Administration. Paul Unruh explained:

A dollar a day, I think it was, to work on the roads. My grandfather went a couple of times, and if he went to work there, he didn't get to do anything on the farm. So his excuse was "I'm not going to take President Roosevelt's money and stand there on a shovel handle." He said "That's all they do. They get the shovel, and they lean on the handle all day long and they get a dollar."

Well, that wasn't exactly true. There are a lot of projects they built. That was my granddad's way of opting out of it because he didn't like that type of work, work for fifteen minutes. He wanted to work eight hours a day.

Jesse Unruh, his parents, and Paul lived in a two-room house—made of wood slats nailed to a frame—on a small cotton farm outside the town of Swenson. The house was on a dirt road and surrounded by a barbed-wire fence. On the front porch were an old rocker and a few straight-backed wooden chairs. Inside, there was a room for eating and cooking and another, a combination living room and bedroom for Isaac and Nettie, who shared a large double bed. Paul and Jess slept in a small bunkhouse with water-stained wallpaper a couple of hundred feet from the house.

A big rock fireplace in the bedroom heated one-half of the house, and a large wood stove in the kitchen warmed the other. An icebox kept food cool with ice bought on the Saturday trips to town. Milk was kept in the window cooler, a box with screens on the side. They grew most of their food. Flour, sugar, and other staples were bought in town on credit.

The family was so poor that Unruh wore his shoes until there wasn't much left of them. He and his brother-in-law, Webb Johnson, bought a pair of shoes and alternated wearing them. Paul Unruh said, "My granddad was reduced to farming with horses, reverted back to horses and plows, rather than tractors, because he couldn't afford to buy a tractor. The only car we had was broken down half the time. He had to use horses and a wagon to go to town to buy groceries. . . . We had no inside plumbing, no running water, no phone, no electricity. It was just a very basic miserable existence."

They were isolated intellectually, even from the news. They did not subscribe to a newspaper and for much of the time had no radio. "My grandfather had bought a radio that ran on a dry cell battery," Paul Unruh said. "When the battery died, he didn't have money to buy a new battery. So we were without a radio." News came from neighbors and visits to town. "You got word of mouth, like politics, that kind of a thing," Paul said. "It was almost like the day, I imagine, when people came west, the homesteaders, the settlers."[19]

The family were prisoners of the relentless poverty of the sharecropper system and the debts that came with it. The crops they brought to the cotton gin produced barely enough money to pay overdue bills at the grocer's and buy seed for next year's crop. Years before, a life of debt had been assured for the Unruhs with the failure of a rural bank, part of a wave of rural bank closings that presaged the Depression. This one cost Ike his meager life's savings and drove the family into destitution. The failure was crushing to Unruh's father, who had had great faith in banks, and he never completely recovered from it. "He drank quite a bit," said his grandson, Paul. "I think with all the hard knocks, he just didn't know any other way to go. So he would drink."

Isaac was short and violent. "His father was very volatile and small," said Virginia. "He would erupt and become very violent. . . . He would beat on them when they were kids. . . . He beat on [Jesse Unruh's] mother, too. He lost his temper around persons, animals, it didn't matter."[20] When Isaac's sister was beaten up by her husband, the much smaller Unruh followed him into a barn and beat him badly. Although illiterate, he could compute farm transactions in his head. He trained bird dogs. "The first thing he'd do was give them a little taste of bird shot," Paul said. "He was cruel about that, but when he got through with those dogs they were very well trained. People loved to have him train their dogs."

Jesse Unruh fought Ike over his cruelty to animals. When the father beat a colt with a chain for lying down while pulling a plow, Jesse grabbed him and threw him down on his back. "Last time I saw him, he was chasing Jess across the field, headed for the house," Paul said.

Jesse's mother, Nettie Unruh, suffered the mental and physical scars of the oppressive life of a sharecropper's wife. One of her legs was deeply scarred after it was ripped by a barbed-wire fence. With no doctor available, she packed the wound with salt and wrapped it with cloth. When the leg swelled, she poured iodine on it. She was overwhelmed by the routine of bare existence, picking cotton during the harvest, growing vegetables, and caring for pigs and cattle. She hauled water from the well, heated it on a wood stove, and laundered clothes in tubs, using a washboard. She baked bread in a steaming hot kitchen. In the morning, she made corn meal mush. For dinner, she cut it into squares and fried it, serving it with Karo corn syrup, and peas she grew in the garden. Occasionally, they had bacon or ham from the pigs they raised, pork she cured herself. But often there was no meat. She cooked huge pots of homegrown pinto beans, refrying them by the second or third day. She made and mended clothes, sewing by the dim light of a kerosene lamp. She taught her children arithmetic and reading, working with them at the kitchen table with papers and pencils and playing games with them. Like wives all through the cotton belt, she was the unsung center of the family.

Cotton, the historian Rebecca Sharpless writes, "could not have been cultivated without women's active participation in agriculture and in caring for other family members who worked in the fields. Women depended on cotton agriculture and cotton depended on women."[21]

Despite the farm's poor output, the father stubbornly stuck it out. "The Unruh place was regarded as the sandiest of the sandy," said Howard Green, who went to school with Unruh.[22] Green would later become a Texas state legislator himself. Isaac gave the banker who owned the farm a third of his cotton crop in return for the privilege of farming the land in a period when the Depression drove the price of cotton down to 4 cents a pound. The system was not actual slavery but kept the farmers firmly in another kind of bondage.

As a boy, Unruh rose early every day, put on his old clothes, mended by his mother, milked the cows, fed the animals, and had breakfast before boarding the bus for the early morning ride to Swenson School, which took up to an hour, or sometimes more if the rain had washed out the roads. After school, Unruh cut firewood and rounded up the cows his father had allowed to wander after they had been milked. "His friends, a lot of his friends, didn't have to do that," said Paul Unruh.

His life may have been hard, but Jesse was popular. "He had personality and a knack for making friends," said Paul. "All the guys he ran around with, they'd seek him out instead of him seeking them out. They'd come to the house to visit him and get him to go places with them."[23]

"I remember him quite well," said Howard Green. "He was large. Very little athletic ability. Not too well coordinated. Big voice." But with his size, he was good enough to play on the high school football team. He was well informed. In classroom discussions of current events, "Jesse would always reveal something Roosevelt said. He followed it very closely. Roosevelt was his hero."[24] He was county declamation champion.[25]

"He was a popular boy, highly respected because of his intellect," Green remembered. "All the girls admired him because he was so smart. Maybe some of the boys were jealous. I don't know." Unruh, Green, and another student, Robert Moore, were friends. "He, Jesse, and I were extremely interested in history," Green said. "We read a lot." A teacher took an interest in Unruh and gave him a summer job on her family's farm.[26]

As top male student in his high school graduating class, Unruh was eligible for a scholarship for his first year of college. He enrolled at Wayland

Baptist College, a small school about 120 miles from home in September 1939 and remained there until June 1940, when he quit. "I think he found out he couldn't earn enough money to have any kind of existence at all other than go to school and work, and not much of a life at that," Paul said. "I think he got disenchanted." With the war a year away, Unruh tried to join the service. The Army Air Corps rejected him because of his flat feet. "He was crestfallen," said Paul Unruh. "He wanted to be an aviator."[27]

Jesse borrowed $50 from his father, enrolled in an aircraft technical school in Dallas, and learned the sheet metal trade.[28] Then he followed his family to Southern California and went to work as a sheet metal worker at the Douglas plant in Santa Monica.

A family visit back to Texas in 1942 had the unforeseen impact of spurring him into the service after all. Paul and Unruh's father were at the farm—"as my grandfather called it, 'batching'"—while his mother was in California visiting her eldest son, Ervin. Unruh and some friends, young men and women, drove to a nearby town, Paul said, and were in the car drinking whiskey from a pint bottle in a paper bag. A town cop came over. He was a man with a reputation as the local bully. Words were exchanged. "Jess had this bottle in his right hand and when the guy pulled him out of the car, whack, he hit the guy on the side of the head with the bottle. I don't know if it knocked him unconscious or what it did but Jess jumped back in the car and hauled ass and left. He got out of there."

When Jesse got back to the farm, "I was little, but I remember hearing the conversation," Paul Unruh recalled. Jesse had told his father: " 'I got to go back to California.' "

" 'What's the matter? Why do you got to leave right now? Can't you wait until morning?'

"So finally, my grandfather got it out of him what happened. Jess said, 'I think I'm going to join the service. I'll find some place where I can go enlist.' "

The next day, the sheriff came by looking for Unruh. "He left," the father said. "Told me he's thinking about enlisting in the service."

The sheriff smiled. "Well, we certainly can't take him off if he's going to be in the service," he said.[29]

With that unpromising beginning, Jesse Unruh forever turned his back on the poverty of his childhood and started his slow climb upward.

THREE

The GI Bill of Rights

FLEEING RURAL TEXAS AND HIS brush with the law, Unruh enlisted in the Navy, after talking a naval doctor into overlooking his flat feet.[1] He was stationed at the base at Corpus Christi, Texas. There, he met Virginia Lemon. She was good-looking and athletic. "I was a tomboy," she said. "I remember my mother coming out [and] finding me at the top of a tree, and she nearly had a fit."

Like Unruh, Virginia was an immigrant to California, having moved there with her family in 1929. "My dad got tired of farming," she said. "My aunt and uncle were out there, and times were pretty rough. They convinced us to come out." She didn't enjoy high school, but at Los Angeles City College, her friendly manner blossomed.

She went north to the University of California at Berkeley for a year and a half, and then returned to Los Angeles, where she enrolled at USC and majored in physical education. She didn't particularly like the atmosphere of the campus, which was a haven for the community's wealthy; in her view, it was "the University of Spoiled Children."

"Most of the people at SC were snobs," she said. "They were moneyed people." But the supportive head of the department guided her through her academic career.

She and her sister, Gloria, had gone to Corpus Christi to visit their brother, a cadet at the Naval Air Station. "It was hand to mouth," Virginia remembered. "We got a room down there somewhere. We got jobs at the naval base. I worked in the tubing department. I didn't do much tubing work, but I manned the desk." Unruh worked nearby in the metallurgy department. He was an overweight, unmannered country boy, whose most sophisticated experience had been working on the plant floor at Douglas. In contrast, although she was the daughter of a family firmly anchored in the working class, Virginia had grown up in the big city and studied at Berkeley and USC. Even though her family had suffered their own hard times on their Nebraska farm, the pain and misery of Unruh's boyhood had been much worse. She described it to me long after Unruh's death. "How would you feel when you were considered the scum of the community?" she asked.[2]

Given their backgrounds, Jess and Virginia might never have met if it hadn't been for the war. But the war often leveled differences, as it did when they encountered each other somewhere in the vicinity of the tubing and metallurgy departments.

They dated with the hurried intensity of a wartime romance. "He was just a guy," she said. "But there was one thing. I had a feeling there was more to him than with the other fellows. Deep down there was something about Jess that told me he was deeper than that. It was an intangible feeling that he had something special that most people didn't have. . . . There was something well worth cultivating. And I tried my best do it." Was it love? "I suppose," she said. "But it was more friends." From the start, she was bothered by his outbursts of temper, but she felt she could handle them.

Her USC mentor introduced her to a colleague at Stephens College in Columbia, Missouri, who hired her. It was another school for the rich. "Stephens was a very snobby school," she said. But her faculty friend steered her through. "I made a place for me there," she said. "I did very well." Unruh pursued her. He invited her down to Texas for a weekend. Against all odds, she found a place on a plane. "I stayed the weekend and flew back. And he called me on the phone, asked me to marry him. I said, 'Oh, why not?' " They married in 1943, and six days later, Virginia was in the base hospital with influenza and Unruh was headed for the Aleutian Islands, where he spent two boring years. In his spare time, he memorized a book, *Thirty Days to a Better Vocabulary.*

"Those were miserable years in the Aleutians in all that cold," Virginia said. "He said he would never go north again." When the war ended, Virginia met him in Seattle after his discharge, and they traveled to Los Angeles, where she had been hired as a physical education instructor at the University of Southern California.[3]

By now, there was a tremendous postwar surge to the West Coast. A substantial number of these new immigrants were veterans, like Unruh, but there were others. They came by bus or car, by the great transcontinental trains, such as the Super Chief, by riding the rails, and some even by air. In addition to newly discharged GIs, there were civilian industrial workers, farmers, gangsters, actors, the skilled and unskilled, drawn by the sunshine or the dreams that were always part of the western edge of the continent.

Some had a bright idea for a business or simply a willingness to work hard. Others were willing to break or bend the law. They all found a place in Los Angeles, then a working-class city governed by a small number of rich and privileged, who were untroubled by its layer of poverty. The city was racially and ethnically segregated, with blacks in an increasingly crowded portion of South Los Angeles and Latinos on the Eastside. Asians, too, were limited in their housing choices by racial restrictions in deeds, as were Jews.

None of these groups were admitted to the downtown clubs or country clubs frequented by the elite, sheltered in enclaves such as Bel Air, Hancock Park, and San Marino. A corrupt police force, supported by the elite, patrolled black and Latino neighborhoods in a heavy-handed, brutal manner. It was a city best known for flashy movie industry wealth, a city well suited for swift change, a city of hustlers, with a dark, corrupt underside, a city of film noir. Vivian Ringer, then a reporter for the *Los Angeles Daily News,* remembered the gangster Mickey Cohen and his henchman parking their black Cadillac outside the paper. "Then they came stomping up to the *Daily News,* and he demanded better coverage than he was getting," she said.[4]

Most of the people in this quintessential middle- and working-class city had a lot more in common with Unruh than with Mickey Cohen. Unruh was just another GI Bill vet, trying to support his family, pay the rent, and keep the car running—one of millions, unnoticed in a place even then captivated by celebrity. The Sunset Strip, Beverly Hills, and the movie studios were far beyond his reach. He dreamed of success, however, but on different terms.

He was developing a rebellious political consciousness that would influence the rest of his life. As he recalled later, "A good many of my experiences in the wartime Navy made me question a number of institutions which I had previously taken for granted. I refer specifically to the racial discrimination I saw, and to the military caste system that constructed barriers between officers and men. I emerged from the service with a very restive, questioning attitude."[5]

The intensity of his feelings were apparent in an article he wrote later describing his Navy service. Officers, he said, were rotated out of the desolate Aleutians in twelve to sixteen months, while enlisted men had to serve on the island chain for twenty to twenty-six months. Just six officers were assigned to a Quonset hut, but those for enlisted men were crowded with up to thirty. He told of two Jeep crashes, one involving enlisted men and the other officers. The enlisted men's Jeep suffered minor damages, and neither of the two men were hurt. They were demoted. "Of the three officers in the other overturned Jeep, the driver was killed and the others seriously injured," Unruh wrote. "The Jeep was nearly demolished. The drunken driver was buried with full military honors and the other two passengers completely forgiven."[6]

He and Virginia moved into an apartment she had rented near USC. With the housing shortage, finding an apartment was difficult. Even with a snooping landlord, who rummaged through the apartment while Virginia was out, the Unruhs counted themselves fortunate. Eventually, the landlord was so unpleasant that "we had to move to another place," Virginia said. "Of course, we didn't have hardly any furniture. We went to an auction and got a dining room table and chairs." Unruh bought an old car. He was, she said, a fairly good mechanic "and he managed to keep it running."

After observing the young Unruhs in their cramped apartment, Virginia's uncle gave them money for a down payment on a house in Downey, a small city miles southeast of the USC campus. "I didn't like it out there. It was isolated from all my family," Virginia said.

Later, they moved back to Los Angeles. As the family grew, she got a job working nights as a physical education teacher at the Inglewood Adult School, while taking care of the children during the day. "I had trouble with the kids. Bradley, I couldn't control him. He would get up from his nap and crawl out the window. . . . I was afraid he would get out and get hit by a car. And, of course, having the other kids, I was taking care of them. And then I worked at night."

When she was at work, Unruh took care of the children. "He was very good with the kids. He loved them. . . . One summer, he had a job that fell through or something like that, and I had mine, so I'd work and he'd take care of the kids and the house. I remember coming home one day, and there he was with a towel around his middle like an apron and he was shaking out the diapers and hanging them on the line. I can see that yet. Yea, he could change a kid. He could take care of them."

When he was discharged, Unruh had no idea of what he wanted to do. Virginia insisted he attend USC. "I decided he had better go to school, because he had the GI Bill. He hadn't even thought about going to school," she said. "I insisted . . . I just told him if you are going to make anything out of yourself you've got to have a vocation. I had to take him by the hand and get him enrolled."[7]

Enrolling at USC, Unruh became one of 7.8 million World War II veterans nationwide, almost half of the 16.3 million men and women who served in the armed forces, who availed themselves of the education and vocational training offered by one of the furthest-reaching pieces of legislation in American history, the Servicemen's Readjustment Act of 1944, known as the GI Bill of Rights.

Unruh and veterans like him brought California not only a phenomenal birthrate but energy, ambition, stability, and intelligence, becoming the scientists, engineers, lawyers, physicians, teachers, accountants, and skilled blue-collar workers who drove the state's growth. They created businesses and worked the assembly lines in aerospace plants. They bought new suburban homes and automobiles. They energized stagnant politics. They put muscle into weak labor unions. They organized California's long marginalized minorities. Few could foresee the impact this generation of vets would have.

"The GI Bill, I believe, came closer to being a social revolution than any event in American history in the twentieth century," the historian Robert M. Berdahl of the University of California, Berkeley, has observed. "It democratized universities by providing access to vast numbers of young men who never otherwise would have received an education. Equally important, it opened the doors of elite private universities to a much broader spectrum of the population."[8]

Recalling the era many years later, Unruh's classmates were still struck by the seriousness of the GI Bill generation and the impact it had on the university and the world outside. Anthony D. Lazarro, who was one of them, stressed that the veterans had not been at USC "for the fun experience of college. They were there for the serious business of their goals in life and moving on." Lazarro grew up in Utica, N.Y. "My father worked in one of the local textile mills," he said. "We were just plain middle-class, making do." He earned a commission and served on an attack transport in the Pacific, taking part in nine island invasions, including the Marshall Islands, Okinawa, and the Philippines.

"No liberty for three years," he recalled. "My wife was my high school sweetheart, and she had an aunt in LA, and she came out to live with her aunt, hoping my ship would come in." It never did, but she was in Los Angeles when he was discharged. "She said, why not finish school here?" Lazarro enrolled at USC, and stayed there, rising to the job of USC senior vice president for business affairs. Could he have gone there without the GI Bill? "The answer is absolutely not," he said.[9]

"They came back to learn," said Edsel Curry, a Trojan football player and track star who returned to USC after commanding a ship clearing sunken vessels from Manila Harbor during the war. "You mature pretty darn fast when you are in charge of a lot of men," he said. "A lot of things happen." For himself and the other vets, it "was a very serious situation and a lot of them, they had lost two or three or four years. They wanted to get their education and get out . . . I think it made SC grow up."[10]

"It was a sense [of], well, it can't get any worse than it's been, it's going to get better," said Bob Wells, Unruh's close friend at USC and throughout his entire life. "But there was also feeling [that] you had to shape it to make it better. . . . I felt that way. Jess felt that way. All the people we knew. Not everybody. Everybody who had any sense of politics."[11]

Michael Bennett, a preeminent scholar of the GI Bill, observes that the vets "just knew they had a chance to do things no one they knew had done and be people more successful than anyone from their old neighborhood. Those young ex GIs were in their early or mid 20s, a little brash on the outside, insecure on the inside, anxious to make up for years lost to the gods of war, tedium, and terror—with similar stories they soon wanted to forget. Life was waiting; the days of dying were over."[12]

Part of the impetus behind the GI Bill was the fear of postwar unemployment. Economists did not foresee the productivity and expansiveness of post–World War II America, and they felt that sending millions of vets to school would ease the competition for scarce jobs. There were also other, less tangible, factors. Still fresh in the national consciousness were memories of the treatment accorded the veterans who had marched on Washington during the Depression in 1932 seeking immediate payment of a $500 bonus for World War I service, not due until 1945. When the veterans, known as "The Bonus Army," refused to disband, police charged. Two men were killed. Federal troops, commanded by General Douglas MacArthur, drove the protesters from their Anacostia camp.

The mass media continued to find the vets a compelling subject. By 1943, badly disabled veterans were being discharged into civilian life, neglected by a ponderous Veterans Administration bureaucracy. The American Legion, leading the fight for improved benefits, called them the Forgotten Battalion, and in testimony before Congress, the vets told of their disabilities and their failure to get help from indifferent or overwhelmed officials. The stories reverberated in the tabloid mind of Walter Howey, a Hearst editor who was the model for Walter Burns, the ruthlessly scheming newsroom boss in Ben Hecht and Charles MacArthur's play *The Front Page*. Howey sensed a great newspaper story, one that would touch the hearts of Hearst readers around the country. So did his boss, William Randolph Hearst. Moreover, the issue gave Hearst another way of attacking his enemy, President Franklin D. Roosevelt, who opposed giving the disabled World War I veterans their long-sought-after $500 bonus. The vets became a Hearst crusade, both for the bonus and for more comprehensive benefits for those who served in World War II.

An American Legion committee met with experts and in less than three weeks drafted a proposal, with the final version written on hotel stationery by Henry "Harry" Colmery, the Legion's national commander, in a room at the Mayflower Hotel in Washington, D.C. The plan was announced on January 9, 1944, as "The Bill of Rights for GI Joe and Jane." After the bill emerged from the kind of legislative struggle that Unruh would relish many years later, President Roosevelt signed it into law on June 22, 1944. It paid for tuition, up to $500 a year, $100 more than Harvard was charging, plus fees, books, and other educational materials—and a stipend for living expenses. And it provided for low-interest housing loans, guaranteed by the government, permitting the vets to buy the inexpensive tract homes being built around the nation.

The aid did not make for an easy life for beneficiaries consumed with readjusting to civilian and family life, desperate to find housing and part-time jobs, overwhelmed with babies and the ever-present task of studying, exercising skills neglected during the war or never developed before. Unruh's friend Bob Wells came out of the war in poor health. He had been slightly wounded in the Pacific and "came down with every disease known in the Army." When he was discharged, "The things I thought I got over with in the Pacific, they began breaking out again, and I went into the veterans hospital." Sick, in and out of the hospital, strapped for money, Wells would not have been able to attend USC without the $115 a month he received from the federal government, $25 more than the usual stipend because of his sickness.[13]

The Unruhs' life illustrates the strain of those days. Readjustment to civilian life was difficult in any circumstances, and in Unruh's case, it was complicated by his temper. Virginia had gotten a taste of it during their brief courtship, but, now married to him, she saw that her husband

was a very difficult man. He used to go into rages. You would never believe the rages he would go into. He felt like they were looking down on him . . . something would happen and I'd go "Uh oh." I'd cringe and wait for him to blow up. And sometimes he would and sometimes he wouldn't. I just had to weather it through until he calmed down again.

I think it was because of the early years. He was repeating his father's [be-havior], what he had seen around the house, [although] he was a little bit more smooth about it . . . I figured I'd change him. . . . Finally, I think I pointed out to him that he wasn't making himself well liked; he wasn't going to get anywhere if he was going to do that. That he needed to be polite, that he needed to fit into the crowd.[14]

Although he tried to control his rages, Jesse Unruh was cursed by his temper throughout his life.

Beatrice Canterbury Lavery, who worked with Unruh on the student newspaper, the *Daily Trojan,* remembered, "He was not as heavy as he got, but he was built heavy. He was fat and wasn't well toned, like a lot of guys coming out of the Army." And he was "Angry. Angry. Angry. Edgy. And challenging in conversations."[15]

Bob Wells said that Unruh at USC was "pretty much like what he was later. He lived a lot. Very intense. The women didn't like him. They thought he was overly familiar." He was, Wells said, "earthy and he offended a lot of people, particularly some of our sheltered coeds. They thought he was too forward."[16]

He majored in economics and journalism. At first, Virginia said, he wanted to be "a hotshot journalist, that's what he was going to do." But his real interest was campus politics.[17]

By chance, Unruh chose a perfect launching pad for his political career. The University of Southern California was part of the fabric of Los Angeles. It was and still is located in the heart of the city, between the banks, law offices, and corporate headquarters of downtown and the industrial and working-class residential neighborhoods of South Los Angeles. From its earliest days, the university felt an obligation to serve and shape the city. Much of this was accomplished through the School of Citizenship and Public Administration, which became the training ground for city and county governments throughout Southern California, providing them with generations of public executives. In time, a network of Trojans ran government in Southern California.[18]

The Southern California Conference of the Methodist Episcopal Church had founded the university in 1879. A year later, it opened to its first class in a mustard field on the rural outskirts of Los Angeles. One building, the two-story wooden Widney Hall, housed the university's twelve instructors and fifty-three students. The city, started as a Spanish outpost in 1781, was growing fast when the university opened, having doubled its population to about 11,000 since 1870. Its leaders were anxious to put Los Angeles's violent frontier days behind them, and a university was considered important in their drive toward big-city power and sophistication.

By the time Unruh enrolled, homes, apartment houses, and businesses, block upon block of them, had replaced the fields around the university. Widney Hall remained, joined by several larger buildings of brick and stone. None of them were exceptional. But together, they created the feeling of an orderly academic enclave in the sprawling flatlands landscape. Doheny Library, with its stone façade, and, west of it, Bovard Hall, the administration building and auditorium, were the most important buildings on campus. But its real center was a plaza with a statue of a Trojan warrior, Tommy Trojan, symbol of USC's athletic prowess.

When Unruh and the rest of the vets arrived, the university was better known for football than academic achievement. A sense of privilege had long permeated the campus. A powerful minority of young men and women in Greek-letter fraternities and sororities dominated a student political life that was so strong and such a good training ground that some of its graduates easily moved into the world of real politics. The "Greeks" extolled "Christian" values and would not admit blacks, Latinos, Jews, or anyone else who did not fit their mold.

Beatrice Lavery became president of her sorority, Alpha Delta Pi, "and when it came time to be sworn in, the oath said you had to be a white Christian. And I wouldn't read that."[19]

A major force in student politics was a secret fraternity, Theta Nu Epsilon. The June 1947 USC *Alumni Review* observed: "TNE rituals and insignia have a distinct resemblance to those of the Ku Klux Klan. The badge is a gold skull with one red and one green eye, superimposed on two gold crossed keys. Elaborate ceremonies, conducted by black-robed figures under the cover of night, are common and are accompanied by drinking marathons. It is a tradition that glasses are always held in the left hand."[20]

"It really was a secret society," said Joseph Cerrell, who enrolled at USC four years after Unruh's graduation and later worked for Unruh, before becoming a prominent political consultant in California. "It was banned across the country. That made it more interesting. They would stuff the ballot boxes and intimidate voters. But part of the mystique was belonging to the secret society, I mean secret grips and the red and green."[21]

TNE's goal was domination of the fraternity-sorority system and the student government. "They were more interested in controlling the student government and keeping the vets from getting the top position, and that's what Jess was fighting," Beatrice Lavery said.[22]

Unruh became a leader of a group of liberals, most of them veterans, who challenged the Greeks, whose ranks also contained many vets. Unruh's group later became the cadre that launched his first campaigns for office.

Around the same time, Unruh joined the liberal campus veterans' organization Trovets, which had a membership of about 500. It was, he said, "at that time led by older men most of whom were Democrats with strong convictions. With the unrest I felt, I was immediately attracted to their beliefs."[23]

"USC was a rich boy's school," Virginia recalled. "And then all these veterans came in. And I guess Jess saw that he could get them together and make him a following. Which he did. He joined Trovets because these were the people who were not from the rich families. I pointed out the advantage of doing these things. I thought he needed something to put his energies into. Then it was Trovets against the orgs, the Greeks."[24] As Unruh's friend Art Buchwald, later a famous newspaper humor columnist, put it,

> an undeclared class war was going on at USC. The GIs returning home had little use for the fraternity men, since most of the frat boys were not only much younger but considered very immature.
>
> The GIs were intent on getting their educations and starting new lives. Some fraternity people partied, drank, cheated on tests and tried to take over school politics. In those days, the administration catered to the fraternities, knowing that eventually they would be the big financial supporters of the school, as opposed to the independents, who would probably not be heard from again.[25]

In 1946, when Unruh became president of Trovets,[26] he asked that his organization be given a vote on the Student Senate. The fraternities and sororities were opposed. "I am not accusing anyone of being a sponger, but [it] is evidence of a negative attitude on the part of the veteran to say 'I'm a veteran, now help me,'" one fraternity representative said.

Unruh had enlisted Buchwald, who wrote funny pieces for campus publications, to handle publicity for his campaign to gain Trovets the senate seat. Even then, Unruh was highly quotable. When the student body president, Jim Mitchell, opposed making a Trovet representative a voting member of the Student Senate, Unruh said, "the argument that only 10 percent of the veterans belong to Trovets is not valid enough reason for not allowing representation in the Senate. If student body president Jim Mitchell fully believes the argument, then I request that he immediately resign as president because out of 12,000 students on campus during last Spring's election, only 3,000 voted, and of these only about 1,100 voted for Mitchell, which makes him representative of the same percentage of students that we have in our organization."[27] When the Student Senate defeated the plan 10–6, and a student senator proposed giving Trovets a nonvoting seat, Unruh responded angrily: "You are relegating Trovets to the position of an ordinary service group. I term the motion for a nonvoting seat as a direct insult to our organization. Although I cannot speak for the group as a whole, I personally refuse to accept." Unruh and Mitchell finally agreed on a plan, and Unruh was chosen veterans' representative.[28]

Trovets' interests took them beyond the campus. "We were concerned with things like housing, our GI checks, part-time jobs, tuition fees, and the long lines and antiquated registration procedures at the university," Unruh said. "The things which concerned the younger, more affluent fraternity and sorority people were of little concern to us."[29]

The big issue for the veterans was housing. Mayor Fletcher Bowron said, "I have heard enough to convince me that the housing conditions in Los Angeles are more serious than in any other area I have seen to date." "The major problem was adequate housing," said Mike Colicigno, a Trovet member. "Volunteers went through the area surrounding USC, asking homeowners to make rooms or even garages available to house students."[30]

Trovets sought help from the university. Unruh wrote the president, Rufus B. von Kleinsmid, asking for an audience. "I remember Unruh telling the Trovet board that the meeting was short-lived. Unruh was asked to leave the president's office [for arguing with the dictatorial president]," Colicigno said.[31] Despite the efforts of Mayor Bowron, the real estate industry blocked municipal efforts to build low-cost housing. To do so might have broken the rigid housing segregation that kept blacks in an increasingly crowded area in the southern part of the city.

The segregation infuriated Unruh. "My first recollection of Jess is standing on the stairs of the fourth story going up to the *Daily Trojan* in the Student Union building, and he started lecturing me on the restrictive covenants," Beatrice Lavery said. "I remember him asking me, 'Do you know that a black man or a Jewish person couldn't buy any of the properties around SC? There were are restrictive covenants on all those houses.'"[32]

Unruh and others made the issue part of the platform of their new political party, the Independent Students Association. The organization demanded that student government investigate the restrictive covenants that affected between 500 and 600 minority students at USC, a move that was echoed years later by Unruh's Civil Rights Act.

The Independent Students Association, Unruh said, "was rather quickly infiltrated by the radical left, and so we abandoned it." The Communist Party was active on campus at the time, Unruh recalled. He said there was "a general disenchantment with the American political system then, in many ways the same as occurred in 1968. Harry Truman had just become president and there was a feeling that he wasn't much. The Communists were very attractive at that point. They were some of the brightest kids on campus." Most of the campus radicals "felt that the Communists were just a bit like other liberals only a little bit more so. They were out to capture and did capture a good deal of the brighter student leadership and they really pushed me hard. I used to say facetiously that the only reason I didn't join the Communist Party was because I couldn't afford the 10-cent-a-month dues."[33]

Henry Wallace, who had been vice president under Roosevelt, was touring the country in 1947, rallying the Left as he prepared for his third-party campaign for the presidency the following year. On May 19, 1947, he told a large crowd in Gilmore Stadium in Los Angeles: "If I fail to cry out that I am anti-Communist, it is not because I am friendly to Communism but because at this time of growing intolerance, I refuse to join even the outer circle of that band of men who stir the steaming cauldron of hate and fear."[34]

Unruh, on the staff of the *Daily Trojan*, reported on a meeting between Wallace and fifteen young men and women that day. In an article in the next day's issue, he told how Wallace had called for understanding between the United States and the Soviet Union. The Soviet Union, Wallace said, lacked confidence in the West "for obvious reasons" and "must be induced to come into world organizations such as the International Bank and Monetary Fund and the United Nations educational, scientific and cultural organizations." Unruh concluded his story on a note that was sympathetic to Wallace: "Wallace was asked if he believed the present Red witch hunting going on in the United States was a smoke screen which some officials were using to cover up their lack of a constructive foreign and domestic policy. 'This is obviously so,' Wallace said."[35]

Virginia Unruh had her own recollections of that period. "Oh, that was a difficult thing. You had to skirt the Communist Party," she said. "He [Unruh] was very careful to stay out of that."[36]

This was when Unruh broke with the Left. He said, "We realized that the ISA [Independent Students Association] was no longer useful, and we found that a number of fraternity and sorority people did share some of our basic concerns. We then formed a new organization called the Unity Party." Edsel Curry, on the fraternity side of campus politics, recalled the change in Unruh. "I had the feeling he was pretty dogmatic in what he was trying to do, kind of one way. [Then] I felt he realized he couldn't get anything done unless he compromised once in a while."[37]

This period of his life shaped the rest of Unruh's career. The break with the Left aligned him with the centrist elements of the Democratic Party supporting President Truman. Another incident had an impact, too. He ran for the party's nomination for student body president but lost. "We held an entirely open convention of the Unity Party," he said. "Everyone present was allowed to vote. Naturally, the opposition packed the convention, nominated a weak candidate and produced an overwhelming victory for the fraternity candidate for president."[38]

Even John Houk, the candidate who beat Unruh for the nomination, agreed the convention had been packed, at least to some degree. "Obviously there were certain people there who voted in the nominations who were not in sympathy with the Unity Party platform and its general program in behalf of the student body," Houk said.[39]

Unruh said he learned "that it is impossible to maintain a purely democratic internal structure for a political party no matter how ideologically appetizing that idea might be."[40] After that, and for the rest of his life, Unruh stayed away from meetings unless he had arranged the result beforehand.

In his time as a student, he and other veterans had made an impact on USC and, in a small way, showed how they would change California in the years to come. "It was probably the most significant thing Jess did [in college]," Tony Lazarro said. "It probably became the beginning of the erosion of the power structure of the Greeks, and USC has become a more independent, diverse place."

FOUR

Hat in the Ring

IN MAY 1947, THE UNRUHS had one child, Bruce, a four-month-old infant, when they moved in with Virginia's aunt, fifteen miles west of the USC campus. Financial necessity helped dictate their move. Virginia taught, and Unruh, still a USC student, worked nights at the Los Angeles railroad freight yard, tracking freight cars for the Pacific Car Demurrage Bureau, which collected fees for railroads from shippers who didn't unload their cargo on time. "He was always on that fragile thin ice of economic survival," Marvin Holen remembered.[1]

The move also gave Unruh a chance to run for the California State Assembly in the 1948 election while he was studying at USC and working nights at the railroad. A competitive race was shaping up for the Democratic nomination for the assembly district in the area where the Unruhs were now living. "He wanted to try to run for office, to see how it went," Bob Wells said. "I think the most important thing was trying this thing out, just personal motivation. . . . What he wanted was a leadership position. He wanted certain things done. And also he wanted to get away from the goddamned railroad."[2]

Unruh was ready for the opportunity. Student politics had taught him rudimentary political skills, such as public speaking and how to organize people to follow him. He was still blunt and impatient. "Not a very easygoing guy. He didn't suffer fools gladly," said Frank Mankiewicz, a friend from those days, who much later was press secretary to Robert F. Kennedy.[3] But Unruh tried to control his temper. He was a good listener. He was empathetic. Having had so many difficult experiences, he had a deep understanding of other people's troubles.

Embarking on a political career in that particular year was not a simple matter for any Democrat. The Democratic Party was in the midst of extraordinary turmoil, from New York to California, from the Deep South to the farm belt. For a young politician like Unruh, navigational skills were essential. The underlying assumptions of California political life were changing as fast as the state's population.

Democratic registration was increasing, along with an explosion of political participation that is difficult to imagine a half a century later. Wartime idealism had carried over into peacetime life, on the part both of veterans like Unruh and of civilians who had spent the war on the home front. In the 1948 presidential election, pitting President Truman against Republican governor Thomas E. Dewey of New York, 86 percent of California's registered voters went to the polls, far more than in elections in later years.[4] Republicans and Democrats formed local political clubs. Candidates for offices from president to school board needed many volunteers to walk precincts, prepare mailings, put up billboards, and do the rest of the chores necessary for a campaign of that era.

The activity reflected the nation's postwar state of mind. In the late 1940s and the 1950s, the country was as conflicted as Unruh himself. Along with the remnants of wartime idealism, Americans had an unquenchable hunger for automobiles, appliances, nylon stockings, meat, and the other consumer goods they'd been denied during the war. Many believed they had earned a comfortable life after the trauma of the Depression and the war. The Unruhs, too poor for anything but an old secondhand car, yearned for the goods they saw other people buying.

Only a minority of critics, ranging from academics to comics, challenged the conformity and smugness of postwar American life. Vance Packard criticized society's materialism in his 1959 book *The Status Seekers.*[5] He said that the drive for social and material success in the rich postwar economy had left many "badly distressed and scared by the anxiety, inferiority feelings and straining generated by this unending process of rating and status striving." The younger generation's vague and mild feelings of rebellion were also given voice by William H. Whyte. The "organization man," Whyte declared in his 1956 book *The Organization Man,* "must fight the organization. Not stupidly or selfishly, for the defects of individual self-regard are no more to be venerated than the defects of cooperation. But fight he must."[6] The truth was, however, that rebels didn't succeed in big organizations. The adaptable and successful, David Riesman wrote in *The Lonely Crowd: A Study of the Changing American Character* (1950), were the "other directed," those willing to accommodate to win the approval of society and the boss.[7]

Unruh was no conformist. He wanted to be the boss and had no desire to work his way up the corporate ladder. Nor, given his domineering temperament, could he have done it. No American corporation would have tolerated his views of the inequalities of American life. Politics offered a way for him to move up. And politics was accessible. Almost anyone could make a difference, whether he or she was rich or working class. Politics was fun, with parties and drinks between envelope stuffing and precinct walking, a break from the rigors of conformism and status seeking in day-to-day life.

The Unruhs lived in a modest area that was a sharp contrast to other parts of West LA, especially to the large homes in the foothills of the nearby Santa Monica Mountains and around the campus of the University of California at Los Angeles. For the most part, the area was conservative, represented in the state legislature by Harold Levering, a Republican most famous as the author of a state loyalty oath. But liberals lived there too. Some were wealthy, many from the movie industry. Others, less prosperous, lived in houses and apartments scattered around the flatlands.

While the Democrats had no chance of defeating Levering in the fall, the June primary was important to the party. It was one of the countless skirmishes around the country that would determine the Democrats' postwar direction. Would it move leftward? Or would it be centrist, following the path of Harry Truman, committed to the Cold War abroad but supporting liberal economic and social programs at home?

The winner of the Democratic primary for state assembly would appoint members to the Democratic county committee. The committee was almost powerless. But in those days, every contest, large or small, was shaped by the party's ideological battle.

Former vice president Wallace had left the Democratic Party by then and was running for president as a Progressive. But he had substantial support among Democrats, including the district's Left. Wilbur Yerger was the Left's choice for assembly, and Unruh challenged him. Unruh, Wells said, "was angry at Yerger. He had no use for him. For one thing, he was an opponent. The other thing was he [Unruh] thought there was a danger from the Left."

The campaign was run out of Virginia's aunt's house. It was a penniless operation, with a few USC volunteers from the Unity Party and Trovets, which made it difficult to recruit help from the nearby campus of USC's rival, UCLA. Unruh worked on the campaign in the afternoons and evenings, going door to door to ask for support, while still checking freight cars on the night shift at the Demurrage Bureau. Virginia organized the volunteers, making sure there were tasks for them, arranging work space at the house for them, and overseeing their activities. "Most of us didn't know what we were doing," Wells said. Unruh knew he had no chance, "but hope springs eternal . . . he came in very far back in the crowd. There were a number of candidates, and he was disappointed he didn't do better than he did in terms of placing."[8] Yerger won the primary, and the Left got the committee appointments.

Four months after his primary election loss, the Unruh family returned to a much more Democratic neighborhood closer to USC. Unruh and the others converted the political organization they had formed for his assembly campaign into a club they called the Democratic Guild. It was one of many grassroots Democratic volunteer organizations springing up around the state, a phenomenon that owed much to the political participation of veterans. Vets became a driving force in the revival and transformation of the Democratic Party.

"It grew out of SC and to a certain extent UCLA involvement, just a whole bunch of people getting together to see what they could do in politics," Wells said. "To begin with, we weren't even sure that we were going to be a Democratic organization. We had some who said we should work within the Republican Party. The basic people who formed it were veterans. They were people who wanted to improve their communities."[9]

The modesty of the guild operation reflected the simplicity of the era's low-budget grassroots politics. William Collins, the treasurer, reported $228.90 in receipts for the first half of 1951, with $127.50 coming from ticket sales to the annual banquet. Expenditures were $217.06, $30 of it going for renting a hall for six monthly meetings.[10] A donation of just $1 was charged for the guild's fall carnival.

Guild members worried about whether they—an organization of college students and recent graduates—were relevant. "What makes us necessary above and apart from the regular Democratic clubs and organizations?" Wells and two colleagues asked.[11] As part of their search for relevancy, Unruh led a "buzz group" in a discussion that asked: "What does the guild stand for? What are the goals, the aims, the objectives of the guild? Just what should our organization try to achieve?"[12]

The party's ideological split continued. The Democratic Guild was strongly centrist. As a Democratic Guild publication put it, "We are in the words of Sen. Hubert Humphrey, 'Square Deal, New Deal, Fair Deal, Welfare-State Democrats.' As democratic progressives we condemn and oppose all totalitarianism, whether fascist or communist."[13]

Unruh continued his fight against the party's Left, running for a seat on the Los Angeles County Democratic Committee, another contest dominated by Cold War politics. Unruh lost, and his Democratic Guild colleagues blamed "the instructed Left" for his defeat. They called his opponents an "Apparit" (referring to the derisive term used for unquestioningly loyal Communists, "apparatchiks") and said the meeting "furnished classic examples of totalitarian floor tactics."[14] In the one-page, mimeographed guild paper *Stumper*, Wells asserted: "The Communists, having failed with their third party adventure, are seeking to infiltrate the Democratic Party."[15]

In the 1950 election, the guild undertook two tasks. One was campaigning for Jimmy Roosevelt, a son of the late president, who was the Democratic nominee for governor, and for Representative Helen Gahagan Douglas for U.S. Senate. The guild helped organize a parade for Roosevelt in the neighborhoods around USC and a speech on the campus.[16] Guild members volunteered to analyze Douglas's June primary results to help determine where to marshal Democratic forces in the fall. It was a task requiring them to spend hours at the gloomy and uncomfortable office of the County Registrar of Voters. "Dear Guild Kids," Douglas wrote after her primary victory, "Thank you so much for the beautiful flowers. . . . I cannot adequately express my gratitude to you for all the wonderful help you have given me in the campaign."[17] Roosevelt lost to the popular Republican governor, Earl Warren, and Richard M. Nixon defeated Douglas.

The second task was to try to eject Wallace supporters from the Democratic committee in the West Los Angeles district where Unruh had run two years before. The anti-Wallace candidate was Frank Mankiewicz, then a young Democratic activist in the party and a founder of Americans for Democratic Action, a national organization opposed to Communist influence in the party. "I ran because a lot of people in the district wanted to take back the party," he said. "After I announced, I got a call from Jess, and he said he had formed a group, and they had picked an assembly district to help."[18]

Mankiewicz won the party nomination, assuring the defeat of the Left in the fight for central committee seats. But he lost the election in the fall to the unbeatable Levering. Unruh worked in the campaign headquarters and in the neighborhoods with his Democratic Guild colleagues. Subsequently, Unruh managed the campaign of Esther Murray, the Democratic candidate for Congress in the area. His new political connections got him a paid position directing the 1950 census in Los Angeles County.

Unruh and the others had also attracted the attention of anti-Communists in the Los Angeles labor movement, particularly John Despol, a leader of the Steelworkers Union. He encouraged the Democratic Guild, as did two members of Los Angeles's Central Labor Council, Sue Adams and John Donovan. "They were mentors in the true sense of the word," said Wells. "They would come to meetings. We'd go to meetings with them, and afterward we would go out. Over coffee they would tell us about the labor movement, about the Democratic Party, and took a lot of time with us."[19] The advice was invaluable, and it shaped Unruh's direction in the Democratic Party, strengthening his natural instincts toward pragmatic, centrist politics.

By 1952, Unruh was ready for another run for the assembly. In embarking on this campaign, he was confronted with a new situation, something entirely different than the ideological battle he had been waging with the Left. In this race, Unruh was up against the peculiar special interest power that dominated California legislative politics. In this game, Left and Right didn't matter. What counted was money.

On the surface, his district, the sixty-fifth, looked winnable. It was a working-class district, and most of the people in it were not unlike the Unruhs. The majority were Democrats. These neighborhoods were so different from the popular vision of Los Angeles as a glamorous movie capital that they might as well have been in different states. Block after block of modest bungalows and apartment houses, occupied by the sort of middle-class, blue-collar people who comprised the real Los Angeles, all looked pretty much the same.

Many residents were newcomers in this city of transients. And the vast area lacked the long-established institutions that were important to big-city politics—old churches, powerful unions, big ethnic lodges, large, well-settled extended families, and, most important, a strong partisan patronage system that reached from City Hall to the street corner.

In Chicago, New York, or Gary, Indiana, party bosses put their candidates—mayors, aldermen, congressmen, state legislators—on slates that were distributed house to house, church to church, union hall to union hall, cousin to cousin. In Los Angeles, cousins were living a half a continent away, and the church rolls were as changeable as the city's population. Unions, while stronger than in the prewar Depression days, were weak in comparison to those in the industrial Midwest and Northeast. And, most important, political parties, the glue that held urban politics together, were feeble.

The main reason for party weakness was a series of laws put through by the Progressives, who were part of a reform movement that swept much of the country in the late nineteenth and early twentieth centuries in a rebellion against railroads, steel companies, and other industrial trusts devoted to keeping prices up and wages down. In California, the Progressives' target was the Southern Pacific Railroad Company, which had a stranglehold on the shipment of agricultural produce and industrial goods.

The California Progressives did much good in their four most important years of power, from 1911 to 1915. Their program was a compendium of ideas that had been rattling around for years and finally found fertile ground under the leadership of a cantankerous, stubborn San Francisco attorney, Hiram Johnson, who in 1910 was a prototypical California outsider protest candidate. During his populist campaign, Johnson, a Republican and a successful San Francisco attorney, made no pretense of embracing the life of working people. He traveled the state in an expensive and luxurious Locomobile, a car so named because its makers boasted that it was as well built as a locomotive. Still his platform, centering on attacks against the Southern Pacific, was more liberal than that of longtime Republican leaders.

The Progressives backed a state constitutional amendment that gave women the right to vote in 1911. Once in control of the state legislature, they limited child labor and established a minimum wage and an eight-hour workday for women. A workers' compensation law offered protection for the first time against illness and on-the-job injury. Regulation of railroads and other utilities was increased. These were trailblazing ideas, but the Progressives are best remembered for electoral laws, the initiative, the referendum, the recall, and cross-filing, all of which changed the nature of California politics and government.

Cross-filing allowed candidates to seek the nominations of all parties. Johnson had a practical reason for wanting this. His program was too liberal for the Republican Party, but it reflected the views of a majority of Californians. Cross-filing permitted him to cut loose from his Republican shackles and also campaign for Democratic votes. Johnson, before anyone else, saw the implications of what later became an article of faith among California voters—vote the person, not the party.

Johnson and other Progressive leaders also believed parties were at the root of political corruption, through which big business, in general, and the Southern Pacific, in particular, exercised control. "The basic villain, they believed, was the political party, which they deliberately sought to weaken because it seemed the primary vehicle of special interests' political power," the historian Jackson K. Putnam observes.[20]

The Progressives also felt that ethnic minorities dominated political parties. "In the face of Catholic and Jewish immigration, . . . Progressivism reasserted by implication (and occasionally by overt statement) an embattled conviction of the essentially Protestant nature of American society," the historian Kevin Starr notes.[21] Another eminent California historian, Carey McWilliams, says bluntly: "By and large the reform leaders of the Johnson movement were racists, including Johnson himself."[22]

By the time Unruh emerged, the fallacy of the Progressive theory was clear. Progressivism had not produced a legislature filled with high-minded nonpartisans. Rather, the result was a business-dominated legislature that was run by conservative Republicans and Democrats and controlled by lobbyists for corporate interests.

Most of the time, the legislature was Republican under cross-filing. Although between 1932 and 1948, Democrats had a 60–40 statewide registration edge over Republicans, and Democratic presidential candidates carried the state every four years, Republicans generally controlled the state legislature in that period. The reason was simple: when cross-filing began, the Republicans were the majority in the legislature. And cross-filing favored incumbents, who were better known and financed than their challengers.

The newspapers, the most important mass news media of the day, reinforced the advantage of Republican incumbents. With no party labels on the ballot and absent grassroots party organizing or advertising, the newspapers were a dominant force, and about 80 percent of the state's papers were Republican.[23]

By the 1950s, three powerful newspapers—the *Los Angeles Times,* the *San Francisco Chronicle,* and the *Oakland Tribune*—controlled the Republican Party, choosing candidates who fitted the pro-business, anti-union, Cold War–hawk pattern favored by the publishers. I personally saw what Unruh and other Democrats were up against when I worked for the *Tribune* from 1953 to 1960 and knew the owners, Joseph R. Knowland, the patriarch, or—as we called him, "the old man"—and his son, William F. Knowland, then California's senior U.S. senator.

The gentlemanly old man was a mixture of right-wing politics, love of California's natural beauty, and old-fashioned sentimentality, a quirky, highly personal form of conservatism often found among his generation of buccaneers. He opposed big government but, as chairman of the State Parks Commission, he was an architect of the large system of public parks that preserved part of the state's famed redwood forests. Despite his conservatism, he fostered the career of the moderate Earl Warren, the former local district attorney and a Knowland family protégé. Hometown pride trumped political doctrine.

As with the other publishers, Knowland was connected to day-to-day life by his political editor. Knowland's was Dave Hope, a talented newspaperman, generous with his support and advice for young people like me. He and the old man were a team. Supplicants usually had to get past Dave. The editors in charge of news coverage obeyed instructions from Dave or from Knowland's office without question. Watching Hope work at an old desk in the back of the newsroom, pounding away at his typewriter, it would have been difficult for a visitor to sense his great power, an influence also possessed by the political editors of the other papers, Kyle Palmer of the *Los Angeles Times* and Earl C. "Squire" Behrens of the *San Francisco Chronicle*. They were the gatekeepers; they advised their bosses, carried out their wishes, and delivered their messages to the public in slanted news stories. Reporters for the news services, who wrote stories straight, referred to the political editors as "trained seals." There wasn't much of a chance for an underdog Democratic legislative candidate to make an impression.

With parties weakened, legislative power moved to interests ranging from agriculture to labor, from liquor to racetracks to oil, and many more—just the opposite of what the Progressives had sought. The legislature became what McWilliams described as "one of the great commodity markets in America where an astonishing variety of interests bid for favor and preference."[24] It wasn't necessary to be a corporate boss or lobbyist to participate in the marketplace. Veterans, pet lovers, temperance groups, racial minorities, and women's associations lobbied, too, and sometimes made deals with business and union representatives. To get anything done, they had to be part of the system. If you had a bill for the veterans, you'd line up support from the lobbyists for the racetracks or breweries. The perfect illustration of how the system worked can be found in the career of Unruh's Republican opponent in the Sixty-fifth District, John Evans.

Evans was called "Biltmore Johnny," a nickname he had earned by spending much of his time at the long men's bar of the Biltmore Hotel in downtown Los Angeles, several miles north of his district. It was a gathering place for the high- and lowlife of the city's political and business classes at lunchtime and the cocktail hour and a hangout far beyond the means of Unruh, Wells, Holen, and the rest of their crowd, who stocked up at the neighborhood liquor store. A *Los Angeles Examiner* reporter described Evans as "debonair." In a gangster movie of the time, he could have played the mouthpiece, the lawyer ready to free the crooks on bail.

His patron—in fact, his political creator—was a master of California's peculiar special interests politics. His name was George H. McLain, and he was the leading advocate of higher old-age pensions. McLain led an organization of almost 70,000 older Californians, the California Institute of Social Welfare.[25] Its importance extended far beyond the institute's membership. In 1950, when Unruh was beginning his career, Californians over the age of sixty-five constituted a substantial part of the population in the big counties. They comprised 17.2 percent of Los Angeles County's residents. In Alameda County, it was 15.8 percent, and in San Francisco, 17.2 percent. In the more rural counties of Northern and Central California, older people totaled more than 20 percent.[26]

McLain enjoyed the good life. "He has a personal tailor . . . and wears personally tailored suits," noted a writer of the time. His Institute of Social Welfare bought him an Oldsmobile 98, and he owned a half interest in the advertising agency that placed the group's ads for a 15 percent fee, a substantial amount. The institute paid for his liquor, delivered to his home and costing between $200 and $250 a month. He lived in a house with a swimming pool. His bedroom was decorated with a stained glass window of the Virgin Mary and the Christ Child, taken from the old mortuary he had converted into the institute's headquarters. "He did pinch waitresses' bottoms in Sacramento; he did have a whole series of affairs and may still," one observer noted. "He does drink and he must have some social life at the Saints and Sinners Club, the one outside organization to which he belongs."[27]

I encountered McLain in the State Capitol in the early 1960s. Having read about him for years, I felt as if I had run into a famous character from history. He was always dressed in a black suit, white shirt, and dark tie, his hair combed back in a pompadour, his oversized horn-rimmed glasses and mustache drawing attention to a face that had a theatrical quality. The black suits had replaced the checked and striped suits and two-tone suede shoes of earlier years. He looked more like a high-rolling lobbyist than the leader of seniors seeking an increase in their pensions.

He knew how to reach the residents of faceless neighborhoods, including those in the district where Unruh was preparing to run against John Evans. They were not faceless to McLain, whose prosperous family had been thrust into poverty early in the Depression. And he did not need the hostile newspapers. He had the radio.

His warm evangelist's voice reached through the state, opening his broadcasts with a warm, "Howdy folks, are you with me?" Typical was a broadcast in February 1944: "I received a telephone call from a lady who said she was the neighbor of a blind lady and she thought I ought to call on this blind lady and hear her story." At first the woman thought McLain and his assistant, who accompanied him, were county welfare investigators, notorious for their heavy-handed treatment of recipients. "Dear lady," said McLain, "we are not welfare workers, we are from the Citizens Committee For Old Age Pensions. At once her wrinkled face seemed to brighten. . . . She was just as spry and full of hope as all get out."[28]

His broadcasts worked. In 1948, he persuaded California voters to approve a constitutional amendment that increased the state old age pension from $60 to $75 a month, reduced the eligibility age, and, most astounding, named McLain's aide Myrtle Williams director of an expanded State Social Welfare Department. Shocked, business interests and the newspapers immediately launched a campaign to repeal the McLain plan, which succeeded the following year.

Through his broadcasts, McLain carried on a perpetual fund-raising campaign to support his lobbying in Sacramento and a large office in Los Angeles. "He is said to have remarked a couple of years ago, 'Anyone can form an organization in this state if he can cut a hole in a shoebox [for donations].'"[29] He solicited life memberships from the aged, $5 down and $5 a month until the required $75 was reached. Another campaign was "Buy a Brick" to pay for headquarters in downtown Los Angeles. A brick cost $5, and a membership in the organization's foundation $10. In addition to financing headquarters, the campaign promised to buy old mansions for members to rehabilitate for their residences. The money permitted McLain to operate in Sacramento in the same manner as corporate lobbyists. Like them, he had lawmakers in his pocket. Evans was on McLain's payroll, as well as receiving favorable stories in the McLain newspaper. "Johnny Evans of the 65th," was the headline of an article in McLain's *National Welfare Advocate* in March 1945. "John W. Evans—he's that way—Johnny on the Spot—made history at Sacramento when he caused the Legislature to take the first vote it ever cast on $60 pensions."[30]

The genial Johnny entertained legislators on McLain's behalf. McLain had a suite in the Sacramento Hotel near the Capitol, and Evans received $75 a week to entertain them. "The money was certainly not paid on a salary basis," Evans said. "The money was for use in payment of luncheons for members of the Legislature in McLain's rooms while McLain had to go to Washington. . . . I was spending the money for McLain, and the practice was to invite various legislators to McLain's suite at the Sacramento Hotel to eat and talk."[31]

The big lobbyists maintained such suites at the Sacramento or the Senator, the two hotels closest to the Capitol, where they provided food, drink, and card games. Eventually, Evans was charged with bribery for accepting the money. He testified: "Not only did none of the $75 go into my pocket but I'll prove that my home is mortgaged, that I have devoted virtually all my time, energy and income to the cause of the old people for over a decade and that I'm practically broke—flatter than a pancake."[32] The bribery charges were dropped after a jury couldn't agree on a verdict.

New to the district, underfinanced, and confronted with Evans's support from the McLain organization, Unruh didn't have much of a chance in 1952. With a little money and plenty of advice from his labor backers, Unruh began his campaign for the assembly from a storefront on low-rent Vernon Avenue. Unruh was there much of the time. "He encouraged volunteers, he went out and worked precincts, he did just about everything," said Wells.[33]

When she could spare time from the children, Virginia Unruh was at the headquarters, too, handing out assignments, coordinating volunteers, and managing the details, just as she had done in 1948. Wells said that Unruh figured Evans's defeat would be a two-step process, losing in 1952 and winning in 1954. "We talked about [the likelihood of losing] it, just the campaign leadership," Wells said, not wanting to share the insiders' gloomy views with the rank and file. The volunteers put up small posters on telephone polls, and Wells wrote and produced a tabloid newspaper that became a fixture of every Unruh legislative campaign, the *Southwest Democrat*. The *Democrat* was the vehicle to attack Evans. But Evans won both the Democratic and Republican nominations. "Of course he [Unruh] was disappointed," said Wells. "Every candidate believes in miracles."

The next election, in 1954, was different, thanks to a strategic error made by Republicans in the legislature. Long opposed to the Progressives' cross-filing, Democrats, financed by a Democratic oil millionaire, organized a campaign for a voters' initiative eliminating cross-filing, and it received enough signatures to appear on the 1952 ballot. In an attempt to defeat it, the Republican-controlled legislature put another measure on the same ballot, retaining cross-filing but requiring candidates to list their party affiliation on the ballot. Republican candidates would be labeled Republican, bad news for those running in Democratic districts. The Republican measure won.

The change coincided with an explosion of grassroots political activity, marked by the formation of Democratic clubs. So widespread were the clubs that they organized into a statewide federation, the California Democratic Council. The council—it was soon best known by its initials, CDC—became the center of Democratic politics, and its conventions were among the big political events of an election year. Unruh, while believing the CDC was too far to the left, frequented the conventions.

Tom Rees, another World War II vet starting out in politics, remembered meeting Unruh during one of the conventions. "I saw this guy in the parking lot—it was dark—and I think he had a pint of scotch. . . . And he had a top coat on." They started talking. Rees, who also felt the CDC was too leftist, told his new acquaintance, "these guys are so spaced out. They got the martyr trip going. What the hell's wrong with them? They ought to fight tough." Unruh replied, "You bet." Unruh drained his bottle, threw it away, turned to a friend and said of Rees, "Who is this guy? Is he one of us?" He was, and when Rees was elected to the assembly, he and Unruh became staunch allies.[34]

Another young man who passed the Unruh ideological and practicality test was Joseph Cerrell, a college student from New York. When Cerrell enrolled at USC, he soon formed a Trojan Democratic Club, and wanted to campaign for a Democratic candidate. He called the county party office and asked for a campaign near the campus. He was given the Unruh number. Virginia Unruh answered the phone. She said, "There's a meeting tonight at the 4900 block of South Vernon."[35]

That began Cerrell's involvement. The CDC convention was to be held in Fresno, and Unruh wanted to go. He packed Cerrell and three others into his old two-door car and drove them to the convention, 300 miles away. These conventions were a mixture of academic exploration and ideological warfare, drinking, storytelling, horse trading, and sociability. The delegates were intense and intelligent. Subcommittees writing resolutions were like graduate seminars. The resolutions were the heart and soul of a CDC convention, and as delegates debated matters such as recognizing the Communist regime in China, they reveled in arguments that centered upon the party's Cold War split.

Unruh, on the pro–Cold War side of such issues, attended all the meetings and watched with disapproval as more liberal delegates framed the resolutions. Such stands, he felt, had no place in a party faced with the practical task of winning an election. With neither money nor fame, Unruh had little influence at these sessions. "Nobody was buying him drinks from the bar," Cerrell said. "This wasn't a case of some candidate who is about to win."

Unruh and Cerrell returned to the campaign. With his studies at USC low on his agenda, Cerrell devoted himself almost full-time to Unruh's race for the assembly. Campaign technology was minimal. By day, Cerrell stuffed envelopes with brochures, and at night, he joined his SC friends as they "sniped," pasting up outdoor advertisements and tearing down those of their opponents. Both were time-consuming.

For the brochures, Cerrell first typed the campaign message on paper, then, after it was approved, typed it again on a thin sheet of special paper called a stencil. The stencil was attached to a mimeograph machine, the era's version of a copier. Cerrell, turning the mimeograph by hand, cranked out copies. Meanwhile, other volunteers typed addresses, obtained from the county registrar, of voters on sheets of labels. Volunteers then pasted the labels on the envelopes. The mimeographed messages were stuffed into the envelopes, which were stamped and taken to the post office, from there to be sent to potential voters.

Cerrell and his sniping crew worked at night. They put paste in buckets, filled them with water, and pasted their signs on telephone poles, fences, and walls, many of them in places where such posters were banned. "[As] my pay for doing this," he recalled, "we would go over on Crenshaw to the Tiny Naylors and have breakfast at 6 A.M., then go back to school and fall asleep in class."[36]

Wells churned out the *Southwest Democrat*, hammering away at Johnny Evans. He brought up the Biltmore Johnny nickname and recalled the assemblyman's indictment for bribery, although writing it carefully so as to minimize Evans's connection with McLain. "McLain was popular, and there were quite a few elderly people in the district," he said."[37]

The Saturday night before the election, Cerrell and the other volunteers distributed a pamphlet, quoting a news story in *People's World*, the Communist Party daily, which noted Evans had been endorsed by a union. "We put out a thing in red and white, signed by the People Against Communists in Government," Cerrell recalled. "It was a real smear attack, and it was effective."

Unruh was in a good mood. "The more the campaign went on, the better he was looking," Wells said. "He began to get a little notice from the press that the seat was up for grabs."

Unruh raised his own campaign money while struggling to support his family. He had returned to his job of counting freight cars, while Virginia taught school. Some of his contributions came from labor unions. A friend from USC, William Munnell, already a well-connected state legislator, helped. "You know how legislators are," said Wells. "They see a comer. They want him in their corner, and I think that was the important factor. As time went on it became more and more apparent that he would win. We really weren't too surprised."[38]

Unruh's victory was a sign that California politics were changing. Waves of immigration had created a constituency for the Democratic Party, as had the wartime industrialization of metropolitan Los Angeles and the San Francisco Bay Area. Voters knew candidates' party affiliations, because this information was now required on the ballot. The change in the law helped the Democrats defeat Biltmore Johnny Evans and other entrenched Republican incumbents. Volunteers, organized into clubs, provided the energy and workers needed to run the campaigns. In other races, Republicans, too, benefited from the help of volunteers. The result was to give California politics a more partisan edge.

But the marketplace of Sacramento still bustled with trades and favors. Biltmore Johnny Evans had been defeated, but the system that created him remained.

FIVE

The Education of a Rookie

THE FORCES UNLEASHED IN California by World War II were coalescing as Unruh campaigned successfully for his state assembly seat in 1954. By now, the state's industrial expansion, the energy of the veterans, and successive waves of immigration had made California a prototype for mid-century America.

Unprecedented demands were being made on a state government that was just beginning to emerge from its rural past. The University of California, the state colleges, junior colleges, and kindergarten through the twelfth grade all would need more teachers, buildings, and books to accommodate the infant baby boomers, the generation born after the war. The wartime aircraft industry was being transformed into a producer of planes for growing civil aviation, the Cold War military, and the beginnings of the aerospace industry. Agriculture, with its huge factory farms, was demanding more water, as well as fighting union efforts to organize farmworkers. The mentally ill were trapped in the shadows of old state mental hospitals, immortalized by the 1948 Olivia de Havilland movie *The Snake Pit*.

Veterans with low-interest GI loans became homeowners. Developers bought land and devised mass production techniques to build homes inexpensively. The prospect of such development was transforming financial institutions. When traditional banks were reluctant to finance the construction, savings and loans stepped into the breach. Suburbia grew outward from Los Angeles, San Diego, and the cities of the San Francisco Bay Area. It also spread to the orchards and farms of Orange County, even extending into the farmlands of the Central Valley.

Only the motor vehicle—automobiles and trucks—could connect the sprawl. The growth of suburbia and the automobile were intertwined. Freeways were built, and narrow two- and three-lane roads and city streets were widened. In a state where life was increasingly shaped by travel over long distances, oil became more important than ever, sending oil companies searching for new fields. The oil industry, facing declining yields from its inland fields, turned to the tidelands off the California coast.[1]

These huge shifts in so many aspects of life often required changes in state law. Some of the issues were well publicized and easy to understand. Others were so complex, as in the case of oil, that few lawmakers comprehended them. Industry specialists and company lobbyists settled such questions in private. For Unruh, as was true for most people, oil and gasoline were products purchased at a service station to keep a car running. Only after he was elected and served his first term in the legislature, did he see the connection between political power and the gas pump. He would eventually understand the link between politics, the local savings and loan, the supermarket, the farm, and every other business selling goods and services. The connection was in Sacramento, in the chambers of the assembly and senate on the third floor of the State Capitol.

His education began during his 1954 assembly campaign.

A friend from USC, Assemblyman William Munnell, had offered Unruh contributions and advice. Munnell was "the only legislator who had been of any significant help to me," Unruh said afterward.[2] Munnell was not just another assemblyman. He was part of a bipartisan group who were gathering votes for a candidate for assembly speaker, Luther "Abe" Lincoln, a Republican. Lincoln needed the votes of a majority of the eighty assembly members to win.

So important was the job of speaker that Munnell, Lincoln, and the others began the campaign months before the actual election. Legislators traveled the state by car and plane, visiting cities and towns where prospects were running in their own assembly district elections.[3] Trailing them were the lobbyists, often loaded with cash, offering campaign contributions for their choice for speaker. The lobbyists' future, and that of their employers, would be heavily influenced by the result.

The speaker presided over the assembly. But, like the speaker of the U.S. House of Representatives, he did much more. In Sacramento's political marketplace, the speaker was the gatekeeper to the assembly. When oil interests wanted passage of a bill that would benefit the industry, or labor sought an increase in workers' compensation for on-the-job injuries, they had to pass through the man in charge, the speaker. The speaker assigned the bills to committees, where the real work of the legislature was done. Moreover, he chose the chairman and members of each committee. Lobbyists for each interest group wanted chairmen and committee majorities that favored them. A lobbyist's dream was, as they said in the Capitol, to have the speaker in his pocket.

The speaker also shaped the professional lives of the assembly members—and, when called upon to bail out a drunken lawmaker or help hide a messy liaison, their personal lives as well. In assigning members to a committee, the speaker determined whether a lawmaker would have a high-visibility career or be consigned to oblivion. He controlled the Rules Committee, which allocated office space, ranging from suites to tiny quarters adjacent to the cafeteria.

He also decided when committees traveled for hearings away from the Capitol, a prized source of per diem payments, mileage allowances, and visits to the hotels and restaurants of Los Angeles and San Francisco and the golf courses of Palm Springs, all luxuries for the underpaid assembly members. With so much at stake, Unruh's decision to back Munnell's candidate, Abe Lincoln, was critical, more so than he may have realized at the time. By betting on Lincoln, Unruh was also betting that his early choice would propel his Sacramento career to a fast start, with the best committee assignments and other perks.[4]

In choosing Lincoln, the liberal, populist Southern California Democrat Unruh was supporting a Republican businessman whose values and background were very different from his. Unruh's choice was dictated by the partisan lineup of the assembly. In 1954, any Democratic assemblyman wanting a share of power had to support a Republican. Throughout the year, the fall election seemed certain to continue Republican control of the assembly and senate, as well the governorship. Democrats were in such bad shape that they nominated a recent Republican, Richard Graves, for governor against the incumbent, Republican Goodwin J. Knight. Graves was unknown statewide, although well respected among Capitol insiders as the chief lobbyist for city governments. Despite his Capitol reputation, Graves was no match as a campaigner for the extroverted, audience-loving Knight, who, in addition to his political skills, benefited from solid and slanted newspaper support.[5] And despite the partisan difference, Lincoln's political philosophy was closer to Unruh's than that of the other candidate, H. Allen Smith, a conservative Republican.

The contest between Lincoln and Smith for such a powerful office reflected the politics and issues of mid 1950s California. Both Lincoln and Smith favored policies that would promote population and business growth, which were important to Lincoln's home-building and development business. He was also the author of a huge highway construction bill.

But Lincoln and Smith differed ideologically, mirroring the divisions in the Republican Party.

Lincoln, from Oakland, across the bay from San Francisco, had learned his politics from Governor Earl Warren, a moderate Republican, who resigned in 1953 to become chief justice of the United States. Warren had lived in Oakland, where he began his career as district attorney of Alameda County. As a young Republican volunteer, Lincoln got to know him and to admire his skill in navigating between conservative and moderate factions of the GOP, as well as an electorate that was becoming more Democratic. A master of hiding his feelings behind a deceptively genial exterior, Warren had survived assaults from the Republican Right and from the lobbyists and their bosses to become one of California's most successful and popular governors. Mindful of Warren's coalition-building skills, Lincoln had learned the Capitol game, waiting for his chance to change it. "I was what I thought of as a moderate Republican," Lincoln said.[6]

Lincoln's district included a large number of blue-collar Democrats in working-class Oakland, where liberal Democratic politics were emerging after decades of domination by the Republican newspaper, the *Oakland Tribune*. With party affiliation now designated on the ballot, Lincoln befriended this increasingly active part of his constituency, as well as the labor unions that were sparking the Democratic revival. A substantial number of his constituents, like Unruh, were immigrants from the Southwest drawn to the West Coast by wartime industry.[7]

Smith, a former FBI agent, represented Glendale, a Los Angeles County suburban city that was a Southern California Republican hothouse, a center of the party's growing conservative movement. While the arrival of wartime industry had increased union membership and power in Southern California, the Los Angeles area, particularly suburbs such as Glendale, remained centers of anti-union sentiment, fueled by the union-hating *Los Angeles Times*. With Lincoln as speaker, there would be a better chance for Democratic legislators and their labor allies to win approval of some of their proposals, which included civil rights legislation, child care centers, improved care for the mentally ill, and increased aid to the needy, aged, and blind.

Moreover, Lincoln was a reform candidate, standard-bearer for a group of Republicans and Democrats who, two years before, had installed one of their own, James Silliman, as speaker. Silliman was now running for lieutenant governor, and Lincoln was the reformers' choice to succeed him.[8] The business lobbyists in general backed the more conservative Smith, figuring he would be friendlier to their clients. Lincoln's antilobbyist stance was to Unruh's liking, fitting in with his campaign against the lobbyist-controlled, Biltmore-bar-loving Johnny Evans. In a campaign brochure, Unruh proclaimed that Lincoln stood for "Honest, sober, uncorruptible [*sic*] representation" and "Unrelenting vigilance against pressure politics and lobby legislation."[9]

The reform movement that Unruh embraced had begun as a revolt against the strong lobby control exemplified by a legendary figure, Arthur L. "Artie" Samish, the representative of beer, liquor, racetrack, movie, bus, and railroad companies.[10] By 1954, Samish had been put behind bars in the McNeil Island Federal Penitentiary in Puget Sound for income tax evasion. But the legislature was still much the same body Samish had fashioned.

Looking back on it much later, Unruh said Samish was "the master lobbyist . . . virtually the boss of the California legislature."[11] Lincoln put it more precisely, recalling the situation when he was elected: "It was not comfortable to be a junior assemblyman. The group in control was led by the speaker and the majority leader. They had close ties with various lobbyists, particularly . . . Samish. . . . There was tremendous pressure on freshmen to become part of their operation, to a point where you couldn't be assigned a secretary or an office or get support for your bills unless you were part of their team."[12]

Samish enjoyed being called what he titled his autobiography, *The Secret Boss of California.* He was a 300-pound, six-foot-two-inch man with a big face and an expression that ranged from shrewd to thoughtful to mischievous to downright intimidating. Samish's bragging, especially in an interview by Lester Velie in *Colliers* magazine in 1949, proved to be his downfall. Velie wrote that as a photographer, illustrating the story, he was shooting pictures. "The big man disappeared into his bedroom and soon emerged with a dummy, togged out as a bum, its wooden feet poking from tattered hobo's shoes . . . he plunked the dummy on his lap. 'That's the way I lobby,' he said. 'That's my legislature. That's Mr. Legislature. How are you today, Mr. Legislature?' he inquired of the dummy." And that's how he was photographed.[13]

Even after his power was gone following his income tax evasion conviction, Samish knew how to make a deal. So I learned when I interviewed him in the course of reporting on one of his old political associates.

The Samish I met was an older version of the vibrant fat man of the *Colliers* picture, still big and charming as he held forth in the San Francisco office where he had operated at the height of his power. He wasn't especially forthcoming, but I was pleased, nevertheless, to be interviewing such a famous rogue.

At the end of the interview, he wondered if he could ask me a question. "You know," he said, "I've done a lot of favors for the Chandlers, gotten a lot of bills through the legislature for them." The Chandler family owned the newspaper that employed me, the *Los Angeles Times,* as well as vast amounts of Southern California real estate. "I bet you have," I replied. He said the *Times* had never reviewed his recently published book. "Do you think that's fair?" he asked. No, I agreed. The memoir of such an important figure deserved a review. I returned to Los Angeles, and I spoke to the book editor. I wrote a generally complimentary review of the entertaining and enlightening book, tempered by my feeling that Artie hadn't told it all.

Samish, with his system of "elect and select," maintained his cadre of loyal legislators with campaign contributions, legal fees to lawyer legislators, and other payments. He also used fear. "Locked in the big safe in my outer office are the black books I kept on every senator and assemblyman," he said. "My staff and I found out everything there was to know about the lawmakers, and I mean everything. It all went into those little black books. Come election time, they could prove mighty handy."[14]

It was a corrupt system that was as typical of Sacramento as the summer heat. Legislators were poorly paid and often broke. Some were in the habit of prowling restaurant bars looking for lobbyists—cynically called pigeons—to buy them a meal. This was known as "the pigeon walk."[15] "The legislature was miserably underpaid and [that] made them really, really dependent on their outside income," Unruh said. "This made them more dependent upon, more importantly, members of the Third House, the lobbyists, who were always around willing to pick up a tab."[16]

Years of such freeloading and worse had left the legislature captive to the lobbyists and their employers. In the late 1930s, the situation had turned so scandalous that the local district attorney launched an investigation, headed by a detective, Herbert L. Philbrick, who wrote a detailed report that makes fascinating reading more than a half a century later. Among Philbrick's revelations is the story of Assemblyman Charles Hunt, who had worked sporadically as a railroad fireman. At the end of his first session in 1933, Hunt announced to his wife, Anna: "I am going to get all I can, anything above $25 for my vote influence." At the end of the 1935 session, he handed her $5,000 in cash. Nothing came of Philbrick's report, which was published in a daily legislative journal but later eliminated in a revised version.[17]

Assemblyman Ralph Dills became a legislator a year after the report was released. He recalled the contrast between the lawmakers' poverty and the luxuries offered by the lobbyists. "We had no air conditioning in those Assembly chambers," he said. "It was hot, no committee rooms with air conditioning, no room for the legislators at all." In Sacramento, he lived in motels. "Buckets of blood. They were way out of town. You know those transient motels? That's all I could afford." But it wasn't entirely grim. "The lobbyists were very, very generous with their meals and taking you places," he said. "They'd have a train and run us over to Reno and we'd go over there and gamble and we would come back the same night or stay over there if we wanted to."[18]

John Moss, an assemblyman who later was elected to Congress, remembered a night in 1953, two years before Unruh arrived. It was at the end of a legislative session, and lobbyists filled the assembly gallery. "It was late at night and they were carousing," Moss recalled. "I didn't think they were funny; I thought they were disgusting. There'd been too much drinking as there frequently is at the tail end of a session." Moss demanded that the speaker, Sam Collins, who was regarded as being controlled by the lobbyists, clear the gallery. "He wouldn't turn my mike on; he wouldn't recognize me. So I stood on the floor, and I just roared until he had no alternative but to recognize me. I decided if you don't recognize me, you're not going to proceed." Finally, Collins cleared the gallery.[19]

To an outsider, the Capitol scene was a mess, an unmanageable collection of greedy lawmakers and manipulative special interest lobbyists, all pursuing their own goals—for the legislators, a meal, a trip to Reno; for the lobbyists, a bill that would save their employers millions. The always-perceptive Samish saw the Capitol for what it really was—an entirely manageable system of interests and individuals whom he could manipulate. Possession of such knowledge, and the ruthlessness needed to use it, put him in control.

It was, as the journalist Gladwin Hill said, "the clever manipulation of disparate interests." Former state attorney general Robert Kenny described it to Hill: "Samish invented the invisible lobby in California. If a legislator tried to move against the banks, then the oil companies, insurance companies, trucking concerns and railroads all would join in helping out the banks. It was a system of mutual aid."[20]

Yet it was more. Although Unruh would not have liked to be compared to Samish, he came to see the legislature in the same way Artie did. Unruh, too, understood that the legislature was a collection of individuals, each with foibles, weaknesses, and strengths. Just as important, these individuals were part of a system in which interest groups, sometimes allies, sometimes foes, were bidding for the lawmakers' support. To master the legislature, to be the boss, the leader had to control the manipulators and the manipulated.

Samish was the most famous lobbyist. But other interests were more influential in the legislature than his beer, bus, and racetrack clients, and they had more sway over the state's economy. These advocates, however, were more than happy to surrender the spotlight—and the accompanying heat—to Samish.[21]

Of all the interests in the mid 1950s, none was more influential in the Capitol than oil, then providing much of California's wealth. It was a turning point for the industry. With the decrease of inland oil sources, oil prospectors were looking offshore, where the tidelands fields had been put into play when President Dwight D. Eisenhower signed the Submerged Lands Act. His action ended decades of controversy between the states and the federal government over control of oil in the tidelands, submerged land within the territorial boundaries of the United States. The law gave California jurisdiction from the surface to the ocean bottom in an area extending three miles beyond the coastline.[22]

The potential of the tidelands oil fields was huge. Joe B. Hudson, an oil company geologist, told a meeting of petroleum geologists during this period that more than 10 billion barrels of oil could be found in the California tidelands.[23] Yet the state clearly had a role, both to regulate the drilling and to obtain revenue from the oil. "The state now had to bring order to its domain," Robert Sollen writes. "Free of effective control, the offshore oil industry had ravaged coastal resources. It polluted air, land and water, created a visual blight and left dangerous and unsightly debris as each field was depleted and abandoned."[24] Lou Cannon writes:

> Two kinds of companies competed for the offshore oil fields, the majors or Big Oil, which generally ran integrated oil-well-to-service station operations, and the independents, or Little Oil, which discovered and drilled for oil, selling it to refiners. California immediately became the battleground for a fight between Big Oil . . . and Little Oil. Little Oil was big by any commercial standard except in comparison with such economic giants as Standard and Shell. In addition to those companies, Big Oil included the giants of Signal, Union and Texaco. Little Oil included Pauley, Wilshire and Superior.[25]

The Superior Oil Company had been founded in 1921 by William M. Keck, one of the West's most successful oil prospectors, or wildcatters, and a stalwart of the oil lobby. Keck was supporting Smith for speaker in the race in which Unruh was supporting Lincoln.[26] Smith seemed to be the best choice for the oil men, given his conservative philosophy and his home in Southern California, site of the offshore fields.

Keck had the knack of finding oil in areas passed over by the less lucky and skilled. As an example, there's the story of Keck and Andrew Joughin, who had a strawberry and wheat farm in Torrance, several miles south of Los Angeles. It was at the height of the 1920s Los Angeles oil boom, and wildcatters were searching the hills and flatlands for drilling sites. Joughin tried to interest wildcatters in exploring his farm, but none offered a deal except Keck and his partner, who leased 600 acres. The partner sold half his share. Keck's instincts were better. He retained his 300 acres, and his 46 highly productive wells were considered one of California's most successful oil-drilling projects.[27]

Keck operated in Sacramento with the same kind of aggressiveness, helped by two men who became part of the folklore of Sacramento lobbying. Unlike Samish, Keck's attorney Harold Morton and lobbyist Monroe Butler have left no autobiographies. Nor did they make Samish's mistake of bragging to journalists. But their footprints through the Capitol are preserved in the memories of the legislators who had to deal with them.

Morton was a domineering, demanding man who worked out of his office in downtown Los Angeles. Democrat Allen Miller, a lawyer running for the assembly in Los Angeles, encountered him in 1952 when a friend, who was a lobbyist for the funeral and cement industries, offered to introduce him to Morton. "Well, I've heard of him and who he represents," Miller replied. "I don't know I would particularly like to have a contribution from him."[28]

Miller said Morton "was making inroads for Keck and the so-called independents in influencing the Senate. The scuttlebutt around was that a lot of the guys in the assembly were on the take from Morton and the Keck interests." But the friend persisted. Miller, wanting to meet on his own turf, offered to treat Morton to lunch at the University Club in downtown Los Angeles. "No," said the friend. "I don't think Mr. Morton wants to work that way." Morton wanted Miller to come to his office, which would put him in the role of supplicant rather than luncheon host. Miller declined, but after several such discussions, Miller's friend finally persuaded him to visit the Morton office.

Miller recalled: "Mr. Morton told me, 'We need men of your caliber in the legislature. We need men of your integrity . . . I want to help you.'" Morton, he said, fumbled in his drawer "with hundred dollar bills. And finally he came up and gave me a package. It turned out, I think, there were either five or 10 hundred dollar bills." Miller said he would have to report the contribution. "Well, most of the fellows just don't want to do that," Miller remembered Morton saying.

After he was elected, Miller voted against one of Morton's bills. Morton, who was waiting in the back of the assembly, asked the sergeant at arms, Tony Beard, to bring Miller over. "I never saw a man so livid in the face. He called me 'double crossing, double dealing' and said 'I thought we were friends.' . . . So you can't tell me that [those who make] contributions to campaigns don't expect quid pro quos," Miller said.

Not all the lobbyists were so publicly demanding. But polite or rude, they all were determined to defeat Lincoln, as Unruh and several newcomers learned after their election in November 1954. Unruh's friend Tom Rees, the newly elected Democratic assemblyman, said, "I would have assemblymen call me up and kind of hint I could get all these things if I switched my vote to Smith. I was considered a Lincoln vote. Votes were switching around, guys were going one way or another. They were going around the corner to make a deal on chairmanships."[29]

Rees recalled a visit from a lobbyist representing one of Samish's old clients, the beer industry. "He was a real old time lobbyist, he really looked like a lobbyist. . . . He had these jowls, this soulful look and these big bug eyes that would stare at you.

"Right after the campaign, I was really broke," Rees reminisced. "He said, 'That was an interesting campaign and I would like to help you with your deficit,' and he peeled off several hundred dollar bills, I forgot how many. Staring at my eyes, he slowly pushed the one hundred dollar bills toward me across my desk, and I slowly pushed the hundred dollar bills back to him, saying 'I'm sorry, we didn't have a deficit, so we don't need the money.' It really killed me because I could have used some rest and relaxation. I was flat broke. I couldn't even go to Palm Springs."[30]

Unruh had similar experiences when he, firmly in the Lincoln camp, arrived in Sacramento. He described them in an illuminating *Reader's Digest* article in 1960, "This Is How Payola Works in Politics," by "Assemblyman X" (actually Unruh), as told to Lester Velie, the *Colliers* magazine writer who got Samish to talk. Unruh said, "At the capital, I found both sides— good government rebels and Third House—scrambling frantically to switch the few votes that would decide the issue. Lobbyists who had formerly shunned me now showed great concern for me." One offered to pay his campaign deficit, which Unruh estimated at $300. The lobbyist said, "don't give that $2,000 deficit another thought." Just vote, he said, for the lobbyist's candidate for speaker "and we'll take care of it for you." It was only later, when several other lobbyists "also offered to clean up my '$2,000 deficit' that I realized I was being offered a bribe."[31]

The count for Lincoln and Smith tightened, with Lincoln's tally showing him ahead, as the election of speaker neared. Lincoln offered the post of majority leader to a Republican "who was kind of known as a lobbyist Samish type," Unruh said. "Lincoln bought [him] pure and simply by giving him what the other side . . . had already promised to somebody else, and that was the chairmanship of [the] Public Utilities and Corporations [Committee], which in those days was very important because they had railroads and the truckers, and those were two big, important lobby groups."[32]

Election day for speaker was Monday, January 3, 1955, the first day of the legislative session, and Unruh's first day on the job, although he had visited Sacramento to prepare for it.

Lincoln nervously kept score on a tally sheet as the voting proceeded. Weeks before, he had had 51 pledges, "But I knew that I wasn't going to get 51 votes. I did hope to get 44 or 45. When they got down to my name, I could see I had lost a couple already and I had over halfway to go. I was forced to vote for myself which didn't seem right to me at the time, but as I look back now, I could say it's done all the time."[33] The AP reporter wrote: "There were chuckles throughout the chamber when Lincoln voted for himself—it was that close—and when it became Smith's turn to vote, his name was called twice. Then he voted for himself.[34]

"When Assemblyman Jesse M. Unruh voted for Lincoln, he announced that it was the 40th vote." The forty-first came from one of the most talented of the reformers, Republican Caspar Weinberger of San Francisco, who had recently led a cleanup of the corrupt administration of state liquor laws and would eventually be secretary of defense under President Ronald Reagan.[35]

Weinberger's vote put Lincoln in the speaker's office. Lincoln "was very nice to me," said Unruh, whose friend Munnell had "produced my vote and a couple others." Munnell's reward was chairmanship of the assembly's Finance and Insurance Committee, one of the legislature's most coveted "juice" committees, so called because of the big campaign contributions—juice—that could be squeezed from businesses needing to pass or kill legislation.

Munnell appointed Unruh chairman of a subcommittee. The appointment put Unruh in the legislative game and was a signal that he was a young man worth cultivating. As he put it in the Assemblyman X article: "My first two years were the happiest I've known. A freshman's life is a fine uncomplicated thing. Most lobbyists don't know you well enough to expect anything from you. They are sizing you up in the hope of future favors." As for himself, "As a pure (and priggish) freshman, I'd pass up the town's finest restaurant—where lobbyists took lawmakers—and grimly eat my bacon-and-tomato sandwich at a cafeteria." In fact, a colleague said of Unruh's cafeteria meals, "He ate everything."[36]

As his choice of a dining spot showed, Unruh's immediate concern was money. He had little, and a wife and four children to support. He was paid $300 a month plus a small per diem when the legislature was in session. He moved into a $50-a-month room at the Elks Club, a fifteen-story building that had towered above Sacramento since 1925. The elegant ballroom, art deco lobby, gymnasium, and large basement swimming pool were remnants of a simpler time when the Elks and similar clubs had been an important force in the life of a city like Sacramento, then still very much part of rural California. The small, spare rooms were used by visiting Elks and impoverished legislators.

Unruh would recall this period of his life in an unpublished memoir he was to write thirty years later. The language is stilted, not the way Unruh spoke, but it does give a picture of his life then:

I was elected to the California legislature when I was quite young, before I made any money whatsoever and with a large family. [During the summer, he returned to his job in the rail yards counting freight cars.] This was a very unsatisfactory arrangement [but] necessary because we simply did not have enough income to exist. . . . We had a particularly difficult time when it came to deciding whether to move my family to Sacramento or not. If you did not take your family to the state capitol in those days you were faced with the dilemma of trying to get home on weekends [on] over 400 miles of not very good highway and eight to 10 hours each way. That meant if the legislature adjourned on Friday noon, it would be late Friday night before you got home and necessitated leaving around noon on Sunday if you were to get any kind of sleep before the session began again on Monday.[37]

On the rare occasions his family visited him, "We would put a pallet down on the floor and my wife or I would sleep on the pallet with one of the kids and the other would sleep in the bed with the other kid." But mostly he was away from the family for the six months of the session. "To move a family to Sacramento and maintain a second home for a large family such as mine was an almost impossible expense for us so I lived the life of a single man," he said.[38] He increasingly enjoyed it, and Virginia saw their marriage beginning to slip away:

> Getting up there and getting back home was a problem. We didn't have the money for him to fly. He used to have to drive up. And somebody else went with him. And they would drive up there and he would come back at the end of the week. And then it would end up it seemed like there were some weeks he didn't come back. He just stayed away. Things got kind of difficult then between us. That's when it started to come apart. And then there was a girl up there, too, that was clinging around. Yeah, he liked the ladies.

Eventually, Unruh got an apartment. "I think he had a girlfriend, too," Virginia said. "That was a source of tension. I was stuck at home with the kids and he was flying high." They argued, but "it didn't do much good. . . . He was stubborn and difficult. He kept having these girlfriends on the side and that didn't sit too well, with me sitting at home with all the kids." Yet they remained married. "We just barely stayed married. That was because of the kids. What would I do with a house full of kids by myself? I couldn't take care of them and work [to] support them. . . . If that had happened, he would take off on his own. And I'd be left holding the bag. I'd be working and taking care of the kids, both."[39]

As a single man, Unruh roamed through a male-dominated society where lobbyists and legislators were big men chasing underpaid secretaries. Life was not all bacon-and-tomato sandwiches in the cafeteria. His rough, blunt, profane, blue-collar manner fitted in well around the Capitol. He was smarter than most of the legislators. And he could be friendly and sociable, interested in what made a colleague tick, always trying to figure out the system. He liked to drink, to sit around with the veterans—many of them like him, crude, foulmouthed, and fond of alcohol—and learn their tricks. He had a wicked, clever sense of humor. Even the conservative old-timers enjoyed his company.

Take, for example, an evening in his first term with a tough and powerful veteran, Senator Earl Desmond, who represented Sacramento. Hoping to get some publicity in the Los Angeles papers, Unruh had introduced a bill to outlaw draw poker, which was, and is, legal in California. Draw poker parlors were a tradition in Sacramento, which still retained a trace of the frontier town it once was. As a result, Unruh's bill attracted the disapproving attention of Senator Desmond.

One night, Desmond ran into Unruh and his friend Assemblyman Tom Rees at Bedell's, a restaurant and bar a block from the Capitol that was a hangout for lobbyists, legislators, and reporters. Desmond confronted Unruh over the poker bill. The story of the evening was told by Rees in an oral history, one of many oral histories that provide a view into the California legislature that is far more graphic, human, and enlightening than the usual academic studies or newspaper stories of the day.

"He had balls of brass," Rees said of Desmond, "and he was head of the Governmental Efficiency Committee in the Senate. That was the committee that would kill your bills. If your bill was sent there you just said, 'Hail Mary' and said good-bye to it. He didn't care who it was; he had no fears. And he was a very conservative Democrat. He didn't even recognize the assembly, and especially young assemblymen."

Rees said Desmond "had had a few belts." He offered to show Unruh and Rees some poker parlors.

And so we went with him, and we went into some of the toughest places I have ever seen. . . . Desmond was okay in the first couple places. They knew him; he was drinking his Old Crow. [Then] We went into one place and the owner didn't know who Desmond was. [Desmond demanded that the owner] set up some God damn whisky . . . the bartender was not laughing. . . . We really felt we were going to have to fight our way out of that bar when the place got raided. Of course they all knew Earl Desmond and one guy from the sheriff's department said, "Senator, I'll take you home. Can you guys take Desmond's car?" We were in no condition to take Desmond's car but Unruh said "Oh yeah, no problem." So we get Desmond's car and followed this captain . . . back to Desmond's place out in the suburbs. I think Jesse knocked over something and then the captain brought us back to Sacramento.

"We woke up the next day feeling terrible," Rees said. During the legislative meeting later in the morning, Desmond came into the assembly chamber, bringing with him Hugh M. Burns, the president pro tem of the senate, a kingpin of the legislature. Desmond shouted, "Where the hell are Unruh and Rees? Those bastards drank me under the table last night. Where are you? I want to take you out to lunch."

"So we went to the Senate lunching place and were the honored guests of Earl Desmond and Hugh Burns. That's what it takes to get to know people in Sacramento."[40]

As he made acquaintances and friends, Unruh analyzed the situation from his vantage point as a junior member of assembly speaker Lincoln's team.

The Capitol was still a political marketplace, Unruh realized. The same men tossing cash around during the speakership election continued to prowl the Capitol halls and hang out at the Senator Hotel. Many years later, Unruh described the legislative politics after Lincoln became speaker. Life, he noted, had changed from the immediate post-Samish days. He said, "the most powerful interests . . . were not as interested in getting things through the assembly . . . as they were in seeing that things didn't get through the legislature and, by and large, what most of the business interests tried to do in those days, having had some very good years before that and having had Artie Samish build in the kind of tax advantages that the liquor industry and the wine industry and beer and horseracing enjoyed, they were not so much concerned with fighting an offensive battle as they were in defending what they already won and they were spectacularly successful in that."[41]

If Unruh couldn't beat them, he could at least figure them out and turn the system to his own advantage. He made friends with lobbyists. One of them was Charles R. Stevens, lobbyist for four oil companies, Standard, Shell, Richfield, and General Petroleum. Stevens was the highest-paid advocate in the Capitol.[42]

Another of Unruh's best connections occurred unexpectedly. One day, a courteous man with the manner of an accomplished salesman visited Unruh in his office. He was Robert M. DeKruif, right-hand man to Howard Ahmanson Sr., owner of Home Savings and Loan Association, two insurance companies, and a bank, as well as being a fund-raiser, adviser, and friend to Governor Knight. Ahmanson was a pioneer in California's postwar savings and loan industry, which financed much of the state's housing construction in the growth years of the 1950s, 1960s, and 1970s. But despite Unruh's position on the Finance and Insurance Committee and his potential influence over savings and loan and insurance legislation, DeKruif wasn't calling on him for help with these many enterprises. His request was more modest.

A friend of Ahmanson's, Howard Edgerton, another savings and loan owner, was deeply involved in supporting the aging Los Angeles County Museum of Science and Industry, located in Unruh's district in Exposition Park, adjacent to USC. Edgerton wanted Unruh to introduce legislation, backed by the governor, to modernize the old museum. He had asked the more influential Ahmanson for help, and Ahmanson had dispatched DeKruif to Unruh's office.

Unruh was, DeKruif remembered, dressed inexpensively. Despite his rough, unschooled manner, Unruh had a charming way about him. Unruh was seated at his desk, and DeKruif stood. "I was trained as a salesman by Howard Ahmanson, and I used to call on ten people a day to try to get their insurance business" said DeKruif. "Howard would never let me sit down. He said never sit down. And give them one constructive thought and get out." DeKruif made his pitch and left. The short visit was the beginning of Unruh's long friendship with DeKruif and with Ahmanson, who, over the years, had many occasions to call on Unruh for help with legislation much more directly related to his business.[43]

The visit was part of the education of a rookie, although Unruh was better schooled than most of the new legislators. USC student politics, his battles with the Left, his tutelage by union friends, and his assembly campaigns had taught him the fundamentals. But the twists and turns of the Capitol were new, and as his first session drew to a close, he pondered the lessons. He still burned with anger over discrimination and the power big business had over working people like him. Months in Sacramento had awakened him to the challenges faced by the state, of the need for schools, child care centers, mental hospitals, and higher taxes to pay for it all. He had also learned about the many interests standing in the way of reaching those goals.

His friend Bob Wells remembered talking to Unruh when he returned home from the session. "The next day or the day after he came over, and we ran out of booze, and he and I went to the liquor store to get some more. And he was talking all the way there about what he found out in the first session. He said 'It's easy to be a hero. You can get up there and talk a lot. Come back and be a great liberal. Or a great conservative. And [with] your core constituency, [you] get a lot of applause when you appear before them. But none of those people are effective. And I mean to be effective.' It seemed to me that this was the biggest lesson he learned."[44]

He saw the tension inherent in trying to appeal to liberal Democratic activists in his district, and outside it, while becoming a leader in a legislature so dominated by lobbyists and their corporate and union bosses. The pragmatic, even cynical, course he chose permitted him to accomplish much. But it limited Unruh, too, throwing him in with men he would have scorned a few years before.

SIX

Segregation and the
Unruh Civil Rights Act

IN THE MID 1950S, Californians liked to brag that their state was different from the Deep South, free of Jim Crow segregation. But in truth a web
of laws, judicial decisions, regulations, and customs in California had the
effect of segregating whites, blacks, Latinos, Asian Americans, and, to a
lesser extent, Jews.

A good example of how racial segregation worked in that era can be
found in the district Unruh represented in the assembly and the neighborhoods around it. The area was full of racial tension, even violence, after
African Americans began to move from an overcrowded ghetto to neighborhoods that provided better homes, yards, and public schools. Counter-
ing the discrimination was the civil rights movement, both in Los Angeles
and across the country. The movement began in the 1940s, with demonstrations against housing and job segregation and the frequent police bru-
tality that supported such practices. The historian Josh Sides writes:

> Most Americans did not recognize its [the movement's] presence until the late
> 1950s . . . [but] for urban blacks, especially in the western United States, the
> dramatic events of the 1960s were the culmination of at least two decades of
> struggle for equality. Leading that struggle were the thousands of African
> American migrants who had defiantly left the South, determined to finally
> and fully share in the country's new prosperity. The act of migration itself was
> the cornerstone of the new movement, bringing black people intent on equal-
> ity to cities where that equality was conceivable. Further infusing the ranks
> were returning black veterans, emboldened by military service during the
> war.[1]

The veterans also brought idealism, energy, and fearlessness to Mexican
American neighborhoods. During the war, Mexican Americans had found
themselves targets of a deadly combination of hostile police, courts, and

press. When the body of a teenager was found near an open reservoir, named Sleepy Lagoon after a popular song, 300 Mexican Americans were arrested, and 23 of them were charged with murder. The press was inflammatory in its coverage, the judge oblivious to the defendants' rights. One of Los Angeles's first civil rights organizations, the Sleepy Lagoon Defense Committee, fought back, and the defendants were acquitted and freed in 1944.[2]

In 1943, servicemen went on a rampage in Los Angeles against Mexican Americans wearing zoot suits—long jackets with wide shoulders, pegged and pleated trousers, long key chains, and wide-brimmed, flattop hats. Police arrested the zoot suiters rather than the servicemen, and, as an example of the slanted news coverage, the *Los Angeles Daily News* delightedly reported "zoot suit . . . gangs of hoodlums continued to lose their trousers to service men, and in many cases nearly lost what was in 'em."[3]

With the veterans a driving force, Latino community leaders built on the organizing done on behalf of the Sleepy Lagoon and zoot suit defendants. They formed civil rights and political organizations, including the Asociación Nacional México-Americana, the American GI Forum, and the Community Service Organization.[4]

The development of the civil rights movement in black and Latino communities would in later years shape California's political development. But in the mid 1950s, Unruh focused his immediate attention on African Americans, by far the largest minority group in his predominantly white district.

Unruh's attitude toward them was shaped by his boyhood. He had been outraged by white treatment of blacks in Texas and Kansas. The anger he had felt about segregated housing during his years at USC remained with him when he was elected to office. Yet growing up in Texas gave him an understanding of the views of southern and southwestern working people, and led him to view the civil rights movement through a cautious filter. He knew his boyhood friends and his generation of southwestern immigrants—a growing part of the California electorate—would shy away from, if not implacably oppose, the civil rights movement. Civil rights, to Unruh, were not an academic or judicial exercise, or something to be discussed in liberal salons. Rather, they were part of a daily struggle of working-class neighborhoods like the ones that Unruh represented, and he had to walk the line between his personal beliefs and the conflicting feelings of his largely white constituency.

At the outset of his career, some African Americans were suspicious of the big man with the Texas accent and wary attitude toward their movement.

A friend from Unruh's early political days said that Unruh's relations with African Americans were not easy. "I am not going to tell you Jesse Unruh was a racist, but I just want to remind you where he was brought up, the environment [in which] he was brought up," said Joe Cerrell. One of Cerrell's jobs in Unruh's 1954 campaign was to deal with African American newspapers. "None of these people liked Unruh," he said. "They saw him as a phony liberal. They knew his background. They never thought he was a civil rights liberal."[5]

But Unruh was a person who saw that the economic obstacles faced by minorities were not too different from ones he'd faced when he was a boy. "Jess used to say . . . the black people and us were one as bad as the other," his nephew Paul said. "I told him except for one thing. We were white." Even as a boy, Unruh was deeply troubled by treatment of blacks, Paul remembered.[6] "From the time I knew him, I would say civil rights was an overriding priority [of his]," said his friend Bob Wells.[7]

But the political and social atmosphere in which he operated did not favor civil rights activism. Whites lived in one world and California's minorities in another. Because neighborhoods were segregated and the newspapers ignored minorities, most whites heard little about incidents involving racial discrimination.

To put Unruh's attitude in perspective, take my own experiences growing up in the San Francisco Bay Area during this period. I was unaware of the problems facing blacks. I thought California was an open and free society, with opportunity for all. I noticed, but was not especially troubled by, a sign at our suburban public pool that said "Colored Patronage Not Solicited." I was one of just a few Jews in our public schools, but except for an occasional remark, I never experienced anti-Semitism until I enrolled at the University of California at Berkeley and saw how religion and race segregated fraternities and sororities. We Jews had our own fraternities and sororities and were not admitted to other clubs.

White California lived in an atmosphere of benign ignorance. I began to truly understand this in the first days of my career in the 1950s. The newspaper where I worked printed no news of blacks in our city—either good or bad. I once covered a horrible murder-suicide in a housing project in West Oakland, the black section of the city, involving the deaths of a father, a mother, and their children. My editor asked their color. I said black. He held his thumb and index fingers about an inch apart in a manner that signified he wanted a very short story, befitting people whose deaths were not deemed worthy of notice. Reports I filed on racial battles in the public schools went unprinted. Nor did the paper employ blacks.

This sort of journalism was widespread in California and, in fact, the rest of the West. When J. Edward Murray, managing editor of the *Los Angeles Mirror,* assigned Paul Weeks to do stories on the black community in the mid 1950s, some of Weeks's colleagues criticized him to his face. "Paul, the way you are writing those stories, you would think you were part nigger," one of them said. In the 1950s, the *Los Angeles Times* would not send reporters into black neighborhoods.[8]

The *Mirror* was owned by the much bigger *Times,* and Weeks said that Murray's inclination to investigate Los Angeles's social problems was risky because of the attitude of "his *Times* overseers . . . as I recall the *Times* frowned on the series I wrote for the *Mirror* on the blacks moving into LA, their problems with employment, housing and education." When the *Mirror* was closed in 1962, Weeks moved to the *Times.* Frank McCullough, one of the managing editors, told him: "We're doing a pretty good job covering the situation in Mississippi and Alabama, but would I look at what we're doing in our own backyard?" Weeks said blacks were "at first suspicious of anyone wanting to put anything in the white press about them. And I didn't blame them." He recalled reporters covering the police "characterizing murders, rapes, and so on among blacks as misdemeanor crimes," not worthy of coverage. "When the crime became black upon white, it could reach headlines."

Weeks got into trouble with his bosses when he protested the ejection of a black reporter working for an African American newspaper, the *Sentinel,* from a meeting of a segregationist organization. Eventually, Weeks was taken off the civil rights beat. When he left the beat in 1964, he told his editor, "This town is going to blow up one of these days, and the *Times* won't know what hit it." His prediction came true a year later in the Watts riots.[9]

State politics was white, too. Even though African Americans and Latinos were an important part of the Democratic Party's base, the party was led by whites. I encountered few African Americans or Latinos when covering Democratic politics in the early 1960s. When Unruh was running for the state assembly in 1954, three members of the Young Democrats complained to the council because it had not backed a black for assembly in a neighboring district. "For some 500,000 Negro citizens in California and 18 million in the U.S. there is a lack of political representation," they said. "That this situation is on so wide a scale and over so long a period of time indicates the seriousness of it."[10]

Whites led the most liberal Democratic organization, the California Democratic Council. No African Americans were among the CDC's thirty-eight directors in 1961, and no president of a congressional district council was black.[11] The CDC was committed to civil rights, but its leaders' main concerns were Cold War issues, such as disarmament, recognition of Communist China, and détente with the Soviet Union.

James Q. Wilson noted in 1962 that "at CDC conventions and conferences very few Negroes are in evidence even though the total attendance may number three or four thousand people from every part of the state and those Negroes present are usually seen keeping to themselves, outside the flow of events at the meeting."[12] Mervyn Dymally, then a young African American leader, recalled picketing a CDC convention because there were no blacks on the executive committee. He described the CDC leadership's attitude as "saying, in effect, look, we are pure, we are for civil rights. We are for Dr. King. We are for fair employment practices. We are for fair housing, et cetera. Why do we necessarily have to have a black in the executive council to prove we are liberal?"[13]

Blacks had limited power, even under Unruh's liberal speakership. Dymally was an assemblyman elected in 1962 in a Los Angeles district that Unruh had created in the 1961 reapportionment to ensure the election of an African American. Dymally was appreciative of what Unruh had done for him and was a loyal follower. But, he said, "I strongly resented the fact that, as close as Unruh and I were, his inner working circle was still all white . . . there were only three blacks in the Assembly but political integration is something I felt strongly about. . . . In the context of black politics I was close to Unruh. But in the context of the leadership . . . I wasn't part of Unruh's operation . . . I was part of his outer circle."[14]

Labor was ambivalent. The AFL-CIO supported legislation to ban discrimination in hiring.[15] Even so, a substantial number of union leaders and members were hostile to integrated workplaces. "In postwar America, the much-celebrated solidarity and communion of unionized workers was as often a barrier to integration as it was a facilitator," Josh Sides notes.[16]

In 1949, the Unruh family had moved into a neighborhood where one in three residents was black.[17] Their new home was in a two-story frame apartment house on the eastern edge of the Sixty-fifth Assembly District he later represented, a few blocks from USC. It was a pleasant neighborhood of small bungalows, apartment houses, and larger homes, all of them with yards and access to better public schools than were available in the Central Avenue ghetto.

White resistance to black newcomers in the area was strong, and it reached from adults down to children. Three years before, white and black teenagers had fought in front of a malt shop across from Manual Arts High School, near USC. A police officer told the Los Angeles County Human Relations Committee that "there has been an antagonistic white group south of Exposition Park which has banded together to keep Negroes out of their community through restrictive covenants. The adults may have communicated their attitudes to their children."[18]

Near the Unruh apartment was Figueroa Street, a broad boulevard that was the unofficial barrier to black migration westward. The migration west was spotty, slow—contested all the way by white residents. It took courage and determination for Unruh's black neighbors to move across Figueroa.

West of the Unruh apartment, block after block of modest homes reached westward to the hills separating the Los Angeles flatlands from the sea, many of them based on the California Craftsman design, although on much smaller lots than the more elegant Craftsman houses in Pasadena. Modest, perhaps, but they were at the heart of the LA home-owning soul, explaining the intensity with which whites and blacks fought over possession of them.

A few miles east of the Unruh apartment, the black Central Avenue area was miserably overcrowded, a condition that began with the great migration of blacks from the South to obtain the aircraft plant and shipyard jobs that opened up to them during World War II. A militant newspaper publisher, Charlotta Bass, who owned the *California Eagle,* an African American community paper, remembered it with a fury that remained many years later when she wrote her memoirs. "Due to the great influx of Negro people at that time, especially from the South, housing conditions were at their lowest level," she wrote. "It was pathetic. Negro families who came to work in the war industries were forced to live in old garages, broken down storefronts, deserted railroad coaches, thatched tents—all without sanitary conveniences."[19] As Bass put it: "Is it a crime in America for a Negro, or Jew, or Mexican or Chinese to live next door to a man who is none of these?"[20]

Covenants in property deeds restricted the sale or occupancy of homes in most of Los Angeles and surrounding cities to whites. In practice, the restrictions extended to guests. Bob Wells and his wife were evicted from an apartment south of USC when an African American friend visited.[21]

The areas around USC, including parts of Unruh's assembly district, were the sites of intense fights over civil rights, as African American families sought to move out of the Central Avenue ghetto. "Many Negro families were driven from their homes," wrote Charlotta Bass. "Crosses were burned by the Ku Klux Klan in front of people's homes who were sympathetic to the Negro homeowners as well as before the Negroes' homes themselves." The author well remembered one morning when she opened the doors of the Eagle office and found KKK written on the sidewalk in letters a foot high.[22] Not long after World War II, some of America's greatest black entertainers, including Hattie McDaniel and Ethel Waters, had to go to court to defeat the West Adams Improvement Association's efforts to drive them from their mansions on Sugar Hill, an affluent neighborhood where both blacks and whites lived.[23]

Most of the battles were fought in more modest areas. If Los Angeles ever preserved monuments to its civil rights movement, many of them would be the homes of African Americans who moved into white neighborhoods. Half a century later, most of them still look the way they did when they were at the center of the storm, block after block of single-story bungalows on small lots, working-class homes for working-class people, the houses still neat, surrounded by their small yards, although thick burglar-proof bars on windows and doors attest to the increase in crime. The residents—blacks and Latinos—remain strongly blue-collar, very much like the whites who once lived there.

One of the most notorious cases of housing discrimination occurred during the early days of World War II. In 1942, Henry Laws and his family were ordered by a court to move from the home they owned in a predominantly white neighborhood on East Ninety-second Street, five miles south of the USC campus, south of the Central Avenue ghetto. The Laws, both working in war plants, had moved into the house with their daughters, Dolores Laws and Pauletta Fears, whose husband, Antone, was in the Navy and had been wounded in the 1941 attack on Pearl Harbor. The Laws's son Alfred was in the Army.

The Laws were unaware of a restrictive covenant in the deed. A real estate firm, apparently wanting to gain possession of the house, brought suit against them. Judge Roy V. Rhodes ordered them out of their home, a decision that was upheld in a second trial. The husband, wife, and two daughters moved out but had trouble finding another place and had to live in their automobile for a time.

At that point, Laws placed a telephone call to Charlotta Bass at the *California Eagle.* "What do you think we should do?" Laws asked Bass.

"Do?" replied Bass. "What should you do?'" Her voice furious, Bass said,

"You go back into your home and stay there. We'll fight this damnable condition until hell freezes over."[24] They moved back into the house and said they were willing to go jail rather than move.

Their plight attracted wide attention in the black community and beyond. A biracial organization, the Home Protective Association, was formed, with Charlotta Bass as chair. But on November 30, 1945, Judge Allen W. Ashburn ruled they had to leave their home or go to jail. Again, they declined. More than 1,000 demonstrated in front of the house the Sunday before their scheduled arrest. But, as Mrs. Bass reported, "The police car finally came, however, and Mr. and Mrs. Henry Laws, and their daughter, Pauletta Fears, were taken to jail. Dolores was not home at the time, and so escaped the indignity." Antone Fears and Alfred Laws returned from the service to find their family in jail. Eventually, the family won its battle and remained in the house when courts began ruling against racial covenants.

The jailing of the Laws while their son and son-in-law were in the service illustrated the gap between the idealistic goals espoused by America in the war and the way things actually worked. "Young men serving their country . . . began asking questions," wrote Bass. "Why, they asked, should I fight to preserve a democracy that permits parents, sisters and wives to be jailed because they dare to live in their own homes?" said Bass. "Why should I bear arms in defense of a democracy like this?"

The same point was also eloquently made by Superior Court judge Stanley Mosk. In a decision in 1947 finding racial covenants unenforceable, Mosk ruled in favor of three African American families buying homes in the all white mid-Wilshire section of Los Angeles. He said: "Our nation has just fought against the Nazi race superiority doctrine. One of these defendants was in that war and is a Purple Heart veteran. This court would indeed be callous if it were to permit him to be ousted from his own home by using 'race' as the measure of his worth as a citizen and a neighbor."[25]

The U.S. Supreme Court overturned racially based restrictive covenants in a Missouri case, *Shelley vs. Kraemer* (334 U.S. 1), in 1948, but the decision did not stop resistance to integration in Los Angeles neighborhoods. Just months after the decision, a bungalow on a narrow lot just east of Figueroa, in a neighborhood that had become majority black, was damaged by arsonists. A burning cross greeted an African American physician when she bought a home west of Figueroa in 1949.

When Bessie Woods moved into a house she bought west of Figueroa early in 1950, neighbors called on her. While they, personally, had no objections to Negroes, they said, others did, and they advised Woods to move.[26] Leimert Park was a residential neighborhood on the western edge of the assembly district Unruh would one day represent. A home was trashed there one afternoon while the African American owner was briefly away during moving day.

"Clear out or face the consequences," warned a note placed on the door of a home on the southwestern edge of the assembly district after Angus and Ursula Bates, African Americans, purchased the frame story-and-a-half bungalow on West Forty-second Street. More warnings came in the next twenty-four months, followed by the burning of a small cross on the backyard lawn.[27]

William Bailey, a black junior high school teacher, moved into a single-story Spanish mission–style house in a predominantly white neighborhood half a dozen miles west of black Los Angeles. Moving west meant being closer to the ocean, cleaner air, better schools. Across the street was a two-story duplex, just sold to an African American fireman by the white owner, Bernard Hartstein. At 4 A.M. on Sunday, March 16, 1952, bombs shattered both the house and the duplex and broke windows on twenty other residences on the street. Nobody was injured, but the homes were badly damaged.[28]

On January 7, 1953, Dale Gardner, the executive secretary of the Los Angeles County Human Relations Committee, said that resistance to integration was centered in the working-class area south of downtown, an area that included USC and Unruh's future assembly district. "Several improvement associations and protective organizations have endeavored by various means to stop the westward movement of Negro families in that area," he said.[29]

A crowd gathered when blacks bought one of the bungalows on South St. Andrews Place late in 1952. Denied the use of Christ Lutheran Church, the white demonstrators gathered in a vacant lot to talk about how African Americans could be kept from the neighborhood.[30] Resistance continued into the late 1950s.

When blacks moved into a two-story home in the white Crenshaw area, notes warned them they would be bombed. When neighbors heard of a home owner selling to blacks in View Park, a hillside area to which African Americans were beginning to move, residents held a meeting to try to stop the sale, and rocks were thrown at the house.

Housing segregation was not the only outrage inflicted on minorities. Discrimination was sanctioned at high levels of government. In 1948, the

Los Angeles County counsel ruled that the county could sign contracts with hospitals and sanatoriums, paying them to provide care for the ill, even if the institutions discriminated. Even small steps against segregation by official Los Angeles met with intense resistance. A month before Unruh was elected to the state assembly in 1954, the Los Angeles City Fire Commission held a public hearing on Mayor Norris Poulson's proposal to end Fire Department segregation into white and black firehouses. Off-duty firemen and police officers blocked the entrances to the hearing room, refusing to allow African Americans to enter. George L. Thomas, who reported on the hearing to the Human Relations Committee, said that when he complained about the exclusion, one of the blockaders said, "There's one of you in there already and that's enough." Thomas commented, "Here in the United States of America—at least in one little corner of the U.S.—was totalitarianism at work."

In August 1944, at the height of World War II, Armando G. Torrez told the Human Relations Committee: "We know that right here in Southern California in some of the schools, we have separate classes for the Mexicans; that we deprive Mexican youngsters of the use of public plunges except on the day water is to be changed, the excuse on investigation being that these youngsters were dirty and would contaminate the water."[31]

Such incidents were rarely reported by the newspapers of the day. Even though white defiance of the law was occurring in and around his assembly district, Unruh did not take up the civil rights cause until his friend Marvin Holen showed him a small story in a newspaper.

Holen, an orphan, had been raised in a foster home in Los Angeles. He commuted to UCLA by hitchhiking, served as a Marine combat officer during the Korean War, and graduated from UCLA law school. While working as a page at the CBS studio in Los Angeles, he became friends with a fellow usher, Sam Hartog, a GI Bill student at USC and a member of Unruh's college political gang. That led to a friendship with Unruh. Holen, like Unruh, had not been involved in the civil rights movement.

"It started in October or November of 1958," Holen said. "I was sitting on the floor of a friend's house reading the *Herald*. I ran across a small item which said the state supreme court okayed the refusal by the Hollywood Professional School to exclude a black girl solely because of her race. . . . So I told Jesse about this, and his visceral reaction was strong. We thought about it, and we decided to put in a bill in the legislature to do something about it . . . this was just Jesse and myself."

By 1958, Unruh was a rising young legislator. He had used his position as chairman of a Finance and Insurance subcommittee to hold well-publicized hearings in Los Angeles and San Francisco. Holen, just out of UCLA law school, was special counsel to the subcommittee. Unruh had also distinguished himself as Southern California chairman of Attorney General Edmund G. Brown Sr.'s successful campaign for governor, leading to a Democratic sweep of statewide offices and control of the legislature.

Early in the 1959 session, Unruh became chairman of the most important committee in the assembly, Ways and Means, which handled every bill that might affect the budget, a source of immense power. He brought Holen to Sacramento with him as consultant to the committee. They became part of an administrative-legislative team committed to passing liberal programs that had long been on the Democratic agenda. The major administration civil rights bill, long espoused by civil rights organizations, was for creation of a Fair Employment Practices Commission to stop discrimination in employment.

Unruh and Holen moved into a three-office suite in the Capitol, along with Unruh's secretary, Marian Cerrell, mother of Joe Cerrell. Holen and Unruh shared a two-bedroom motel suite.

One of Holen's first tasks was to write a bill correcting the wrong visited on the African American girl denied admission to the Hollywood Professional School. Speaking of himself, Holen said, "this novice, this uneducated ignoramus in the law sat down to write this thing." He worked alone. "We were not part of any establishment," he said. "We came from nowhere."[32] Holen met with an attorney on the legislature's legal staff and drew up a bill that banned discrimination in a wide variety of institutions, ranging from private schools to restaurants, that served the public. "And we introduced it to a stunning silence," Holen said. "Nobody noticed it."[33]

Nobody, that is, except Franklin Williams Jr., president of the San Francisco chapter of the NAACP. He told Holen he appreciated Unruh's introduction of the bill, but that it didn't have a chance.[34]

Holen felt Williams was "looking down his nose at me," wondering about the motives of a legislator and his aide who had had little connection with the civil rights movement. "He was coming from a movement, from long hard work, from fund-raising efforts, from organizational efforts, from negotiations, from careful calculation of support and opposition . . . I just wandered in from left field. Jesse Unruh just wandered in from left field."

Holen, in his naïveté, thought the measure was a surefire winner. He was unaware of how many civil rights bills had been killed in the legislature. If he was shocked by Williams's pessimism, Williams was equally surprised by

Holen's ignorance of the civil rights movement. Williams explained that he and his organization had been working for a considerable period of time on a minor revision of some civil rights measures on the books, and that that was about all that could be expected from the legislature.

The few legislators who noticed may have believed the bill was an effort by Unruh to appease his African American constituents, or a publicity stunt, nothing worth serious attention. But by then Unruh, although not yet Big Daddy, was on his way to becoming a power to be taken seriously, and he was better connected than most lawmakers. "Jesse loved to carouse," Holen said. "He stayed out very late at night. I mean he'd come banging into the motel at 2 o'clock in the morning. He enjoyed his colleagues, they enjoyed Jesse."

When the bill was ready for its first committee hearing, opponents began to surface. Religious schools, cemeteries, fraternal organizations such as the Elks, and real estate dealers were among those demanding to be removed from the long list of groups named in the bill. At that point, Holen wrote and inserted a key phrase, declaring that Californians are entitled to equal accommodations "in all business establishments of every kind whatsoever." Holen recalled: "It was the broadest way that I could think of saying something. Remember, I never practiced a day of law. This was my way of speaking."[35]

"A lot of the members, in the committees particularly, began to think we were serious," said Holen. "Because Jesse was becoming more serious. Jesse was becoming a more serious power center. And we seemed wedded to this thing for some unknown reason."[36] By then, the NAACP's Frank Williams was also looking at the bill with more interest. Holen was struggling over language that would satisfy the growing number of critics when Williams dropped in to see him. He told Holen that he had a friend, Nathaniel Colley, who might be able to help.

Colley, on his way to becoming one of California's most influential African American leaders, was a graduate of Tuskegee Institute and, after rising from private to captain in the Army during World War II, distinguished himself as a student at Yale Law School, where he was known for his writing ability. He began practicing law in Sacramento in 1949 and six years later persuaded a white friend to buy him a lot in a restricted area called South Land Park. "When my mom would check on construction, she would let them think she was the maid," said Colley's son, Nat Jr. "After we moved in, there was a cross-burning on the lawn, but it was a fairly quiet experience after that."[37]

Colley looked at the bill, sized up the problem that Holen faced—the need for broad language that would overcome opponents' efforts to nibble away at sections of the measure. He came up with the words "All persons within the jurisdiction of this state are free and equal." This phrase, plus Holen's "business establishments of every kind whatsoever'" turned out to have the impact of broadening the bill far beyond the expectations of both supporters and opponents.

After passing the assembly, the bill moved on to the state senate. Rural counties controlled the senate in 1959. The forty districts were apportioned on the basis of geography, rather than population. It was designed to assure a voice for lightly populated rural counties. The "cow counties'" interests were protected, but their strength in the senate gave rural lawmakers a great influence—a veto, in fact—over legislation affecting the fast-growing urban and suburban portion of the state. And while a few liberal senators had been elected in 1958, the senate remained hostile to civil rights legislation. Such bills were sent to the senate Governmental Efficiency Committee, known as the graveyard for bills the senate leadership opposed.

That's where Unruh's civil rights bill landed. And there it stayed for three or four months. Holen recalled senators assuring opponents that the bill would never leave the committee. "We kept trying for a hearing and we somehow couldn't get it set," said Holen.

One afternoon, Unruh and Holen were standing near the secretary's desk when she completed a phone call to the senate Governmental Efficiency staff, inquiring when the bill would be considered by a committee. "Well," she said, "they've now taken it off [the schedule of bills to be heard] again." Unruh, Holen said, had returned from lunch "so maybe he had had a few drinks . . . and puts his 'grim mouth' on, nods his head up and down and says, 'We'll show them. Take every senate bill off the hearing schedule. Every senate bill.'"

Like so many of Unruh's decisions, this one was made quickly, probably under the influence of alcohol, the result of instinct and gut feelings rather than well-planned strategy.[38] It was also a sign of Unruh's growing confidence in himself, and in his skill as a legislator. "As the session wore on, Jesse began to accumulate authority, appreciate it and enjoy it. He was learning how to use it," Holen said. "This is the bill that was the crux of [his] education—the Unruh Civil Rights Act."[39]

Unruh well understood the power he held as chairman of Ways and Means. The committee had to approve any bill that involved state spending. The power gave the committee and its chairman enormous influence because most of the legislature's bills had to pass through it. By holding up the senate bills—on scores of subjects, ranging from important statewide proposals to the local projects that are the bread and butter of a legislator's life—Unruh had elevated himself to the ranks of a major power player.

The senate, which had always treated the assembly with disdain, had to deal with Unruh and his bill. The senate leaders relented, gave the bill a committee hearing, and sent it to the floor for a vote. But they waited until the final night of the legislature, a chaotic time when scores of bills are up for vote, many of them hurriedly amended. The Unruh bill came out of the committee looking very different from the original proposal, breaking the agreement Unruh thought he had with the senate leaders.

At first Holen felt the senators had severely weakened the bill. They had removed the list of the kinds of businesses covered by the measure. But they inadvertently left in Holen's phrase "in all business establishments of every kind whatsoever." As he dashed across the Capitol from the senate to the assembly, hurriedly reading the measure, he realized that with his phrase retained, the bill was even broader than he had envisioned.

Holen showed the senate version of the bill to Unruh. "He was so angry," Holen said. "I mean his face was red. He was really enraged. This was something that he really cared about and he'd been double-crossed, which was as bad as anything else. And I kept saying, "'I think they've done themselves in. I think it's much broader.'"

"Are you sure?" said Unruh. Holen replied, "Jesus, Jesse! What do you mean 'Are you sure?' I think so."

"Okay," said Unruh. The bill was passed and signed by Governor Edmund G. Brown Sr.[40]

Even after the bill became law, the Unruh Civil Rights Act attracted comparatively little notice. Public and media attention went to the legislation creating a Fair Employment Practices Commission, which was a major part of Brown's legislative program. But as the years went on, the Unruh Act evolved into California's most powerful civil rights law, gaining in strength as courts broadly interpreted Holen's fortuitous phrase, making the measure apply to any business "whatsoever." It gave minorities a weapon against discriminatory landlords and real estate companies. It banned discrimination against a number of groups, including the disabled. Later legislatures expanded the act to include gays and lesbians.[41] The impact was greater than Unruh and his friend Marvin Holen had ever anticipated.

Unruh had created an institution of government that would remain in place long after he was gone, providing a way for generations of Californians to pursue their rights. Neither he nor Holen thought they were engaged in institution building when they introduced their bill at the beginning of the legislative session. But as the years passed, the importance of their contribution became clear. Government's role was to provide accessible systems people could use to improve their lives. Throughout his career, one of Unruh's great contributions would be his conceiving and building such institutions.

Holen, at the time, thought that the new law would convince African Americans that Unruh was fighting for their rights. "Boy, he really showed those black constituents of his that he was out there for them," Holen said.

Unruh's instincts told him differently. He remembered the blacks' mistrust of him, just as he recalled the racial divide he'd witnessed in Texas. He carefully watched the demographics of the Sixty-fifth Assembly District. He sent assistants to report on the area, block by block, charting the change, much of which was occurring along Vernon Avenue, a thoroughfare that ran through the heart of the district. A neighborhood at Vernon and Figueroa Avenues, in the eastern part of the district, had been almost 10–1 white in 1950. It now had a majority of African Americans, as did nearby neighborhoods. To the west, a neighborhood around Crenshaw Boulevard and Vernon Avenue, all white in 1950, was about a third black. In parts of the district, the change was huge. In 1950, a neighborhood of bungalows at Vernon and Denker had 4,292 whites and so few blacks that they were combined in the census report with "nonwhites." By the end of the decade, the neighborhood was split between 1,686 whites and 1,486 blacks.[42]

Unruh wasn't sure of black support. When it came time to realign the boundaries of legislative districts in 1961 to reflect the demographic changes reported in the 1960 census, Unruh, by then speaker of the assembly and its absolute master, had the district's lines redrawn to assure that it would remain white by a large majority. As Professor Leroy Hardy of Claremont McKenna College, an authority on reapportionment who helped draw the lines, said, "the population makeup was increasingly white and the bulk of the black population was shifted to other districts."[43] All that remained of the old district was a long strip, four miles long and two to three miles wide, that included USC and was adjacent to Exposition Park and the Museum of Science and Industry. Thus Unruh remained the man to see in Sacramento for the university and its prominent board of trustees, and for the leaders of the museum, including its rich political donors. In other words, he fled African American voters but held onto his contributors.

Unruh the idealist passed California's strongest civil rights law. Unruh the pragmatist knew the story wasn't over. He understood, although he did not share, the bigotry and fear of his white constituents as they moved from his district. So, always the practical politician, he followed them. He comprehended the depths of America's racial divide, and he knew it would remain a central dilemma of American politics for decades to come.

SEVEN

Fair Housing and White Backlash

By 1963, EVENTS AND TECHNOLOGY were burning the matter of racial injustice deep into the American consciousness. The technology was television, and the events were a series of momentous developments in the civil rights movement.

These developments transformed the nation's politics into something far different from the local competition for votes in neighborhoods and maneuvering in the Capitol that Unruh had learned just a few years before. The powerful images of southern protesters and the violent resistance they encountered lifted the civil rights movement high on the media agenda. As the journalism scholar Edward Bliss Jr., who was part of the era as editor of CBS's *Evening News* anchored by Walter Cronkite, puts it, "Network accounts of what was happening nationalized awareness."[1] William A. Wood of the Columbia Graduate School of Journalism, observes: "Suddenly men and women all over the country were as close as across the street to the crucible of revolution. Whites everywhere were awakened and shaken up."[2]

In April, Police Commissioner Bull Connor used police dogs and fire hoses against demonstrators in Birmingham, Alabama, and Dr. Martin Luther King Jr. was arrested. Governor George Wallace stood in a doorway to prevent the desegregation of the University of Alabama, and that night President John F. Kennedy delivered a speech on all three television networks announcing his civil rights legislation. A day later, on June 12, the civil rights leader Medgar Evers was shot to death outside his home in Jackson, Mississippi. In August, more than 250,000 participated in the March on Washington to support the civil rights bill. And on September 15, terrorists exploded a bomb in the Sixteenth Street Baptist Church in Birmingham, Alabama, killing four young girls and injuring twenty others. Reporters, producers, cameramen, and sound crews, elbowing their way into the heart of the action, covered these events. In the intensity of combat, they may not have known they were shaping national policy, but they did—just as they would in Vietnam a few years later. Their stark images of the civil rights movement are imbedded in the national memory, as important as those of the two world wars and the Great Depression.

No longer was it possible for politicians and editors in the North to ignore the civil rights movements that had been growing in their communities for a quarter of a century without the attention or blessing of the mass media. The rosy glow of self-deception that had hung over white California—a mood well captured by a 1962 special edition of *Look* magazine devoted to the state, then on the verge of becoming the nation's most populous—was disappearing. "Historians may someday point to the California of the 1950s and 1960s as the state where the twin ideals of equality and freedom were first successfully realized," T. George Harris wrote at the time. "The political message of California is now clear: The needy minorities of the past are becoming the prosperous majorities of the future. The have-nots now vanish into a society of near equal haves."[3]

Look's assessment was far too optimistic. In the very next year, the energy generated by the southern movement invigorated California's own civil rights organizations and began to pierce white smugness. In South Central Los Angeles, more than 50,000 filled the old Wrigley Field baseball park in May, a crowd that extended onto the field and into the parking lot, to hear Martin Luther King. The programs distributed to the audience had pictures of Birmingham's police dogs. "There comes a time when people get tired of being trampled over by the iron feet of oppression," King said, in the same words he had used during the Montgomery bus boycott.[4]

The demonstrations in LA were hard for the media to ignore. The movement's immediate target was the Los Angeles Unified School District, a large and segregated school system that included Los Angeles and neighboring smaller cities. Periodically, through the spring and summer, African Americans marched on district headquarters, sought admission to de facto segregated, predominantly white schools and filed lawsuits demanding desegregation. While the targeted schools were several miles southeast of Unruh's district, the impact of the demonstrations was area-wide, and the Los Angeles civil rights movement finally made it to the top of the news agenda.

The *Los Angeles Times* put the story of a planned march in May on page one with the headline "LA Declared Target for Total Integration." The Reverend Maurice Dawkins, pastor of the People's Independent Church, one of the African American community's most activist congregations, said,

"We are not just asking for a small specific adjustment but a total community integration.[5]

The drive for integration of the Los Angeles school district met with the same furious resistance that had confronted African Americans' efforts to buy homes in Unruh's assembly district and the neighborhoods around it. The resistance centered around the small, working-class, predominantly white suburban city of South Gate, just five miles southeast of Unruh's district, which had been settled largely by immigrants from the Midwest, the South, and the Southwest. These people shared Unruh's rural heritage and the drive for economic security and a better life that had brought him to California. South Gate was part of a belt of similar small cities southeast of Los Angeles. One of them was Hawthorne, where Unruh had moved in with his brother before World War II, joining the war workers commuting to the aircraft factories. If any politician understood the hopes and fears of these residents, it was Unruh.

South Gate was the center of resistance because South Gate High School, part of the Los Angeles district and almost entirely white, was the target of a lawsuit seeking its integration with Jordan High School, a mainly black school in nearby Watts. As the integration effort intensified, "whites began to fight back," the historian Becky N. Nicolaides notes. "From Santa Monica and Long Beach to the San Fernando Valley and Hollywood, whites mobilized an opposition movement. South Gate's citizens were at the center and they typified broader white resistance—particularly working-class resistance—to racial integration in Los Angeles."[6]

By then Assembly Speaker Unruh had become a figure of legendary power, and his nickname, "Big Daddy," was now as well known as his given name.

Unruh felt he had already dealt with the concerns of black Californians with the enactment of his Civil Rights Act. "We've just about done for the minorities; at least we've put the laws on the books to do for them," Unruh told T. George Harris of *Look*. "Now we have to work on the problems of the majority, on the quality of life in the state."[7]

He was the undisputed boss of the assembly. As a young reporter covering that house, I used to stop in Unruh's office in the morning. By 9 A.M., the room was full of people seeking favors from the boss. The most powerful business lobbyists, the biggest labor union officials, the minor bosses who got out the vote for Unruh candidates—all of them waited. Sitting there, watching, eavesdropping on bits of conversation, I tried to understand what made this man so powerful that he could turn all those big men in the waiting room into the meekest of supplicants.

Late in the morning, he walked the short distance to the assembly chamber. Unruh rarely presided, leaving that to a colleague. He restlessly roamed the floor, talking to the other legislators, occasionally sitting down in a vacant chair for a confidential chat, checking the mood of a house that he knew was volatile. He was a commanding individual, not only because of his size, but also because of the way he carried himself. He was confident and enjoyed being in charge, as if every day in the assembly chamber reminded him of how far he had come. He rarely spoke during debates. But when he did, rising from his seat in the rear of the chamber, the restless crowd of assembly members stopped chatting and listened. It wasn't just that he had the votes to push almost anything he wanted through the house. He was faster on his feet, smarter, wittier, more logical, and more eloquent than any of his colleagues. When Unruh spoke, it was a performance not to be missed.

His power, his personality, and his view that the legislature might already have done what it could for civil rights were all in play in the long debate over the most important bill of 1963, a proposal to give the state power to act against property owners who discriminated in the sale or rental of homes and apartment houses, a measure supporters called "fair housing." The name rankled the opponents, who considered the plan most unfair.

The legislation would give the state authority to step in and prohibit discrimination because of race, color, religion, or national origin in the sale or rental of housing. It would be a powerful weapon for minorities trying to break the color line. Judicial decisions had banned discrimination. Unruh's own civil rights act had forbidden the housing industry from engaging in biased practices. But the aggrieved had to go to court to press their rights. The proposed law went much farther, allowing them to bring the investigatory power of the state down on the heads of property owners. Violators faced criminal penalties. A maximum penalty of six months in jail and a $500 fine awaited those found guilty of refusing to rent or sell to minorities. In other words, jail was a possibility for those who discriminated in housing sales or rentals, a practice that had been considered a right in white neighborhoods.

Unruh's attitude toward the open housing bill was complicated—too nuanced for the simplicities of political debate. He retained the same sense of outrage he'd felt against bigotry since boyhood, saying in a speech:

> No man can stand before you and say that injustice and prejudice do not exist. No man can claim that the ghettoes are not there. No one can pretend that any Negro who can afford it can live anywhere he wants in California. I

think about myself and where I came from and where I am now. The journey has been long and hard. But the road was open. The education to pay for it was financed by the federal government under the GI Bill of Rights. Our democracy did a lot for me, the son of an illiterate sharecropper. Perhaps the most it did was to allow me to believe the wonderful stories about what life could be in our great country. This hope allowed me to believe that I could make something of myself, that I would not always be poor and perhaps hungry. I would not deny this hope to any of our children. If I am not my brother's keeper, I refuse to be my brother's jailer.[8]

Yet Unruh was skeptical of the proposed housing legislation. "There is no question in my mind that you cannot legislate into existence good human relations, nor can you abolish cultural or physical differences by making them against the law," he said. Punitive laws "are necessary in the sense that they represent the least we can do to assure minority group members we mean business about their rights as guaranteed by the Constitution. They also assist those majority group members who want to do what is right but lack the courage to be out of step with their neighbors." But they "cannot and will not materially affect the everyday existence of individuals in our society which is after all the object of our concern. Punitive laws at best guarantee equality of opportunity—they cannot provide equality."[9]

This was not what most backers of the measure wanted to hear. They saw the proposal as both a legal and a symbolic step forward. But such symbolism was foreign to the pragmatic Unruh. He viewed racial injustice through the prism of his own life. Education, beginning when his mother taught him to read at the kitchen table, had raised him from poverty. A mentoring teacher in high school and a determined wife who enrolled him in USC had helped him acquire the skills that raised him from working-class anonymity to the fame and power he craved. Education was more important than regulation, especially for African Americans, who, he felt, still were affected by the horrors of slavery. In a speech at Los Angeles State College, he insisted:

If the educational and economic gap is not closed or narrowed, few Negroes are going to take advantage of a fair-housing law to break out of the de facto housing ghetto in this economic class segregation all of us live in today in California. One of the myths frequently indulged in by those who are guilty of wishful thinking about this question is that there are no differences of aptitude, capability or intelligence between minority and majority group members. This is simply not true and the trouble with maintaining this myth is that it is too easy to check the facts and disprove it. We cannot lie to one another and to ourselves about this problem and hope to solve it. Acknowledging that there are differences does not, however, support the opposite myth propounded by bigots looking for scientific underpinnings for their need to feel superior. They contend erroneously that these admitted differences are biological or hereditary. This is certainly not true, either.

It is just over 100 years since slavery was abolished in the United States. There are people alive today whose parents were slaves. This is a short period in the history of human affairs. We have never adequately taken into account the long run effects of the institution of slavery.[10]

Unruh also knew the fears and prejudices of white working-class men and women. From his own experience, he understood society's great racial divide. He believed that the laws on the books were working, and he was concerned that Californians were not ready for more. Time would prove him right, but in 1963, his views were not popular among liberal Democrats and leaders of the civil rights movement.

His caution was very much in line with that of the president he admired so much, John F. Kennedy. Kennedy, as a presidential candidate, had telephoned Coretta King when her husband, Martin, was imprisoned in Georgia. JFK's brother Robert F. Kennedy called a judge to try to secure King's release on bail.[11] The phone calls were considered an important reason why Kennedy was able to carry the African American community on election day by a 70 percent of the vote to his opponent's 30 percent.

Robert Kennedy and his staff intervened on behalf of southern demonstrators with dedication and personal courage. But the Democratic administration was restrained by fear of losing southern states in the 1964 election and by the power of southern Democrats in Congress. Only after almost half a year of freedom rides and other demonstrations in the South, met by violent assaults by local law enforcement officers, did President Kennedy go on national television to announce his civil rights legislation. "Now is the time for this nation to fulfill its promise," he said. "The events in Birmingham and elsewhere have so increased the cries for equality that no city or state or legislative body can prudently choose to ignore them."[12]

In California, the civil rights movement, inspired and empowered by events in the South, focused its attention on the legislation that both sides knew would be hardest for white home owners to accept, the housing bill. Two years before, the Democratic administration had not shared the movement's determination or priorities. "Civil rights did not have pride of place in Governor Brown's 1961 message to the California legislature; it was listed ninth—among the 'myriad problems of growth' in a 10-point program," the political scientist Thomas V. Casstevens has observed.[13] That year, an antidiscrimination housing bill, introduced by Assemblyman Augustus Hawkins, a Los Angeles Democrat and one of two black legislators, passed the assembly but died in the senate. By 1963, Hawkins had moved on to the U.S. Congress, and a new bill on housing discrimination was introduced by another African American legislator, William Byron Rumford of Berkeley.

Rumford and Hawkins rose to leadership positions while accommodating the white world. They walked a line common to ambitious African Americans of their generation, the Jackie Robinson generation. Robinson was the black athlete who integrated major league baseball, masking his fiery and competitive nature behind an agreeable façade. If the legislature was a boys club, Rumford and Hawkins had to be two of those boys—not, perhaps, part of the innermost circle but trusted and liked by the most powerful legislative leaders and lobbyists.

Rumford, a pharmacist and drugstore owner, acknowledged his hard road upward. He said, "Well, I guess I've always been a barrier-breaker in a sense. It just has fallen [to be] my fate, really, more than anything else, and I've been a very persistent kind of a guy all my life. I just carried through something that I had to overcome. It was like getting accustomed to going down the track or hurdling; it's just another hurdle."[14]

Unruh had appointed Rumford chairman of the assembly's influential Public Health Committee, which wrote air pollution control and other health-related measures. He was also a member of the Derby Club, an elite inner-circle organization of legislators and lobbyists (who paid for the weekly lunch and drinks) presided over by a conservative and powerful Democratic senator, Randolph Collier, who chose the members.[15]

After Hawkins was elected to the assembly in 1934, defeating a black Republican in South Central Los Angeles, he linked up with business lobbyists to whom ideology and skin color were unimportant. Alone, but unwilling to operate on the margins, Hawkins learned how to become important, even powerful—through the lobbyists. "The influence of the lobbyists was very great," Hawkins said. "Keep in mind I first went to Sacramento earning only $1,200 a year . . . lobbyists became important because there was always one—or several—inviting you to dinner and to spend the evening, you know, at the cocktail lounge and then food. This went on in a very lavish sort of way."[16]

As Samish showed, the major lobbyists were undemanding except for the votes that affected their employers. Samish didn't care if lawmakers voted for old-age pensions, just so long as they voted for liquor too. This was not difficult for Hawkins, who explained:

> Most of the things that I campaigned for or against were a reflection of my own district. I never supported taxes on liquor or cigarettes ordinarily because my district didn't want me to. I was never against horse racing because people in my district believed more in having horse racing than those who didn't want it. With the number of liquor stores in my district, for me to put a tax on liquor was politically unpopular. So most of the issues that some were lobbying for or against were, more or less, not of any embarrassment to me.

As a result, he was an Artie Samish vote on the matters that were important to the lobbyist's liquor store, distillery, brewery, and racetrack clients. "The things I voted for he was lobbying for," said Hawkins.[17]

Such relationships, and Hawkins's openness about them, offended some of the postwar Democratic newcomers. "He was a fighter for all liberal causes and individuals," said Allen Miller, a Democrat who served in the assembly from 1953 to 1959 and had been a Lincoln supporter.

> But he also accomplished his ends by—in my opinion—taking substantial contributions from monied people, lobbyists who had an axe to grind. His philosophy was that, "If I can take this in order to accomplish my ultimate ends, so what's wrong with it?" . . . I'm sure he voted when he could, without hurting his long range views, for the oil interests . . . and some others. Horse [racing] and so on. I think he felt in order to accomplish his long-range ultimate ends, that he could afford this. This didn't compromise him in his mind, at all, with respect to his accomplishments.[18]

Hawkins's civil rights advocacy was irrelevant to Samish, far off the Samish agenda.

In the first months of the 1963 legislative session, Rumford was optimistic about his housing bill. "I think we have an excellent chance to get the bill through this time," he said. "I feel California, certainly one of the most liberal states, should retain its position as a leader in the [housing] field giving all Americans the right to have access to all things available to all Americans."[19]

Attention turned from Sacramento to Berkeley, home of the oldest of the University of California's campuses. Berkeley for years had been governed by conservative city councils, dominated by merchants and the real estate business. But a new liberal council majority, in an effort to break up segregated neighborhoods and promote integrated schools, had just passed a fair-housing law. The ordinance, the first of its kind in the state, prohibited discrimination because of race, color, religion, national origin, or ancestry in the sale, rental, lease, or other transfer of housing accommodations. It imposed misdemeanor penalties for violations and created a Board of Intergroup Relations to investigate, conciliate, and hold public hearings on complaints of discrimination.[20]

But opposition was strong, and the measure's foes saw statewide implications. The real estate industry and other conservatives led the opposition to the Berkeley law. A member of the California Real Estate Association, the state's leading opponent of fair-housing legislation, said, "If we can beat the ordinance in Berkeley, we're certain it will hammer the final nails into the coffin [of the Rumford housing proposal]."[21] The measure was approved by the Berkeley City Council, but opponents immediately gathered enough signatures in the city to put a referendum on the ballot, giving voters a chance to overturn the law.[22]

Unruh quickly grasped the danger to the state's proposed open housing law—and to the Democrats. To him, it was a tip-off to what white voters would accept. In a speech two weeks after the bill was introduced, he said the legislature "should take a long look at the state level if the [Berkeley] ordinance is soundly defeated. If it is defeated badly, it may well be a warning signal." After his talk, he expanded on the sentiment while talking to reporters. "I don't want to hoist a storm warning on this," he said. "There is still a great deal of discrimination in California and legislation may be needed to fight it but we have also come a fair way in this field. I would not like to jeopardize what we have done already by precipitous actions for the future." Californians must be educated, he said, on "why it is necessary to live together and to do it rather than telling them they must live together."[23]

He was looking far down the road, beyond this particular bill. He could see race beginning to splinter the New Deal coalition. He knew that the white union members, an essential component of the coalition and part of his own political base, would tolerate no state interference in what they considered their right to keep their neighborhoods white. He was trying to navigate between them and people like his longtime supporter Loren Miller, the Los Angeles attorney and NAACP legal leader, who had long fought segregated housing in his city and was part of the legal team that had persuaded the U.S. Supreme Court to overturn discriminatory housing covenants in 1948.

Miller was not happy with the speaker's words. "I do not believe that the fate of statewide legislation should be made to depend on the outcome of a local issue," he wrote Unruh.

> California cannot and should not rest content in the halfway house on the road to equality. It must either move forward or it will regress. Refusal of the legislators to consider and enact fair housing legislation will not constitute a "breathing spell" but rather a turning back from a task undertaken four years ago. You have played an important role in the progress that has been made in those four years.
>
> Your defection at this time would involve far more than a mere personal action. It would be a signal that the surge toward equality has petered out and your example would be followed by many others.[24]

Governor Pat Brown was also caught between the forces divided by race. Reporters wanted to know what he thought of Unruh's comments. It was early in the session, but even then signs were appearing of the split between the two. Brown said:

> Without disagreeing with the speaker, let me say this, that I don't think it's time to go slow at all nor to go faster. I think we have to look at a situation of the minority groups in this state not being able to find good housing, and I think that proposals that we've made are fair to all the peoples of the state. . . . I intend to use all the powers of governor to see that no longer are people that are good Americans refused decent housing in the state of California by reason of the color of their skin or their race or religion. I feel very strongly about this, and I haven't discussed it with the speaker but in previous conversation I know that he agrees that fair housing would be a good thing. Now whether this specific legislation he agrees with or not is something that I intend to discuss with him at a very early moment.[25]

Nine days later, at another press conference, a reporter asked Brown, "How serious is the breach between yourself and Speaker Unruh on the question of civil rights?"

"I don't think there is any breach at all," Brown replied. "Mr. Unruh and I meet at least once a week and discuss these things. But we all say things that are not always understood. There's no breach between the speaker and myself and I'm very, very thankful that I have a man as strong as Jesse Unruh as speaker of this legislature. He's certainly not a rubber stamp but there's not a governor in the United States that has [a] more loyal speaker than Mr. Unruh." Brown added, in a remark that prompted the reporters to laugh, "If he's ambitious, so was Caesar."[26]

By now, civil rights were at the top of the liberal agenda, and Tom Carvey, the president of the California Democratic Council, taking advantage of a chance to attack his foe, said Unruh had in effect issued "an open invitation to the real estate lobby to pour its resources into the Berkeley referendum."

Unruh, under assault, wanted more information and knew he could find it by examining the mood in Berkeley. Early in the spring of 1963, he contacted a political pollster, Don Muchmore, and asked him to survey public opinion in Berkeley. Unruh had an insatiable appetite for public opinion polls and any other source of political information. He studied Muchmore's statewide polls and those of others. He even polled his own assembly district, where he never faced significant opposition and where he was personally familiar with every block. He had the curiosity of a good reporter plus an economist's belief in data. He also listened to current gossip and solicited advice from many people. On some Sundays, he'd drop in on his nephew, Paul, by then a blue-collar aerospace worker, and talk politics. He made his judgments based on such information, interpreted though his own experiences in life.

Polling as Unruh had ordered, Muchmore found that the Berkeley housing proposal was in trouble. The pollster acknowledged that polling for racial feelings "is perhaps the most difficult one of all about which to determine attitudes and opinions since it involves deep rooted beliefs which require extensive sampling." Even with those limitations, Muchmore surmised that the proposal was losing. Of course, minority votes—overwhelmingly African American—favored the measure 97.5 percent to 2.5 percent. There was a small but noticeable drop-off among student voters—the Berkeley student body was predominantly white—of 83.3 percent in favor to 13.3 percent against, with the rest undecided. Sentiment turned sharply with a category called "other voters"—those who were neither minority nor students—with 62.4 percent opposed. This group was largely white but probably included some Latinos. When it came to party, something of great importance to Unruh, Democrats backed the measure 64 percent to 32 percent. But if the substantial number of black Berkeley Democrats were removed from the Democratic sample, the margin of support would undoubtedly have declined. Republicans were opposed 62.4 percent to 32 percent. When Muchmore computed the answers of everyone who responded to the poll, the housing measure passed by 3 percent, but when he weighted the responses by figuring in factors such as his predicted voter turnout and apportioning the undecided, he found the measure was 8 percent behind.[27] That, plus the weakness in the Democratic support, gave Unruh cause to worry.

On March 27, the assembly Governmental Efficiency and Economy Committee, under Unruh's firm control, held a two-and-a-half-hour hearing on Rumford's bill in a room crowded with almost 400 spectators. "Before the economic and social problems of race relations approach the magnitude of those faced in several eastern cities, we must dilute the ghettos," Attorney General Stanley Mosk testified. "Integration is a fact of the twentieth century. It will come as surely as tomorrow. Our only choice is whether it will be forced upon us or attained through orderly public action. I therefore urge adoption of Assemblyman Rumford's bill as an excellent example of orderly public action."

Along with the attorney general, representatives of the NAACP, the California Commission for Fair Practice, the AFL-CIO, and the Northern California Council of Churches spoke up for Rumford's bill. James D. Gorforth, who said the Rumford bill would depress the home-building industry, represented the California Chamber of Commerce, the state's major business organization. Also opposed was the California Real Estate Association.[28] Both organizations were powers in the Capitol.

On April 2, Berkeley voters overturned the city's fair-housing law, just as Muchmore had anticipated, by a vote of 22,750 to 20,456. The racial divide was sharp. More than 90 percent of African Americans favored the measure, while 63 percent of whites were opposed.[29] Just as troubling to the advocates of fair housing was the composition of the Democratic vote opposed to the law, which tended to be retired or working class—two groups at the heart of a coalition important to the Democrats since the New Deal.

Unruh studied the returns and concluded that the bill should be amended. Rumford got the message. He said, "Mr. Unruh and several other legislators pointed out to us that the people weren't ready for the fair housing bill and that we would have an awful time trying to get it through."[30] He agreed to an amendment to his bill removing misdemeanor penalties and the maximum sentence of six months in jail and a $500 fine. A second amendment exempted owner-occupied homes and small multiple-unit dwellings. Owners of such homes had been the heart of the resistance to housing integration, as Unruh had seen in his own district. "One never gets what he wants in the legislature," Rumford said. "We had to take what, more or less, we could get under the circumstances. I would say the bill was not as strong as I would have liked to have it but the legislature itself is a platform of compromises."[31]

The amended bill passed the assembly in a bipartisan 47–24 vote. "The issue is very simple," said Assemblyman Charles Garrigus. "Does any man with property have the right to use that property to degrade his fellows? No, he does not." The Republican leader in the assembly, Charles J. Conrad, in opposing the bill, brought the issue down to the level of an individual property owner who would be covered despite the measure's exemption. Consider, he said, the case of an elderly owner of a six-unit apartment who declined to rent one of the units to a black person. Refusal would bring action by the state. Renting, however, might prompt his other tenants to move.[32] Conrad's assumption of widespread white bigotry was ugly, but even Rumford supporters worried that he was saying out loud what other opponents were afraid to say, and that this unspoken racial prejudice would doom the bill in the senate.

In the senate, the measure was assigned to the graveyard, the Committee on Governmental Efficiency, a conservative, business-oriented body that listened to the lobbyists who hung out in the office of the senate president pro tem, Hugh Burns. The chairman was Luther Gibson, a conservative Democrat, part of the ruling clique headed by Senator Burns and supported by business lobbyists. Gibson published a newspaper in Vallejo, a Navy town on the northwestern edge of San Francisco Bay whose economy centered on its naval base and shipyard. Most of his committee's work was done in secret, and when he presided at public sessions, where private decisions were ratified, he always seemed to be in a cranky mood.

Knowing that the committee members met privately before the session, John Quimby, then a young assemblyman, who had a wicked sense of humor, decided to poke fun at the members' secretiveness. "I laid out my various papers and stuff and cleared my throat and getting ready, put both hands on the rostrum and leaned into the mike and said 'Well fellows what did you decide?'" he recalled. Gibson, amused, had the committee approve the bill.[33]

Such collegiality was rare in the committee. Joseph Gunterman, who was lobbying for the Rumford bill on behalf of the Friends Committee on Legislation, a Quaker group, said, "That was the graveyard and the most noted corpse in the graveyard was supposed to be the fair housing bill."[34]

In the assembly, Unruh had shaped the bill to what he thought was possible and made sure that it had more than enough votes to win. In the senate, he had no such power.

Unruh's counterpart in the senate, Burns, from the agriculturally oriented city of Fresno, was a conservative Democrat. He had a big, broad, friendly, wrinkled face. Morning visitors to his office were offered a coffee and brandy. In his declining years, he often recited the old gag: "If I had known I was going to live this long, I would have taken better care of myself." He was a great friend of lobbyists for racetrack, liquor, beer, wine, oil, and other interests. The *Los Angeles Times* Capitol columnist George Skelton remembered going to Burns's office for an interview in the mid 1960s "and finding four influential lobbyists, representing liquor, oil, insurance, racing, playing poker with the senator's chief of staff. They stayed there all through my interview, listening and dealing. And I later learned that's where these lobbyists camped much of every day, a de facto part of the Senate leadership team."[35]

Unruh had cultivated Burns since his first days in the legislature, although they were ideological opposites. The senator opposed the housing bill. To Burns, the message of Berkeley was clear. "When non-whites organize for equal rights and equal opportunities no right thinking persons can disagree. But the public has shown by its attitude now that it is not in favor of granting any special privileges to minorities by removing the rights of one group and giving [them] to another."[36]

Unruh and Burns shared a streak of extreme pragmatism and a mutual admiration of how each had mastered the game of politics. Around this time, they had begun holding weekly news conferences together. The event had started out as an oddity but became a regular Capitol feature. There was good chemistry between the two. Unruh was usually deferential to the older man, showing a respect that countered the low regard in which some senators held the speaker. And the novelty—and the presence of the legislature's two top leaders—assured a good crowd of reporters and coverage every week. The reporters enjoyed these events and soon started calling them the "Hughie-Jesse Show."

Like Unruh, like all good political leaders, Burns had excellent antennae when it came to his colleagues. He needed them. Unlike in the assembly, where Unruh was in complete charge, Burns led a collection of independent barons, the chairmen of the most important committees. "He pushed things but none of them lorded it over the other[s]," said Gunterman.[37] Burns's natural inclination was to oppose the Rumford bill. But he survived by giving chairmen great power over their committees and wielding his own influence in subtle ways—a word here, a conversation there, a message relayed through a third party, and, always, a willingness to compromise. Burns was conservative but too practical to be an ideologue.

His conservatism was also tempered by a change in the senate. By 1963, the senate, long the repository of California rural conservatism, was slowly responding to some of the new currents in the state. The smartest politician in the senate was a liberal, George Miller Jr., the chairman of the Finance Committee, who fitted in well with the lobbyists and old-timers who ran the house. But Miller also had a broad vision of the state's future, tempered by his experience and realism. He was formidable in debate, with a growling voice and sharp eyes. Outside the senate, he was one of the organizers of the 1953 Asilomar conference that led to the creation of the California Democratic Council.

"He just had a good ear," said his associate, Don Bradley, a Democratic political strategist who worked with Miller to bring new blood into the senate. "He knew what people were talking about and what would sell and what wouldn't. He's as good a politician as I ever ran into. He's a very practical guy, but he wasn't venal at all."

Miller and Bradley engineered the election of several liberals to the senate, a move that changed the ideological complexion of the house to some degree and made possible the enactment of much of the Democratic legislation of the late 1950s and early 1960s.[38] They organized campaigns in rural counties, which had a disproportionate share of power in the senate. Looking for candidates who were smart and fairly liberal, usually attorneys, who had chosen to live and work in small towns instead of more lucrative big cities, they sent a skilled political manager, Van Dempsey, on talent-hunting expeditions. Bradley recalled:

Van would go down and nose around and find somebody who had some prominence and was a Democrat. We would work on him and try to get him to run and offer him some assistance because the process of a normal average citizen going out, deciding he wants an office, and putting it all together himself is a difficult thing for them to do. They don't know how, and they're not sure how they'll be received. We could help them with getting other people in the party to support them, that sort of thing.

It was sort of fraudulent almost. We would get somebody mildly interested and then take them to Sacramento. Miller would escort them around and tell them what a great job it was and the help they were going to get and everything and persuade them to run.

Bradley laughed as he told the story. But he added, "we did persuade an awful lot of very good people to run for office."[39] They were smart and sophisticated men who preferred small-town life.

The new blood had little influence with Senator Gibson's Governmental Efficiency Committee. A month after the housing bill had been sent to Gibson's committee, it had still been denied a hearing, the fate of previous civil rights measures. But this was a different year. Public opinion, shaped by the scenes from the South, would be a factor. John Quimby, representing a district with large numbers of steelworkers, could see the impact. The events were seared into their minds, he said, referring to "the publicity, and the public knowledge, the pictures of the dogs on the folks back in the South and the fire hoses from Bull Connor, and the president calling out the troops and George Wallace on the steps on the college and those kinds of things."[40]

On May 29, ten men and women and their children showed up at the Capitol, where they sat down around the rotunda on the second floor and announced they would not leave until a fair-housing bill was passed. The group, which soon would grow, had been organized by CORE, the Congress of Racial Equality, which the year before had extended its operations to California. CORE had been founded in Chicago in 1942, aiming to protest segregated public accommodations with nonviolent demonstrations. By 1961, CORE had taken its place among national civil rights organizations by sponsoring interracial groups riding segregated interstate buses in the South, expeditions known as freedom rides. In spring 1963, CORE picketed segregated housing tracts southeast of Los Angeles and staged a hunger strike at the Los Angeles school district board headquarters to protest segregated schools.

The tiny Capitol sit-in would scarcely have been noticed on the streets of Los Angeles, where civil rights groups were marching across the city to protest school segregation. But in the closed world of the Capitol in Sacramento, the presence of the protesters was remarkable. They brought with them sleeping bags, air mattresses, blankets, guitars, and a baby-bottle warmer, all of it piled around the rotunda. Each day they sang "We Shall Overcome." More than 300 participated over the next few weeks, one group staying for two or three days and then giving way to another. More than 40 percent of the demonstrators were students.[41]

Their quiet demeanor and their inexpensive, tidy attire were a contrast and, in a real sense, a rebuke to the lobbyists and legislators, especially when they were returning from lunch on the corporate or union tab. One night in particular showed the gap between the legislators and the demonstrators. The legislators and lobbyists of the Derby Club held an annual banquet. Everyone wore formal attire and their derby hats. After dinner, the custom was to march through the Capitol to the other side of the building and cross the street to renew the party at another hangout, the Senator Hotel. On this particular occasion, they passed by the demonstrators, graphically illustrating the difference between the in-crowd and the protesters.

"These people sitting on the floor will not, I am sure, help the progress of the bill," said Senator Burns.[42] Assemblyman Rumford wished they would go away. He recalled years later, "I had felt that we were able to get the legislation that far without that kind of assistance and I had asked them to leave. But they did not. They remained there throughout with their children. . . . Many of the senators were upset about it, saying this was an attempt to threaten them and that type of thing. . . . If they were trying to help me, as far as I was concerned, this was a poor way to do it!"[43]

This was the prevailing view in the Capitol at the time. Observing the demonstrators every day, I saw it differently. They were camped just a few steps from our AP office, and I would exchange pleasantries with them as I walked by. It was unusual to encounter someone from the outside world in our tightly knit society of politicians, bureaucrats, lobbyists, and reporters. The politeness of the young demonstrators and their small children struck me. They brought dramatic tension to the story. They were also a reminder that the fight over Rumford's bill was part of the national civil rights narrative, and this was on my mind as I wrote my stories. I felt I was recording history, that I was reporting something big. And by becoming part of the story, the CORE demonstrators also sent a message to the world outside the Capitol that the fair-housing bill was slowly being strangled in the privacy of the senate Governmental Efficiency Committee.

News coverage increased when Marlon Brando and Paul Newman flew from Los Angeles to Sacramento on June 11 to support the demonstrators. Earlier in the day, Gibson delayed the scheduled hearing on the bill for two days. "I'm not sure there will be any bill," he said. Newman and Brando, accompanied by Assemblyman Dymally, shook hands with the demonstrators and chatted with them. "Stick with it, fella," Newman told one of the demonstrators. Then they went outside to greet a newly arrived contingent of CORE marchers, some of whom had walked the eighty-four miles from Berkeley to Sacramento.[44]

With CORE members in the audience, Senator Gibson showed no signs of buckling on Friday when the senate Governmental Efficiency Committee finally held a hearing on Rumford's bill.

Rumford asked Gibson when the committee would act.

"The bill is still under submission. We still haven't made up our minds," Senator Gibson replied, in his curt manner.

The CORE members laughed loudly. "I will clear the room if there are any demonstrations," said Gibson. "We are trying to act with our hearts and souls and in the best interest of the people of California." He refused to tell Rumford when the committee would vote

"I no longer care to discuss this with you personally," Rumford told Gibson.[45]

At about 6 P.M. that night, about ten of the CORE group left their encampment around the rotunda and walked down the hall to the senate chamber and lay flat on their backs in front of the massive wooden doors at the main entrance. Each one carried a small sign declaring "Call Out AB 1240," the number of Rumford's bill. State police dragged them away, but they were replaced by other CORE members, who had earlier found seats inside the senate chamber on passes given them by friendly senators. They, too, were dragged off. "It was a symbolic protest," said Mari Goldman, a CORE member. "The Senate committee blocked the bill. Our members decided to block the entrance to the Senate with our bodies."[46]

But this affair was bigger than Gibson and his committee. California's fight over Rumford's bill had become a national story—and, with the demonstrators, a visual one, big enough to warrant the attention of the Kennedy administration. During this period of limbo for the bill, Senator Gibson received a phone call from Washington. It was President Kennedy's secretary of the Navy, Paul Fay. Fay was a friend of Kennedy's. He had served with him during World War II, and after Kennedy's death, he wrote a memoir, *The Pleasure of His Company*.[47] When Fay spoke, even Gibson listened.

As Gibson recalled it, Fay talked mostly about the senator's efforts to assure the construction of six more nuclear submarines at the Mare Island Naval Shipyard, an economic bulwark of Gibson's district. In the course of the conversation, Gibson said, Fay "touched on the fair housing bill briefly but there was no implied threat to keep the submarine work from the West Coast if we don't recommend the bill." To anyone who understood the language of politics, however, the threat was clear: no housing bill, no submarines. Just in case Gibson didn't get the message, Governor Brown made it even clearer. "I think the President feels very strongly about a fair housing bill," he said.[48]

"All this time they were attempting to deal with me privately and to get me to subject myself to their amendments which would have nullified the act entirely," Rumford said. "I refused to go along with them and we made a few more amendments which we thought would be acceptable to their committee."[49] Finally, on the last day of the session, Gibson's committee approved the bill. But it was done in such a way as to kill it. With a long agenda of bills awaiting senate approval, chances were the senators would not reach the Rumford measure before the mandatory adjournment of the legislature at midnight.

In the assembly, Unruh took action. He announced there would be no vote on bills from the senate until that house had acted on the Rumford measure and other assembly bills. This forced the senate's hand. At 11 P.M., with pressure mounting, Senator Edwin J. Regan, a Democrat who had grown up in San Francisco, but had decided to practice law in the mountain town of Weaverville, rose to ask for a vote. Burns, unhappy with Regan, denied the request. But Regan demanded a vote on his motion. Up in the senate gallery, the lobbyist Joe Gunterman, who had worked so hard for the bill, thought there was no way Regan could succeed.[50] But he did, by a 20–16 vote on the procedural issue, clearing the way for a vote on the housing bill. "There is no room in California for two classes of citizens," Regan said during the debate. The bill passed 22–13.[51] "I was very much surprised and really delighted," said Gunterman.[52] The assembly quickly concurred in amendments made in the senate, and Governor Brown signed the bill into law.

The exultation felt by Gunterman and the bill's other backers was short-lived. Although it was not apparent at the time, enactment of the housing law marked the peak of post–World War II liberalism in California. Never for the rest of the century and beyond would the liberals again have such influence. The power of public opinion that had elevated civil rights to a national cause prompted a reaction by those who felt that their own rights—of property, school choice, and eventually access to higher education, the professions, and a variety of other jobs—were being denied. For everyone moved by the powerful televised images of the civil rights movement, there were others who were frightened or angered. The following year, the real estate interests that had unsuccessfully fought the Rumford bill in the legislature would continue their efforts by offering the voters a measure to repeal the new fair-housing law. The ballot measure, Proposition 14, was approved, although later and unpopularly overturned by the liberal state supreme court. But the overwhelming vote for Proposition 14 showed that Unruh's fear of a voter backlash had been justified.

The vote marked the beginning of the conservative revolution, a movement that was fueled even more in later years by other events and images— the Free Speech Movement in Berkeley, the Watts riots, protests against the Vietnam War—all blending together in nightly news broadcasts. Unruh, the reluctant warrior on behalf of the Rumford Act, would become its energetic defender during the initiative campaign. But he campaigned with a sense of foreboding, knowing that the Democratic Party, California, and his own career would never be the same.

EIGHT

Animal House

THE NIGHT THE RUMFORD fair-housing bill passed the legislature, Unruh had used all of his skills and knowledge to save it from defeat. His ability to wield his power on this and a variety of other issues made him, in the view of Herbert L. Phillips, the political editor of the *Sacramento Bee,* the legislature's "most effective and powerful member."[1]

During this period, Unruh insisted that a portion of the state's highway construction funds be used for urban mass transit. His legislation created a state arts commission.[2] The lobbyists, who had formerly reigned supreme, now curried favor with him. His young consultants, assigned to important committees, generated research that questioned policies advocated by lobbyists, the senate, and the Brown administration. From their offices emerged innovative ideas on transportation, water management, education, mental health, and all of the other difficult issues that are usually the preserve of the bureaucracy and a few interest groups. Some of the consultants later went on to greater accomplishments. Ronald Robie, for example, became state director of water resources and later an appellate judge, and Rose Elizabeth Bird, chief justice of the state supreme court. Because of Unruh and the team he had assembled, the assembly had outgrown its reputation as a collection of shabby second-raters and now was the source of far-reaching, creative legislation.

But only a month after his success on the Rumford bill, Unruh's career had a serious setback due to his own misbehavior. This unfortunate episode, known as "the lockup," would be a legend for years. It took place at the end of the session when Republicans refused to vote on the state budget unless they could see the details of a school-financing bill.[3] At that point, Unruh— in a fit of temper exacerbated by alcohol and drugs—invoked a parliamentary rule and refused to let lawmakers leave the assembly chamber until they voted. They remained locked up for the entire night.

No single event in Unruh's career did more to give him the reputation of a political boss—"Big Daddy" in the worst sense of the name. No event captured Unruh's duality, the brilliant, far-seeing political leader, on the one hand, and the undisciplined chief of a hard-drinking, card-playing, woman-chasing bunch of assemblymen, on the other.

The behavior of Unruh and his followers was worthy of the Delta House fraternity in John Landis's 1978 film *Animal House*. Surrounded by yes-men who cheered him on, Unruh underestimated his opponents and ignored and antagonized more sober, longtime friends who tried to save him from himself.

To understand how all these elements combined to do so much damage to Unruh's reputation, it is necessary to recall the ribald atmosphere of the assembly of the 1960s.

The male-dominated social order in Sacramento mirrored the rest of American society. Toughness was considered a manly virtue. Unruh did his best to personify it, and his acolytes followed him without question. Wives usually were left at home with the children. Assemblyman and later State Senator James Mills recalled Unruh saying at a dinner with friends, "You have to remember that a considerable percentage of the women around the Capitol are unattached and working in a building where a lot of the men are also footloose because their wives are hundreds of miles away taking care of the kids."[4]

The dual lives—wife and family at home, girlfriend in Sacramento—went unrecorded. We journalists did not report on the private lives of public figures. Reporting on sex was off-limits for television and print news, as was exposing drinking and the rest of the life in Sacramento's Animal House. Editors and reporters did not see a link between public and private conduct. Everybody bought into the culture. Permitted their privacy, the lawmakers ran wild.

Something else shaped conduct: the lowly status of women. It was long before the era of feminism. So prevalent was the belief in feminine inferiority that it even infected women who succeeded. One of the most successful women politicians of the era, U.S. senator Maureen Neuberger of Oregon, sadly noted: "From my own experience, I have found that women perpetuate the prejudices against themselves. They denigrate their own abilities and are uncertain they can deal with the problems of the cities, of taxation and international diplomacy. Is there something in the national mores that makes us think that women are unable to help direct the ship of state?"[5]

The status of women in the 1950s and early 1960s would be foreign to later generations. "Young women who come of age in the twenty-first century may not even recognize the America that existed before the feminist revolution . . . no women ran big corporations or universities, [no women] worked as firefighters or police officers, sat on the Supreme Court, installed electric equipment, climbed telephone poles or owned construction companies," the historian Ruth Rosen writes.[6]

In Sacramento, this translated into "an intensely masculine culture in which women—especially beautiful young women—were sexual tokens of power, a currency of exchange and an emblem of possession," the political scientist Beth Reingold observes.[7]

Unruh summed it up well in a frequent admonition to colleagues. Discussing lobbyists, he said, "If you can't eat their food, drink their booze, screw their women, take their money and then vote against them you've got no business being up here."[8] In other words, women were another perk in the influence package, along with alcohol and money. The atmosphere was not unique to Sacramento. When Jeane Kirkpatrick studied women legislators eleven years later, she noted:

> Not a few students of state government have said that the political culture of the state house resembles that of a locker room. Their point is not merely that legislators are overwhelmingly male. Men's Sunday School classes are also male but they do not—normally—share the macho culture of the locker room, the smoker, the barracks. Apparently, state legislatures do. . . . Among the folkways of state legislators none appears to be more widely shared than the tradition of the *masculine* legislature.[9]

Unruh discussed these issues euphemistically in an otherwise thoughtful book written after he was speaker: "Unlike the other branches of government, the legislature has a definite social atmosphere. Mutual respect and the sense of common purpose are the very substance of legislative activity. It is natural, then, that Americans begin to regard the legislature as a kind of exclusive club with unwritten rules and customs which all members respect; this can be a productive atmosphere in which to work."[10] He didn't give a hint of the riotous nature of the 1960s legislative society.

In this society, of course, there was no place for gay men. "To be gay in the Capitol was to hide, was to lie, was to conceal, was to deceive," said Lee Nichols, who was an aide to both Governor Brown and to Unruh in the 1960s and at the time was a closeted gay man. "In fact, it almost didn't make any difference whether you were gay or not, the suspicion was sufficient."

Driven underground by fear of exposure, gays—legislators and staff members—met hurriedly and fearfully. "In the Capitol you cruised one of two men's rooms, one on the second floor and one on the sixth floor and almost any time of the day there was someone in there," Nichols said. "I don't suppose there was any day that I was hunting for sex that one of those men's rooms didn't produce." Through it all, he was "desperately afraid, desperately afraid."[11] Disclosure meant disgrace and loss of a job. When two of Governor Reagan's staff members were accused of homosexuality in 1967, they were quickly fired.[12]

To many in the heterosexual community, the pleasures provided those in power were irresistible. John Quimby reveled in the legislative life. When he was elected to the assembly in 1962 at the age of 25 and reached Sacramento on his first airplane ride, he was awed. He had been a radio disc jockey and news reporter before being elected to his local city council. He walked on crutches, the result of polio, and didn't have much money. He remembered waking up one morning in a lobbyist's hotel suite. "I thought if there is a heaven it can't be much of an improvement over this," he said.

Lobbyists supplied prostitutes to the legislators. Quimby said the main procurer was a musician in the lower bar of the El Mirador Hotel, across from the Capitol. The bar, known at the time as "the snake pit," was a favorite hangout for legislators, lobbyists, and reporters.

"He was the contact guy," said Quimby. "He had all the girls, he had the stable . . . lobbyists in those days would partake of that service on behalf of members. And I don't know where these young women came from but they were expert prostitutes, and there was quite a bit of that, quite a bit. I got to tell you I participated in it myself a lot. I'm not proud of it. But, what the hell, I don't see how you can avoid it. It was an element."

Late in the day, Quimby said, a legislator might suggest going over to the El Mirador "and pick up a couple of pigeons. . . . What that meant was let's go find a couple of lobbyists who have expense accounts and have dinner, in other words get somebody to buy our dinners . . . two or three guys sitting around having a drink. There would be a little bit of a crowd gathered, and then you'd go off somewhere . . . and have dinner." During the evening, a legislator or lobbyist would suggest finishing off the evening with women, "occasionally, not every week, but once in a while there would be the availability of several of those ladies . . . somehow in the course of the evening, somebody would ask for it or he'd [the lobbyist] suggest it, it depends on how the evening went. . . . By the way, never once . . . and I would have known, did Jess have anything to do with that. Whether or not he felt that he just didn't want to run the risk of getting involved or whether he always had so many of his own ladies, . . . he didn't want anything to do with it. . . . Stuff like that would start to occur, he was gone."[13]

Whether it was prudence or the availability of willing companions that kept Unruh from the prostitutes, it certainly wasn't fastidiousness. His conversation was often crude around women, especially when he had been drinking. My wife, Nancy, recalled an especially raunchy stunt he enjoyed performing in front of women. At a party one night, Unruh stuck out his extraordinarily large tongue to demonstrate that he could touch his nose with it, a trick he managed to make lewd and suggestive. Another time, on the day a friend of ours, a respected journalist, revealed her separation from her husband, Unruh called her up for a date, an invitation she declined. Later, when she told my wife about it, she laughed, but it was clear that she was more shocked than amused.

Jaci DeFord got a taste of Unruh's crude side one evening at a party at Frank Fat's, a Chinese restaurant and bar a few blocks from the Capitol that was a favorite hangout. Unruh walked in and a mutual friend said to him, "I want you to meet Jaci." Jaci recalled, "so he looked at me and said 'I want her.' . . . I thought 'who is this guy? I know he's the speaker but what is this thing? I want her'?" Later they began dating, "but not necessarily alone because you never went any place alone with Jess, but with a group of guys." Once Unruh and his friends were talking about music. "I had been married to a musician and I was sort of chiming in about East Coast jazz and West Coast jazz, and Jess looked over at me and said 'Don't be so knowledgeable.' I wasn't sure exactly what he meant . . . I think what he was saying [was that] this is not really a place for a woman . . . in this kind of society, don't participate, just sit and listen."

Decades later, such comments would have probably provoked a sharp reply from a woman. But this was the early 1960s and men got away with such behavior. Women were grateful for small favors. "There would be times afterward when Jess would ask me about the evening . . . It made me feel incredible that this extremely intelligent man was asking my opinion," DeFord said.[14]

His attitude toward women was evident in his dealings with Yvonne Brathwaite Burke, a beautiful and intelligent young woman who was elected to the assembly in January 1967. Three and a half years had passed since the lockup, but the rowdy Animal House spirit still prevailed in the Capitol. Burke was the first African American woman in the legislature, after defeating Unruh's choice in the 1966 Democratic primary and then moving on to election in November. Another woman, March Fong, was also elected that year. Early in her term, Burke said, Unruh

> asked if I would come into his office. The thing I remember is he didn't sit behind the desk. I sat down on the sofa. He came and sat down across from me in a chair, and he said, "Well, I didn't want you here, but you're here . . . tell me what committee you want. . . . I'm going to give you a committee, . . . I'll give you whatever committees you want."
>
> And so I picked out my committees, and he gave me those committees, made me vice chairman of one of them, and he said to me, "I know that your district is next to mine . . . if you go home and tell what you see going on here, I will spread rumors about you that you will never get over." . . . I assume that [this meant that] if I went back and told about all the mistresses and the women and activities that were going on there and some of the money things, they were going to destroy me.[15]

The first year, she recalled, "I had responded to an invitation to the assembly event, the party, I think they called it a stag but I assumed that it was [for] . . . all members, and both March and I responded." The sergeant at arms came over to Burke, who was seated at her desk, and made it clear she was not invited. "Well," he said, "I just put a case of liquor in your car and . . . you can have your own party wherever you like."

"The next year, I said, 'Don't send me any liquor, I'm going.' " She and Fong went, Fong bringing along some small children from Chinatown to entertain. That was not the kind of entertainment the hosts had in mind. They decided the children would open the show, and then be hustled out so the real entertainment could begin. But first, the children had to put on their costumes. "March was furious. They had them in the dressing room with strippers, and the strippers were taking their clothes off . . . she got all the little kids together and got them to sing and got them home."[16]

During the evening, Jess approached Burke in the company of the famous San Francisco topless dancer Carol Doda, who had enormous artificially enlarged breasts. Unruh had Doda lean over Burke, her breasts over the assemblywoman's shoulders, "and he got a camera and he took a picture of her hanging over my shoulder." The photograph, she assumed, would be used if Unruh ever carried out his threat to ruin her reputation. "[It] said to me he was not joking."[17]

Burke's experience gives a picture of Unruh the bully lording it over his small world in his office and at social events, embarrassing a young woman who had had the temerity to oppose his candidate in a Democratic primary election and to win. It illustrates the kind of rough, undisciplined style that had contributed to the lockup. It is one of the ironies of Unruh's career that his personality and behavior overshadowed the seriousness of the policy issue at stake.

The central issue behind the lockup was important, involving an underpinning of America's democracy, the education of all of its children, poor and well-off. By 1963, the system of financing of public education no longer met the needs of a state that was becoming increasingly less rural. Urban and suburban districts were beginning to show the first signs of the huge gap between rich and poor that so dominated the political and economic landscape later in the century. Once local school boards had built schools and run them pretty much to suit town, city, or county tastes, financing the operation with local revenues. But as urban poverty increased, concentrated in black and Hispanic neighborhoods, the disparity between poor districts, such as those around Watts, and rich ones—Beverly Hills, for example— became extreme, and a movement grew, strongly backed by Unruh, to share the wealth among school districts.

To Unruh, education was the best way to deal with California's postwar transition from a largely rural state and help educate poor minority children, most of whom lived in the cities. He had made this point during the Rumford housing bill debate when he said that, while the bill would right wrongs, the law alone could not raise poor African American and Latino children from the poverty of their surroundings so that they could one day afford to own a home.[18]

Revising the financing of public education, closing the gap between the affluent and the poor, was a central theme of Unruh's political life. In pursuit of that, he was intolerant of resistance. He had a vision; he had power, and he was determined to use it. To Unruh, what followed was more than an exercise in pure power. Rather, he felt he was using his power to help people and doing it in a way that fascinated him, slipping unnoticed provisions into complicated legislation to accomplish his goals.

The school financing issue was part of the significant amount of uncompleted business left by the legislature after it passed the Rumford Act. The session's unfinished work required the governor to call a special session beginning the first week of July. He placed the uncompleted final state budget and the school spending issue on the agenda.[19]

From its beginning on July 8, the special session was difficult, marked by disagreements between the assembly and the senate on matters other than the school bill. The senate had killed the governor's tax proposals in the reg-

Unruh, in his Navy uniform, with his bride, Virginia.

As a young man, Unruh wanted to be a pilot, but his flat feet kept him out of the Air Force. He ended up a sailor stuck in Alaska during World War II.

Unruh in cap and gown after his graduation from the University of Southern California in 1948.

PHOTO COURTESY OF VIRGINIA UNRUH.

Unruh on the University of Southern California campus in 1948. His friend Bee Canterbury Lavery recalled that he was "Angry. Angry. Angry. Edgy. And challenging in conversations."

PHOTO COURTESY OF BEE CANTERBURY LAVERY.

Before his election to the California State Assembly, Unruh worked nights and took care of the children while his wife worked days. "He was very good with the kids," Virginia Unruh said. "He loved them . . . he could change a kid. He could take care of them."

PHOTO COURTESY OF VIRGINIA UNRUH.

Unruh presenting a bill at a California State Assembly committee meeting in 1962, early in his tenure as speaker of the assembly. His plan would have given California's big urban areas greater representation in the state senate. PHOTO COURTESY OF AP/WORLD WIDE PHOTOS.

Unruh chatting with President John F. Kennedy in 1962. Unruh managed Kennedy's presidential campaign in California in 1960 and was offered a federal appointment by the president but declined it. PHOTO COURTESY OF THE *LOS ANGELES TIMES*.

Governor Edmund G. "Pat" Brown Sr. and his wife, Bernice, both looking somewhat irritated, listen to Unruh at the Biltmore Hotel after the June 1964 primary. Brown's candidate for U.S. Senate lost to Unruh's, and the split between the two political leaders became almost irreparable. PHOTO COURTESY OF AP/WORLD WIDE PHOTOS.

Despite their differences, Unruh and Governor Pat Brown appeared at a press conference together in October 1964 to urge support for a state park bond issue. Here, the two confer before meeting with reporters. Brown is shielding his mouth to prevent the journalists from hearing what he is saying.

The old Unruh and the new. When Unruh began his campaign for governor against
Ronald Reagan, the media began exploring the difference between the old and the new.
Illustrating such a story were these before and after pictures.

Unruh was proud of his slimmed-down body, as he shows in this 1967 picture.
PHOTO COURTESY OF THE *LOS ANGELES TIMES*.

Unruh, talking to a California Highway Patrol lieutenant, holds a wet cloth to his nose after getting a whiff of tear gas in 1969 on a visit to the riot-torn University of California, Berkeley, campus. PHOTO COURTESY OF AP/WORLD WIDE PHOTOS.

Unruh with Senator Robert F. Kennedy during the latter's campaign for the Democratic nomination for president in the 1968 California presidential primary election. Unruh managed Kennedy's California campaign and was with him at the Ambassador Hotel in June when RFK was assassinated after winning the primary.

Scene at RFK's presidential campaign headquarters at the Ambassador Hotel in Los Angeles just before Kennedy was shot. Ethel Kennedy and Unruh stand on either side of the candidate. Behind Unruh, putting his hand to his face, is Kennedy's regular bodyguard.

A grieving Unruh in his seat in the California State Assembly during a moment silence during a tribute to Robert Kennedy.

Unruh and his wife, Virginia, when Unruh entered the race for governor of California in 1970.

Unruh engages in a shouting match with Henry Salvatore, a wealthy Reagan supporter, and his wife, Grace Salvatori, outside their Bel Air mansion. Unruh and his campaign entourage, riding a bus, had driven to the exclusive neighborhood to deliver an attack on tax breaks for the rich. Unexpectedly, the Salvatoris came out to denounce Unruh.

PHOTO COURTESY OF AP/WORLD WIDE PHOTOS.

Unruh, campaigning for governor, takes his campaign to the Sacramento home of his opponent, Governor Ronald Reagan. He displays a list of the wealthy donors who had bought the home and rented it to Reagan, who had declined to live in the old state-owned governor's mansion. Reagan wasn't home when Unruh dropped by.

Unruh, campaigning for governor in 1970, stands by an old picture of himself, explaining to reporters that Big Daddy is no more. PHOTO COURTESY OF THE *LOS ANGELES TIMES*.

Unruh congratulates Ronald and Nancy Reagan after Reagan's swearing-in ceremony as California governor in January 1967; Lieutenant Governor Robert Finch stands behind Reagan. PHOTO © BETTMANN/CORBIS.

Unruh and Chris Edwards, whom he later married, with President Jimmy Carter at a Century Plaza event during Carter's 1980 presidential campaign.

PHOTO COURTESY OF CHRIS UNRUH.

California State Treasurer Unruh used his control of billions of dollars in state funds
and bonds to spur construction of housing, hospitals, parks, and businesses.

PHOTO BY BOB CHAMBERLIN/*LOS ANGELES TIMES*.

ular session, while the assembly had approved them. But the hard feelings went beyond that. Some of the senate leaders resented Unruh, indignant at the way he frequently boasted of his determination to make the assembly equal to the senate by such moves as increasing the assembly staff. Some were angry at his strategy in the passage of the Rumford housing bill. They recalled how he had used the same tactics in 1959, when he refused to permit a vote on senate bills in the Ways and Means Committee, of which he was chairman, until a senate committee acted on his own civil rights bill. Unruh, for his part, wanted to weaken the senate's domination over fiscal policy. "We're not going to be a rubber stamp for the senate," he said.[20]

Unruh, however, had an ally in the senate. Democrat Joseph A. Rattigan was the author of the school finance bill and, Unruh knew, would be sympathetic to urban California in the fight, even though he was from a rural county. Although Rattigan was more liberal than most of the senate leaders, he was highly respected by them and by the entire legislature.

After being wounded as a PT boat captain in the Pacific during World War II, Rattigan graduated from Stanford Law School and opened a law practice in Santa Rosa, then a small city in the heart of rural Sonoma County. He was elected to the senate in the Democratic sweep of 1958 and became the embodiment of legislative excellence, both obtaining projects for his district and taking on the most difficult statewide issues. As a young legislator, he won passage of a bill creating a state university in his county. He was a major force in the enactment of the Rumford Act and in approval of a huge expansion of welfare to the poor.[21]

Unruh moved quickly to seize control of the school finance bill. He assigned the task to Kenneth Cory, consultant to the assembly Education Committee.[22] Cory was an example of what Unruh had in mind when he built up the assembly staff to provide the members with information beyond what was given them by lobbyists and the Brown administration. "[T]he lack of access to reliable technical opinion puts legislators . . . at a disadvantage in appraising the claims of special interest groups that can and do command expert advice," he said. "[T]his lack of access to independent advice puts local legislative bodies at an immediate political disadvantage in dealing with private interests and certain kinds of executive proposals."[23] Cory was an intelligent, curious man, a generalist with the ability to grasp complex ideas quickly, even in fields that were initially unfamiliar to him. And he understood politics. In fact, he was later elected to the assembly and to the office of state controller.

He and other consultants started devising a formula that would increase urban funds. It was all in the formulas, expressed in obscure terms of statistics and mathematics, and mastery of them was necessary to achieve Unruh's political and social goals. Unruh was well aware that others—experts from the state educational bureaucracy and lobbyists from school districts that would be hurt by the Unruh plan—were hard at work on formulas of their own. Unruh and other legislators could not work their way through the morass by themselves. Without expert advice, his proposal would be buried under a mass of statistics and allocation formulas.

But disputes over complexities did not cause the lockup during the special session of 1963. Instead, opposition to Unruh from an unexpected quarter triggered it—four young Republican assemblymen who weren't afraid of him and were determined to make his life miserable.

Two of them were from small cities in the Central Valley that were market centers in the rich agricultural heartland of California. Robert T. Monagan, a former college athletic director, congressional aide, and chamber of commerce manager, had been elected to the assembly in a district with a strong Democratic majority. He understood his farm-oriented constituents, who had survived the Depression with the help of the New Deal and prospered with federal government–supplied water, but whose basic conservative values were shaped by their southwestern and midwestern backgrounds. John Veneman was a former county supervisor who, like Monagan, was a moderate Republican in the mold of Earl Warren. His district was so strongly Democratic, and so devoid of snow, Monagan said, that "Pat Brown and Jess Unruh were using the expression that it will snow in Modesto before you elect a Republican there. Well, it snowed the day of the election down there, lightly, and he [Veneman] got elected."[24]

The elections of Monagan and Veneman were among the first signs that California was shifting from the Franklin D. Roosevelt legacy of the Depression and World War II to something more conservative, a trend that would help elect Ronald Reagan governor in 1966. Their rural Democratic constituents, many of them veterans of the immigration from the Southwest, had survived hard times and now cast a suspicious eye at the party's liberal leadership and its support for the expansion of welfare. The conservative, sometimes racist, views they brought with them from Oklahoma, Texas, and Arkansas were at odds with a Democratic Party wedded to civil rights, improvement of economic conditions of the poor, and increased aid to urban schools.

Such a movement to the right was not apparent in the early 1960s; only hindsight makes clear what was happening. In 1962, Governor Pat Brown won a strong victory over the Republican candidate, Richard M. Nixon, who had hoped to use the California Capitol as a springboard to the presidency. At the same time, the Democrats increased their majority in the legislature. But Monagan sensed the change in the grass roots and in his large majorities in the Democratic district when he ran for reelection.[25] His instincts were correct. By the beginning of the new century, the Central Valley provided strong support for Republican governor Arnold Schwarzenegger and President George W. Bush, although the latter never did carry the state.

William T. Bagley, the third maverick triggering the lockup, was another kind of Republican, representing the affluent suburbs of Marin County, across the Golden Gate from San Francisco. Marin County still had many farms run by old families, but suburban communities were growing fast, attracting liberal, ecology-minded young families. Bagley balanced his varied constituency with intelligence and a madcap humor. Houston Flournoy, unlike the other three, was a newcomer to California, a Princeton-educated college professor drawn to the state by a job at one of the Claremont Colleges, a small but distinguished group of institutions in the solidly Republican suburbs east of Los Angeles. All four were so popular in their districts that they had nothing to fear from Unruh.

Unruh wasn't used to such Republicans, young, smart, combative, and fearless. In 1961, he had strong-armed and tempted several members of the Republican assembly contingent into voting for the reapportionment bill. He promised favorable districts to Republicans who supported him—and possibly more. "Money, trips, committee assignments, girls, parties, whatever they needed," said Monagan.[26]

Monagan, Veneman, Flournoy, and Bagley were appalled at the control Unruh exercised over the Republicans in the assembly. The speaker considered the Republican delegation part of his fiefdom. He boasted that he selected the Republican leader in the assembly. "I had a personal grip on enough Republicans that, by and large, I could do it," he said. "I always had five or six or eight or ten Republicans that I could principally rely upon. As a matter of fact, for about four years when I was speaker I used to elect the Republican leader. . . . I had enough Republican friends that I could push them into voting for the candidate I wanted."[27]

Monagan was contemptuous of the collaborating Republicans. "They were in the old school. They didn't have the votes. They couldn't do anything. They weren't willing to run the risk of arguing with the leadership," Monagan said. "[In contrast] we were all young and aggressive, and we were ready to roll."[28]

The newcomer Republicans had made their first move the previous year, 1962. With their intimidating energy, they persuaded the other Republicans to take a rare step—refuse to vote for Governor Brown's budget unless he reduced it by $50 million. At the time, the assembly had forty-seven Democrats and thirty-three Republicans, and so Unruh needed seven Republican votes for the two-thirds required for budget passage. To the surprise of the Democrats, the Republicans defied Unruh for the first time and succeeded in delaying the end of that session.

Unruh was furious. He had appointed seven Republicans as committee chairmen on the condition that they vote for the budget. By withholding their votes on the budget, they had broken their promise to him, and this, in Unruh's view, was one of politics' most heinous sins. He blamed Monagan, Bagley, Flournoy, and Veneman.[29] He was determined to get revenge, and he believed he had the power to do so. He'd just demonstrated his control over the Republicans at the beginning of that session when Monagan ran for the post of minority leader. Unruh made sure the job went to a man he could manage more easily, Charles J. Conrad.

That merely angered the four rebels. Flournoy recalled: "When we lost the minority leadership to Charlie Conrad, Bagley, and Monagan and Veneman and I set out to make life miserable for Charlie Conrad" and for his Democratic sponsor, Unruh. "We used to get together daily, usually at breakfast, and it was really almost a 'what are we going to do to Jess Unruh today?' meeting."[30]

Unruh knew that rural counties' senators, who dominated the senate, were opposed to his plan to help the urban districts, and, with Rattigan's help, he wanted to keep the measure under wraps as long as possible to prevent an organized opposition.[31] This practice, of putting a bill up for a vote without allowing legislators to read it, was not uncommon and continues to this day. Rattigan, the author of the bill, and two other senate liberals had gone along with assembly-backed provisions that would shift money to poor urban districts. "They were in on the plot to keep the bill under wraps," said Mills, who was an assembly member of the conference committee.[32]

Unruh intended to try the same tactics when the conference report reached the assembly, rushing it through the house without disclosing to the rural counties' representatives what he had done. He wouldn't let the assembly Republicans in on his plan. "I was afraid that [if] they found out that we had screwed them pretty good so far as the old rural districts were concerned and had taken much of the money for the poor districts, they would back off in their agreement," Unruh said. "So I didn't want to tell the [assembly] Republicans because I knew damn well they'd be running over there telling their Republican senators."[33]

But his tactic provided Monagan, Bagley, Flournoy, and Veneman with an opening.

The four of them lived in an apartment house near the Capitol. "It was a hot Sacramento day," recalled Houston Flournoy. "We went over to the apartment for lunch and were sitting in the pool."[34] Or, as James Mills put it in his memoir *A Disorderly House,* "After they had eaten their lunches, they lounged around the apartment house swimming pool in their trunks, soaking up a little more of the hot soft sunshine and cold hard liquor."[35]

As they sought relief from the Sacramento heat, Flournoy, Monagan, Veneman, and Bagley discussed how to embarrass Unruh. One of them suggested refusing to vote on the budget unless Unruh let them see the school finance bill. Flournoy didn't like the idea. "I remember saying, 'Well, that doesn't make any sense at all. All he's got to do is tell you . . . and then what are you going to do?'" Flournoy said. "But I didn't have any better idea of what to do."

Monagan and the others persuaded their Republican colleagues to go along with the plan. In the debate, Flournoy explained that all the Republicans wanted was to read the school bill before they voted on it. They would not, he said, vote on the budget until Unruh complied with their request. The members cast their votes, punching the green button for aye. There were fifty-one Democratic ayes (one member was absent) and twenty-eight Republican abstentions, three votes short of the two-thirds majority of fifty-four required for passage of the budget.[36] The Democrats voted for a "call of the house," a procedure needing just a majority of the eighty-member house. Under a call, the sergeant at arms locks the doors and brings in the absent members.[37]

Not only did Unruh feel he'd been betrayed by the Republican chairmen who refused to vote for his budget, but he was furious because the delay might reveal how he had succeeded in shifting money to the poor school districts. "That's what had me so pissed off," Unruh said. "They'd [the senate] already passed it and here we were diddling around."

Unruh called his leadership into his office. Drinks were poured. Mills recalls having a scotch and water. Unruh drank gin on the rocks. One of the group was the assembly majority leader, Jerome R. Waldie. At first, he thought Unruh was right in insisting the Republicans vote for the bill. "But then as the hours wore on and it was clear that these guys were not only not going to surrender, but they were having the ball of a lifetime . . . the results in terms of public perception were devastating to the Democrats, and particularly to Jess," Waldie said. Democrats, like the Republicans, were passing the time drinking and playing cards.[38]

Unruh, himself, got angrier when John Quimby, taking a break from a gin rummy game with Democratic and Republican colleagues, came into Unruh's office and reported that the Republican chairmen continued to insist they would not vote for the budget, despite their pledge to him. "Jess' face metamorphosed into a mask of living fury," Mills writes. "He looked upon their breach of faith as a personal betrayal. He stormed out of his office and through the chaos in the [assembly] chamber and out of the great dark main doors into the mosaic-floored halls outside where all of the television cameras had been moved on their tall tripods to do some interviews of members . . . the speaker dumped all over the Republicans [to the press]."

As Mills tells it, Unruh, his voice "like summer thunder," said: "A number of Republicans have given me their solemn word they would vote for the budget and they have been blackjacked by the Republican caucus into breaking their word." The Republican caucus chairman, Don Mulford, standing nearby, told Unruh he was "power mad." Unruh, stalking away, snapped, "That's bullshit."[39]

With the situation moving toward disaster for the Democrats, Unruh left the Capitol to have a drink with a clerk on the assembly desk, Helen Jones. When he talked about the lockup twenty years later, Unruh went into considerable detail about the date, as if, aware of his womanizing reputation, he felt he had to make it clear that Jones was not just a pickup. His account was also a revealing picture of the subordinate status of women legislative employees of the era:

Helen Jones is a very pretty young lady who was splitting up with a husband at that point. Had three small children and was starving to death. We'd gotten her a job on the assembly desk carrying messages, mostly, and she was very pretty, and I was kidding her as I always kid almost all the girls. On the day of the lockup, I said, "Would you like to have a drink with me tonight?" And she said, "Sure." So during the course of the thing when we weren't doing anything, I went over and had a drink with her and later on ended up having dinner with her. We later on became very close friends.[40]

By now it was 6 P.M., and Unruh's tight circle was worried. Someone had told Waldie that Unruh was across the street at the El Mirador bar. "I began getting quite concerned about it," Waldie said.

Waldie was Unruh's man, but he was his own man as well. Waldie was not only as liberal—and as moderate—as Unruh but was also as intelligent and witty. Unruh had met him in 1958 when Waldie was running for the assembly in his hometown of Antioch, a small blue-collar city on the northeastern edge of San Francisco Bay, where the big employer was a steel mill. At that time, Unruh and Tom Rees were soliciting support for Ralph Brown for assembly speaker. The three of them had lunch, and Rees gave Waldie a $250 contribution. That fall, Unruh raised $500 for Waldie. In Sacramento, Waldie said, "We hit it off very quickly and very easily," and they became roommates.

Waldie's Northern Californian political background contributed to his independence. It was distinctly different from Unruh's—more rooted in old hometown and family connections. Contra Costa County extends inland from the northeastern shore of San Francisco Bay, including the factory towns along the bay, as well as expensive suburbs in the inland Diablo Valley. Industrial Contra Costa County had been strongly Democratic since the Depression, but, Waldie noted, "It was never really very socially liberal. Its liberal aspect was limited almost solely to economics and labor issues— totally different than San Francisco."[41]

In Waldie's district, politics were more personal than in Unruh's in Southern California. Waldie's grandparents had been among the families that pioneered Antioch. His dad worked in the mills and owned a workingman's bar that opened at 6 A.M. for the convenience of night shift workers going home. Waldie helped out there. His father was also constable and mayor, until the town barber defeated him. "Probably guys who got their hair cut voted more than guys who drank," said Waldie. His father influenced him to go into politics. He was student body president in high school, junior college, and law school. In short, he had a stable, traditional youth in a traditional town, far different from what Unruh had faced on his way up.

Independent but loyal, and with a better sense of the world outside the Capitol than Unruh, Waldie was worried. He walked over to the El Mirador to talk to Unruh. Unruh was at a table with Helen Jones and one or two others. Waldie sat down. "I told him the thing was getting out of hand, we weren't accomplishing what we'd hoped, and we'd be better off just to lift the call and close the roll and, if we didn't have the votes, take it up tomorrow," Waldie said.

"Unruh said, 'Nope, don't think so. They would have to give in on it.' I didn't argue much with him. He wasn't in the mood to argue." Waldie returned to the Capitol.[42]

Waldie tried again, this time accompanied by a young freshman from Fresno whom Unruh had taken into his group, George Zenovich. "Jesse was screaming," Zenovich recalled. "He was really in a depressed state because he really wanted a budget [the school finance bill]. . . . I remember we were sitting there at the table, and he got a pen and on a napkin started to write out a resignation and, in fact, wrote it out . . . I, of course, told him he was nuts."[43]

Recalling the night years later, Unruh blamed his behavior on a combination of alcohol and diet pills.

According to Unruh, a friend of his had lost considerable weight, helped by biphetamine, a large black amphetamine-related pill used for appetite suppression. Some used the "black beauties," as they were called, to get high. His friend gave him a handful of them. Unruh said:

Well, I took a couple of 'em and I lost seven or eight pounds. And I thought, well, if one of 'em is good in the morning, then one'll be good at noon. So I took one in the morning, one at noon and sometimes one in the afternoon. They did kill my appetite and I was losing weight. . . .

I had no idea what the effects of the biphetamines, the amphetamines were with booze. Neither did anyone else at that point. So when we got into the lockup and we went in and had a sociable drink, that booze hit me about five times as strong as it ever had before. And not only hit me hard but hit me unknowingly and not with any real predictability. So the next thing I knew I was off in the bathroom crying. I don't excuse myself in this whatsoever, but I do excuse myself on the basis that here was this good ol' fat boy trying to take off weight and taking these pills, having a social drink no more so than usual. . . .

Even when I was having dinner, I had more to drink than I probably should have. But again, it was the damn pill.

So the one time that I plead guilty to my judgment being screwed up really royally was during the lockup. I don't think I would ever have been likely to have held the Republicans in all night, let the Democrats go, gone through the kind of beating I did—I knew I was taking a beating even then. But the longer I stayed in there, the madder I got. Finally when my own lieutenants tried to help me it made me that much madder.[44]

That was not the way Waldie saw it. "He wasn't drunk. I knew when Jess was drunk. I've seen Jess drunk. There was no question in anyone's mind when Jess was drunk . . . if he had been over on the floor instead of over in the restaurant he might have had a better sense of what was going on. He might have reacted differently.

"This was a fascinating event because it was so unusual," Waldie said, "and what was unusual about it was the adeptness that Unruh usually demonstrated was absent that night. And he maintains it was because of pills and booze mixing together. I maintain it was just a simple lapse of judgment that escalated beyond his control. . . . Those things unfortunately happen, and I don't buy [that] he was disabled. That's too easy an explanation."[45]

Another of Unruh's allies made the trip to the El Mirador. Tom Bane, the chairman of the Rules Committee, was a man who, to every degree, met Unruh's requirements for toughness. He was Unruh's hammer, his hatchet, but like Waldie, Bane was secure enough in himself to be independent. He told Unruh, as Zenovich remembered it, "You're out of your mind. You've been drinking too much. Straighten up, because I'm telling you that if you don't straighten up, I'm quitting," or words to that effect. "It was very moving."[46]

Waldie and Zenovich tried to work out a compromise with the Republican leader, Mulford. "He was the only one we could talk to," Waldie said. "The other guys were playing poker. The Republicans, they were really partying. There was no anger anywhere on the floor. There was disappointment, and I was probably the most disappointed one on the floor, but it wasn't anger. And they (the Republicans) were having the time of their lives, calling for cots and announcing every half hour some outrageous thing that Jess was going to do. And they had put together a beautiful, beautiful response to this and succeeded far beyond their imagination."[47]

Around 10 P.M., Waldie and Zenovich talked to Unruh again at the hotel. "At that point, he said he didn't give a damn what we [did]," Waldie said. "So we told him we were going to call a caucus [bring Democrats together for a meeting] and put this thing over until tomorrow. He said do what you want to do. But it was clear he was not pleased."

At the caucus, Waldie, as majority leader, outlined a settlement plan. Unruh walked in, sat down, and listened. "Then," Waldie said, "he got up and made a fiery speech about those Republicans, and what do they think they are doing and they had the arrogance. We simply can't allow that to continue. We won't give in at all. On and on. He got cheers and claps and 'Go get 'em Jess.' So I didn't say anything. The caucus ended and everyone went back to playing cards. . . . I was probably more disappointed than mad. . . . Disappointed in his refusal to follow my advice."[48]

"Jerry Waldie slumped on the leather sofa beside me, with his . . . head in his hands," James Mills writes. "He raised his face to look bleakly at Jess for a moment, and I saw there were tears on his cheeks. He had done his best to save his friend from himself and he had failed."[49] It was past midnight. Waldie headed to his hotel, leaving word with the assembly staff to call him. By then, Mills says, Unruh had returned to the Capitol, and "the gravity of the situation and a lot of black coffee were sobering him up. He was wandering around in a state of blinking exhaustion."[50]

The approach of dawn brought sober reconsideration. Democrats and Republicans were looking for a way out. But neither wanted to surrender. Common sense had fled the Capitol. Senator Rattigan, trying to end the stalemate, met with the Republicans and explained the details of the bill. But even his status as one of the authors and one of the Capitol's most respected figures did not shake them from their determination to see the school finance plan in writing. The demand, conceived so casually in an apartment house swimming pool, had been elevated to high symbolic status.

At 5 A.M., Waldie received a call to return to the Capitol. He joined a meeting in Unruh's office, where the speaker had summoned his loyal and worried advisers. This time, the drink was coffee, and rationality returned.

The legislators agreed that the argument for secrecy no longer applied because Rattigan had already told the Republicans what was in the bill. Waldie said that the Republicans, having won the public relations war, might be ready to settle. Why not give them a written summary of the bill? Unruh, drained of anger and stubbornness, agreed. "Will you take care of that, Jimmy?" Unruh said to Mills. Mills awakened the staff and told them to prepare a written summary.[51]

Waldie was right. The Republicans, triumphant in the media, were looking for an excuse to quit, and the staff's written analysis provided it. By noontime, Assembly Minority Leader Conrad—who had turned against Unruh even though he had been the speaker's choice for the job—rose in the assembly chamber and said the Republicans had seen the summary and it met their demands. Enough Republicans voted for the budget and the school bill for passage, and the crisis was over, twenty-four hours after it began.[52]

The session ended. The chamber emptied, but Waldie remained seated at his majority leader's desk in the front of the hall. "I am still pissed and angry, disappointed, the whole gamut of emotions, and Jess comes up and stands before me and says, 'You're upset aren't you?' I says 'Yeah, goddamn it, I am.' And he says, 'You want to talk about it?' I said, 'No, I don't.' He said, 'OK,' and he leaves and I left and that was the end of that."

But it wasn't quite over for Unruh. He still hungered for revenge, still didn't understand how thoroughly he'd damaged himself, despite the successful passage of the school finance bill. "Once we realized how badly we'd been had in the press, the Democrats were really mad," Unruh said. Some of his colleagues, Unruh said, proposed that he strip the rebellious Republicans of their committee chairmanships. That afternoon, the Rules Committee, controlled by Unruh, changed the rules. The majority party would elect the speaker. No more would Unruh have to bargain for Republican votes and trade committee chairmanships for Republican support.

But revenge was not sweet, as he came to realize. "What hurt us most out of the lockup was the guys lost confidence in my insurmountable judgment," Unruh said. "I think they looked at that and saw such a terrible debacle that they decided, well, he, too, is human. Up to that point, whatever Jesse Unruh said went. Jesse Unruh was so potent and had things thought out so well that it was no problem for them to follow him because they knew that he was 99 times out of 100 going to be right, and I had been right. Their fortunes were all built on his and, as a consequence, once he made a bad mistake that showed . . . that this emperor had no clothes on this particular occasion, . . . they began to worry about their own asses, too."[53]

What was the result? Unruh's provisions increasing money to urban districts remained in the bill—and became law. "It really did hold . . . even though we had to go through two days of living misery," he said.[54] The damage to Unruh was considerable, as he admitted. "I knew that Jesse Unruh was in trouble but I also thought it was possible to get out. To this day, I believe we did get out."[55]

As it turned out, the lockup made the Big Daddy title a pejorative, rather than a label of respect and affection, mixed with fear. It became another obstacle in his way to the job Unruh wanted most, governor. Radio station KNX in Los Angeles editorialized that Unruh "had not only locked up his Republican opponents in the Legislature, he had just about locked up the state of California, politically speaking."[56] Newspaper critics took the same line. "The press in general treated that 24-hour session like something out of the Dark Ages," Unruh complained.

As the weeks passed, he saw that at least part of the blame lay with himself. "He was never the same," Flournoy said. When they returned for the next legislative session, "he had lost 100 pounds, and he was a different

Unruh, much more susceptible to compromise. It changed the inner dynamics of the legislature. I went away hating Unruh, loathing the man. When we got back for the next session, it got so you could have a social relationship with Jess even if you didn't agree with him."[57]

He was not exactly a new Unruh, but certainly a modified one. At least some of the time, congeniality replaced bullying, and he included Republicans in some of his most important work. In the coming years, he and his colleagues—Republicans and Democrats—would go on to make great contributions to the state.

NINE

Backstabbing Democrats

IN 1964, RACIAL TENSIONS were increasing in places ranging from Unruh's assembly district in the heart of Los Angeles to the San Francisco Bay Area. At the same time, other social issues were resonating throughout the state. At the University of California's Berkeley campus, students were organizing to support civil rights and fight conservative causes. In Southern California suburbs, conservatives, long marginalized and ineffective, were organizing in living rooms and backyards.

Despite these powerful forces at work in society, Unruh and other Democratic politicians occupied themselves with trivial party feuds, backbiting, and character assassination that brought their worst instincts to the fore. Isolated in Sacramento, they became all but irrelevant to the tide of history.

Unruh's focus had turned inward, to self-examination, and he resolved to clean up his act. Physically, at least, he had changed. The lockup, he told Lou Cannon, had prompted an intense self-assessment. Even before that, he'd been working on improving his physical appearance, so much a part of his "Big Daddy" image. He lost ninety pounds in four months. "I never ate more than a steak and a salad or a hamburger and a salad or meat and a salad without dressing once a day," he said. "For the first month, I think I ate that once every other day. I would go two days on one meal. I did a lot of things in those four months, went back to the White House for a state dinner and toured Southeast Asia for four weeks. I kept on that diet all the while and was on a pretty heavy speaking tour around the state."

The lockup, he admitted, had been "a bad mistake, but in many ways it was a good mistake for me. It probably added ten years to my physical life because it got me so agitated, along with a lot of other things, that I took the weight off. If you learn anything in this life, you ought to learn some things about yourself and I'm sure I've learned some things in adversity that I would never have learned in the flush of victory."[1]

Still his image needed work. "Frankly his image is troublesome in this district," a Democratic activist, Cheryl Peterson, reported from rural and suburban Sonoma County. "Democratic incumbents are frightened about being tied to him," she wrote Unruh's chief aide, Larry Margolis. In much of the area, she said, Unruh was "virtually unknown except as the 'big, bad boss' depicted in the press. . . . Mr. Unruh needs to be known in California and he needs to be known as the constructive liberal leader he really is."[2]

But no matter how much he changed on the outside, Unruh could not conquer the fury that continued to rage within him. His friend Henry Lacayo, a United Auto Workers official, witnessed Unruh's anger in 1964. The Los Angeles County Federation of Labor, locked in an internal fight, refused to endorse Unruh for reelection to the assembly because a majority of directors on the executive board thought he had not fought hard enough for labor bills in the past legislative session. In the broad sweep of Unruh's career, this was a minor matter, having no impact on his assembly race, which he was certain to win. But, even so, he was obsessed with revenge. Lacayo recalled Unruh dug up "a rap sheet of some arrest record" for an official who had been among the Unruh opponents. Unruh intimated he would use the information against his foe. Lacayo recalled Unruh saying, "When people are in the arena with a politician and they're throwing blows they should expect to be hit back."

Lacayo smoothed things over, persuading union leaders to change their vote and back Unruh, which "satisfied Jess's hurt . . . to some degree." But it left Lacayo disillusioned. "You know this was a part of Jess I began to dislike. . . . It really sort of brought down my hero . . . to a degree where he's now mortal like all of us."[3]

Unruh's anger came into play in another matter that turned out to be more important. Unruh was convinced Governor Pat Brown had offered to step aside after the completion of his second term and to support the speaker for the job in the 1966 election. The promise had been made, Unruh said, in 1962 when Brown faced his difficult reelection campaign against Nixon and badly needed Unruh's help in Southern California, particularly in getting out the vote in Los Angeles Democratic precincts. Unruh's friend and colleague Assemblyman Robert W. Crown said he remembered the promise. He recalled being with Unruh in the governor's mansion when Brown, afraid he was going to lose to Nixon, had promised his backing to Unruh. "He asked for help, and he gave Jesse an absolute commitment that he would not run for a third term," Crown said.[4] Brown remembered it differently. "I may have said, work along with me as governor. I know you're able and I know you're ambitious, and I'll help you. But I had other people who were ambitious too, and it would have been a serious mistake to lay my hands on any particular individual. I would have lost all power."[5]

Unruh had seethed over the episode since the week after Brown's defeat of Nixon in 1962. That week, Eugene Wyman, the chairman of the California Democratic Party State Central Committee, had asked his young press aide, Larry Fisher, to write a news release in which Wyman and some other prominent Democrats urged the governor to run for a third term. "Jess blew up," said Fisher, who had started out in politics working for Unruh and remained loyal to him.

From then on, Fisher said, Unruh could not "overcome the anger, the sense of betrayal, the sense of unfairness. And I was with him off and on quite a bit and most of the time. If I was just driving him somewhere, or whatever, and it didn't have to be necessarily private, there could be people around, a good deal of the time, it would come back to what a lying SOB Pat Brown was. There was never any healing of that wound. It was just festering."[6]

Just as it had during the lockout, Unruh's anger overcame his judgment. The consequences were serious, because it was a time when his wisdom and experience were badly needed by the Democratic Party, and by all of California as it entered a period of political and social unrest.

One of the first signs of the social turbulence that would soon grip the state occurred early in the morning of March 7, 1964, when police moved in on more than 1,000 demonstrators who had seated themselves in the lobby of the Sheraton Palace Hotel in San Francisco to protest the hotel's failure to hire black employees. In the broad panorama of the American civil rights movement, the demonstration was not much more than a blip, but it marked a sharp turn for California.

A total of 167 were arrested at the Sheraton Palace and charged with disturbing the peace. Many of them, like Jo Freeman, were students at the University of California, Berkeley. Freeman was the daughter of a school teacher–political activist in LA's San Fernando Valley. "My turn came at 5 A.M.," she wrote. "When the police grabbed the person next to me, I held on. . . . They [the police] didn't do anything to me worthy of coverage, but once outside I was tossed hard into the paddy wagon, landing with a resounding thud, and some pain, on my tailbone."[7]

The night before Freeman's arrest, Unruh had been in Sacramento, also occupied with a matter of civil rights. In his case, he was trying to improve education for minorities in the public schools. Speaking to a dinner meeting of the Association of California State College Professors, he urged support for his latest school finance bill. This was one more example of his dedication to giving minority children an equal chance to get a good education. He had introduced another major bill he believed would better equalize funding between wealthy districts and poorer areas. It was a radical extension of the previous year's plan to increase funds allocated to urban schools, the proposal that had triggered the lockup. This time, Unruh proposed consolidating the state's 1,583 school districts into just 108. Consolidation of the districts would broaden the tax base of the remaining districts, forcing rich districts to share the wealth with poor ones.

Unruh understood that this approach wasn't easily translatable into the language of politics. "Educational finance is a very complicated subject which unfortunately is understood by few," Unruh admitted.[8] But that was the only approach he could find to make the reforms he believed in. He loved digging into an intricate problem and having his staff research it until they came up with a solution, usually in taxing and expenditure formulas that were as complex as the problem itself, just as his assistants had done with the school bill involved in the lockup.

Progress toward racial equality could not have been made without the civil rights laws. But decades after the passage of such laws, the festering inequalities in education remained at the heart of the nation's racial ills. The civil rights laws, as Unruh knew, were not enough without offering greater opportunities for minorities. But the opposition to his district consolidation plan, led by incumbent school board members and other officials who feared losing their jobs, was strong. "I believe that the arguments, raised largely by professional educationalists who feel their duchies and baronies are threatened, are inconsistent with known facts about our society and run counter to the main goals of modern education," he told the college professors in his Sacramento speech.[9]

Eventually, he was forced to drop the bill and—for the time—his efforts to further reform public school finance. This was unfortunate. Although his moderate approach would not have cured all of public education's ills, it would have been a start in reducing financial and educational inequality.

But the University of California students and others sitting in at the Sheraton Palace didn't want to wait for another education bill to make its way through the legislature. They believed immediate action was needed in a society segregated by laws, hiring restrictions, and residential discrimination. They saw civil disobedience as the answer, a stark contrast to Unruh's efforts to work through the legislative process. The students' sit-in, the biggest of several demonstrations against discriminatory San Francisco Bay Area businesses that spring, was unsettling to Californians. The Sheraton Palace, opened in 1875 and rebuilt after the 1906 earthquake and fire, was a revered part of the city's history, and generations of San Franciscans had dined in the splendor of its Garden Court. The invasion by this young and disobedient crowd outraged people from Governor Brown, a San Francisco native, to Jo Freeman's mother. The governor thought the sit-in endangered Palace patrons and set back the cause of civil rights. Despite her years of civil rights and Democratic Party activism in Southern California, Freeman's mother told her daughter she "was not sending me to college to get arrested. . . . That was not the return she expected on her investment."[10]

Most Californians agreed with Mrs. Freeman. This was not what they expected from their huge investment in the tuition-free University of California.

They were surprised by the intensity of the demonstrators, whose ranks included a number of young men and women who had been active in on-campus protests against university policy, as well as off-campus civil rights causes. For the students, the marriage of the two causes was a perfect fit. "Probably the most meaningful opportunity for political involvement for students with any political awareness is in the civil rights movement," said another Berkeley student, Mario Savio.[11] Savio was also among those arrested at the Sheraton Palace. After his release from jail, he traveled south to participate in the Mississippi Summer Project to register blacks to vote, and then returned to Berkeley in the fall, where he became the best-known spokesman for the Free Speech Movement.

As the months passed, civil rights issues, such as fair housing, dominated political debate. But Unruh and other Democratic leaders were occupied with something that had a much more immediate impact on their careers. In September of the year before, President John F. Kennedy had told Governor Brown that U.S. senator Clair Engle was dying of an inoperable brain tumor. He had learned this from doctors at Walter Reed Hospital.[12] In the coldhearted business of politics, Democrats immediately began maneuvering, figuring that Engle was so sick he would have to drop out of the 1964 election, which would give another Democratic politician a shot at the prized U.S. Senate seat.

As speaker of the California State Assembly, Unruh would have been a logical choice for the U.S. Senate. But polls did not show a groundswell of support for his candidacy, and the office did not appeal to him. Patiently waiting his turn in the Senate seniority system, cozying up to old-timers he didn't respect—that was not his style. His eyes were on the governor's office, the seat of power in California.

Even so, he thought the outcome of the competition for the Democratic nomination for U.S. Senate was important to his career. Unruh had given up hope that Governor Brown would support him for the nomination for governor in 1966, and he was determined to make life miserable for the governor. "Certainly, in regard to the governor, he was increasingly sour, and he sort of made up his mind he was going to show the governor who was really in charge and make things happen," Larry Fisher said. "What he was effectively saying to Pat Brown is, 'If you want anything, you've got to come and see me.'"[13] Apparently, Unruh believed such rough tactics might persuade Brown to forget about running for a third term in 1966, leaving the field to the speaker.

But while Unruh didn't respect Brown, he was wary of him. Even if Brown decided against running in 1966, he still had the power to block Unruh's candidacy for the office. According to Unruh's friend Frank Burns, Unruh believed that Brown was determined to elevate his friend and finance director Hale Champion to the office of state controller. This was an elected office, occupied at the time by Alan Cranston, one of the founders and former president of the California Democratic Council. Unruh thought Brown would back Cranston for the U.S. Senate seat held by the ailing Engle. If Cranston won the nomination and the general election in November, the controller's office would be vacant, and Brown would appoint Champion to the job, giving him a highly visible platform from which to run for governor in 1966 in the event that Brown bowed out. Burns recalled:

> Jess was willing to let Cranston go to the Senate, but what he didn't want was Hale Champion being controller. Unruh told Cranston, "You can be senator but I get a free shot at the governorship." The answer was, "No, up yours, Jess, no deal." Jess talked to Cranston. Jess talked to Pat, [and] he said, "Let's not have a big fight here." But Brown's friends didn't want Jess. A lot of Pat's close friends were not friends of Jess's, . . . they regarded him as a barbarian, uncivilized, a Southern California yahoo.[14]

Thus, it became Unruh's goal to deny Cranston the Senate nomination.

Through much of his career, Cranston, who died in 2000, was a favorite of California liberals. He was a founder of United World Federalists, which, during the Cold War, advocated universal disarmament. As the former Cranston campaign aide Harold Meyerson wrote, the organization was "an expression of postwar one-worldism that valiantly battled the Cold War zeitgeist."[15] This is one of the issues that put Cranston at odds with Unruh, who had supported the Cold War since his USC days, when he rejected the Henry Wallace wing of the Democratic Party in favor of President Truman. All through his career, Cranston was a fervent exponent of arms control. In 1984, controlling the nuclear arms race was his platform when he sought the Democratic nomination for president, only to drop out when voters showed little enthusiasm for his candidacy. In addition, there were huge differences between Unruh and Cranston in personality, wealth, class, and geography. Cranston was a rich Northern Californian from the affluent suburbs of the San Francisco Bay Area, where residents generally held Los Angeles in disdain. Cranston was gracious, sophisticated, and reserved to the point of seeming bland and even boring. But this impression was deceptive. He was as ambitious and as aggressive a fund-raiser as Unruh, and he played politics just as ruthlessly. Cranston's own voracious fund-raising eventually blighted his career. He was reprimanded by the Senate for intervening on behalf of the savings and loan president Charles Keating, who had been indicted on securities charges. Cranston and four other senators who intervened with federal regulators on behalf of the savings and loan owner came to be known as the Keating Five.

The other major contender for Engle's job was the state's attorney general, Stanley Mosk. He had been elected attorney general, the state's primary law enforcement officer, in the Democratic sweep of 1958. Previously, he'd been a superior court judge in Los Angeles.

Mosk, who had been born in Texas and raised in Illinois, was an immigrant to California, like Unruh. As a young lawyer, he had campaigned for the 1934 Democratic nominee for governor, the writer and socialist Upton Sinclair. Four years later, Mosk's new candidate for governor, Democrat Culbert Olson, won, and the young man accompanied him to Sacramento as his executive secretary. His reward after Olson was defeated in 1942 was a judgeship.

In the postwar period, Mosk was the first Jew to be elected to statewide office. On the bench and as attorney general, he was a noteworthy defender of civil rights. He handed down decisions banning housing discrimination against blacks. Later, as attorney general, he expanded the office into new areas, most notably setting up its first civil rights and consumer fraud units. He was responsible for breaking the color line in the segregationist Professional Golfers Association, the sport's ruling body, which controlled who could play in the big tournaments. When he was told that Charlie Sifford, an African American, was banned from playing in PGA tournaments, Mosk threatened to use the law to stop the golf association from operating in California.[16]

In many ways, Unruh and Mosk were opposites. Mosk was gentlemanly, a fit and dedicated tennis player, and, said his speechwriter and adviser Tom McDonald, "a little bit shy."[17] Mosk's son Richard, who is now a state appellate judge, remembers that his father "got along with everybody. There was nobody he would speak ill of. Nobody he disliked. Democrat, Republican. That was his great skill, getting along with people."[18] While Brown was put off by Unruh's aggressiveness, Mosk enjoyed being around Unruh and other politicians. Mosk and Unruh shared a love of the political process—the excitement and the way it could be used to help those struggling for a fair break. Their staffs worked together in improving the civil rights and consumer protection legislation Unruh had created in 1959. Both moderates, they were natural allies against Cranston and the California Democratic Council, which they considered too liberal.

Mosk also saw himself as an ally of Governor Brown. He had helped the governor during difficult periods. "I heard Brown say to him, 'Stanley, you've been so great, I'll do whatever you want for you,'" said Richard Mosk.[19]

In the early stages of the maneuvering to replace Senator Engle, Unruh stuck with the popular incumbent until the question of the senator's health could be settled. Engle was a respected figure, a remnant of an earlier California, of the agricultural and mining state rooted in the western frontier. He was from rural Tehama County, in the far northern part of the Sacramento Valley, 135 miles from the Capitol. To the east was the Sierra Nevada, to the west the Coast Range, and in the center was a valley with cattle ranches and farms dependent on the Sacramento River, with its cycle of winter flooding and dry summers. Engle, elected district attorney at the age of twenty-three, understood that his job after he rose through the ranks of elective office was to guarantee water to his ranchers and those like them in other parts of California, and he was remarkably successful in winning approval for federal water projects. He was liberal, but attuned to the feelings of the influential and conservative ranchers and businessmen in his district. As congressman, he voted for the Taft-Hartley law limiting the power of labor unions, opposed by President Harry Truman and organized labor. He was known in the district as "the little giant in politics," and his reputation for independence trumped the Taft-Hartley vote. He even carried the towns in his district where unions were strong.[20] In the 1958 election, he was an invaluable asset to the Democratic ticket, giving it a moderate tone. The prospect of losing Engle from the ticket in 1964, when moderate and conservative Democrats were slipping away, was all but unthinkable.

Trying to find out the extent of Engle's illness, Unruh sent Burns, along with two legislators, to meet with the senator. "[We] talked to him, terrible, terrible. [Then we] came back and reported, not publicly, but to Jess," Burns said.[21] If Engle were unable to run, Mosk's chances were excellent. Polling showed he was the most popular of the potential candidates, although Engle retained a reservoir of support. Cranston trailed Mosk and Engle by a substantial margin.[22]

In February, the California Democratic Council held its annual convention in Long Beach. Cranston was favored to win the endorsement of this organization, which he had helped found. Unruh, although he had little influence in the organization, tried to forestall a Cranston endorsement. Despite the bad news about Engle's health, Unruh sent a telegram to potential delegates on February 21: "If you attend CDC convention and if you are asked to endorse anyone but Engle you should realize that doing so is tantamount to declaring Engle, despite liberal voting record, unfit to run. I do not know if you want to be in that position, and I am not suggesting what you do—just urging you to consider in this light."[23]

Cranston won the endorsement. But the organization's strength had declined, and Mosk was favored to win the Senate nomination despite the CDC's action. Engle by now was out of the race, too ill to run. Not surprisingly, Unruh was backing Mosk and readying his Los Angeles get-out-the-vote organization for the campaign.

It appeared nothing could stop Mosk. The nomination was his to lose, which is exactly what happened. Mosk, a married man with a family, had a girlfriend who owned a Sunset Boulevard strip club called the Seventh Veil. "I was told friends of Stanley helped her buy it," Mosk's aide Tom McDonald remembered.[24] Someone took a picture of Mosk and the woman getting off a plane in Las Vegas, which fell into the hands of the publisher of the Long Beach newspaper, Hank Ridder. Burns recalled: "The information I got was that Hank Ridder had called him [Mosk] in. Somebody had given the pictures to Ridder, and Ridder had a meeting with Stanley and showed it to him and said, 'What's this?'"[25]

The pictures circulated. According to Richard Mosk, "There were rumors that [Los Angeles County sheriff] Peter Pitchess had pictures. There were a lot of rumors: [Los Angeles police chief William] Parker had a file, the FBI had a file, and there were a lot of files."[26] One of Cranston's closest associates, Roy Greenaway, said that an anti-Unruh newspaper publisher, Tom Braden, "claimed that Alan Cranston showed him those photographs. Alan has always denied it, that he had anything to do with the photographs, and I have no way of knowing what is correct."[27]

"Whether it was Cranston or Brown who circulated the rumors of the woman, so to speak, I don't know," said Richard Mosk. "To a certain extent, it was his [Stanley Mosk's] own fault. You know, if this was a problem he should have gotten rid of it in some fashion."

Mosk's aide Tom McDonald said that while his boss was away on a campaign trip, "Pat Brown was calling a lot of Stanley's chief supporters and saying there was a problem and there were pictures, et cetera. He was saying it would be a disaster for the party, and all of a sudden Stanley's support vanished overnight." McDonald explained that the calls were especially damaging because the donors panicked and immediately called Mosk's chief fund-raiser, who happened to be his wife, Edna.[28]

"It was upsetting to my mother," Richard Mosk said. "I'm not quite sure what happened, except that my mother was probably unwilling under the circumstances to go out and raise money. She was really the greatest fund-raiser he had, and I think she did not have her heart in it under the circumstances." Governor Pat Brown told President Lyndon Johnson, "One of these days I'll tell you what I did to get Mosk out of it." The president replied, "Yeah, but I know."[29]

The plan worked. By Monday morning, Mosk had decided to drop out. "I got into the office . . . and Stanley was locked up making phone calls," McDonald said. "He was locked up a couple of hours on the phone, calling people. And he came out and said he wanted to see me. He said 'I'm not running.'" On March 4, Mosk announced his decision. He blamed a shortage of campaign funds but, of course, didn't go beyond that. "I am unwilling to impose on my personal friends to give and to raise that tremendous amount of money," he said. "I am equally unwilling to accept the obligations implicit in sizeable contributions from those who are not motivated by my friendship."[30]

Unruh was shaken. He went to state party headquarters and talked to Joseph Cerrell, then a young political aide. "He comes in the office and he says: 'I'm running for the Senate,'" Cerrell recalled. "'What?' said the shocked Cerrell. 'I'm running for the Senate,' Unruh repeated. 'Why?' asked Cerrell. 'Well, if we're going to lose to Cranston, I might as well be the guy who loses myself.' But he later dropped that idea."[31]

Something more to his liking emerged. "Out of the blue came Pierre," said Frank Burns. He was referring to Pierre Salinger, once press secretary to President Kennedy and now unhappily serving President Johnson. Salinger was a debonair, adventurous man always ready to take a chance. As a reporter for the *San Francisco Chronicle,* he went to jail to gather material for a series on prison abuses. Later, he was an investigator for Robert Kennedy on the Senate antiracketeering committee before going to work for John Kennedy in 1959. He was eager for something new. After Mosk dropped out, Salinger looked to California, where as a young man he had been an active Democrat. Unruh flew to Washington and talked to Salinger. So did Mosk, angry over how he had been forced from the primary.[32]

Unruh's friend Frank Burns said he thought Salinger had decided to run for the office on his own. "Jess embraced the idea, but I don't think he had a thought about Pierre being a candidate, and I am sure a lot of other people didn't either. Pierre was not regarded as a big political strategist. He was regarded as a very good press secretary." For Unruh, said Burns, it "was a very pleasant surprise."[33]

There was, Salinger conceded, "some question concerning my eligibility to run," since he was not a resident of the state.[34] The Republican secretary of state, Frank M. Jordan, challenged Salinger. But Mosk, as attorney general, issued an opinion declaring Salinger was eligible. The state supreme court ordered that Salinger's name be placed on the Democratic primary ballot.

During the ensuing campaign, Cranston attacked Unruh as well as Salinger. Peter Kaye, a political writer for the *San Diego Union,* reported that Cranston's Senate campaign "was directed against Unruh more than Salinger. His organization set up dial-a-number recordings in three major cities whereby callers could get an anti-Unruh message."[35]

The campaign "became bitter and personal, the race being characterized as one between California's last vestige of the spoils system—Cranston's sole control over the appointment of inheritance appraisers . . . and boss rule, allegedly supported by savings and loan money, exemplified by Unruh," according to the political scientists Totten J. Anderson and Eugene C. Lee.[36]

The tactics used against Cranston were effective, and Salinger won the June primary. Among the factors that gave him a boost were his celebrity as President Kennedy's press secretary and Unruh's get-out-the-vote operation. Kaye noted that the voter effort run by Unruh and his African American allies in Los Angeles turned out "a bloc of votes that matched those he delivered in 1962 for Brown against Richard Nixon."[37]

Supporters sent telegrams congratulating Unruh, and exulting in his victory over Cranston and Brown. "Let he who has pointed the finger of blame extend now the hand of credit," said one. "Well done and you did it."[38] But the tough words of the campaign rankled. Unruh had a thin skin. That and his temper made him ill suited for the hot debate of a statewide campaign. In a revealing letter to Morris Weisberger, secretary-treasurer of the Sailors Union of the Pacific, in 1964, Unruh admitted:

> During the June primary, I spent many tortured hours receiving the brick-bats and harpoons from many erstwhile friends and longtime enemies. It was undoubtedly my darkest moment during my political career. . . . But the dawn came up like thunder on June 2 and before the day was over, so were many of my tribulations—at least temporarily.
> . . . It is surprising how many friends I had all along. Interestingly, most of them were terribly busy before June and couldn't seem to find time to tell me, although others had time to say many unkind things. Perhaps it takes less time to be nasty than it does to be nice . . . [but] while the wolf pack was circling . . . you were loud and strong and clear in your position of defense. . . . I have been accused of not forgiving those who have given me a bad time. The accusation is not true. I can forgive easily—I do not, however, forget my enemies but more particularly [remember] my friends. And I shall not forget that you were my friend—when they were very, very few.[39]

It was a time for the primary opponents to pull together. If they had looked beyond their feuds, they might have seen the storm about to envelop them all. Instead, they continued fighting over matters that now seem irrelevant to the crisis in American society. By the summer of 1964, race, more than ever, was a pivotal issue. In California, Proposition 14, the ballot measure to repeal the Rumford Act, was picking up support through the summer and into the fall as voters began focusing on the November election. Salinger opposed Proposition 14, while his Republican opponent, George Murphy, a former movie musical star and Republican Party activist, declined to take a stand. The repeal measure was a clear manifestation of white resentment against the gains of the civil rights movement. Around the country, there were other signs of unrest. During the summer, riots occurred in Harlem, Rochester, New Jersey, and relatively small African American communities in Oregon and New Hampshire.[40] In the spring presidential primaries, George Corley Wallace, Alabama's segregationist governor, received 30 percent of the vote in Indiana, 34 percent in Wisconsin, and 43 percent in Maryland.[41] Yet President Johnson pressed on with his Civil Rights Bill.

On June 1, the Senate passed it 71–29. Senator Engle was wheeled into the Senate chamber for the vote. Dying and unable to speak, he pointed to his eye when it was his turn to vote to signify aye.[42]

Back in California, Unruh and Brown were still squabbling, now fighting over who would be in charge of President Johnson's election campaign. Unruh appealed to Johnson, his fellow Texan, and he and Burns met with the president in the White House.

Burns remembers that Unruh and Johnson got on well, and Unruh had been a guest at the Johnson ranch. The two would talk about their Texas boyhoods, although the lives led by the impoverished Unruhs had little in common with President Johnson's landowning kin. The two politicians, however, had much in common with each other. They shared an ability to dominate and manipulate their peers, an appetite for women and drink, and a Texas talent for conversation and storytelling. And as liberal, populist rural Texans, they both balanced their belief in civil rights with their understanding of the bigotry of the rural South and Southwest and the importance of white voters in those parts of the country to the Democratic Party.

Unruh told Johnson that he'd like at least a piece of the president's 1964 campaign in California, even though custom dictated that such matters would normally be handled by the Democratic governor of the state. It was important for Unruh to be involved. While the broad outlines of the presidential campaign would be shaped in Washington, considerable money from contributions flowed to state organizations for local advertising and get-out-the-vote operations. In addition, Unruh wanted a say in federal patronage after the expected Johnson victory. Johnson, understanding the need to satisfy the conflicting desires of Unruh and Governor Brown, said the two would have to work out their disagreements, but the president would make sure that Unruh shared power with Brown equally and would not be shut out. Unruh was leaving immediately for a trip to Asia, and he asked Johnson who would tell Brown of the presidential decision. Johnson decided to let Burns do it. "I had to go up to Sacramento," Burns said. "Pat was sitting there with a broken leg. He was very nice about it, but you could see he was boiling."[43]

As the feud continued, Unruh sent his aide Steve Smith to set up a presidential campaign headquarters. The governor rebuffed him. In a letter sent by special delivery airmail, Brown said there seemed "to be some misunderstanding concerning the campaign organization." He said his political adviser Don Bradley would be the statewide professional manager and was "already establishing a headquarters and taking care of housekeeping details." Smith, he said, should not set up a headquarters.[44] Bradley said a compromise was finally worked out, but it "didn't work very well. There was an upstairs and downstairs in the headquarters," with the staff split between Unruh and Brown people. "It was a horrible campaign," Bradley recalled, "but it was never in trouble so it didn't make any difference."[45]

As the Democratic National Convention approached in August, the division between Brown and Unruh escalated even more, heated up by a dispute over the seating at the convention of an antisegregation delegation, the Mississippi Freedom Democratic Party. The convention had been planned by President Johnson to be his coronation as the party's nominee. But Johnson, his advisers, and supporters around the country, such as Governor Brown, had not counted on the impact of the Mississippi Freedom Democratic Party and its remarkable leader and voice, Fannie Lou Hamer.

The Mississippi Freedom Democratic Party's mission was to organize disenfranchised blacks for political activity. It aimed to challenge the state's all-white delegation to the Democratic National Convention. As Hamer's biographer, Kay Mills, observes, the Freedom Democratic Party "forced political leaders from around the country to judge the issues this predominantly black group was raising and to take a stand. It offered a vehicle for people from around the country, not just those who had volunteered to work in Mississippi, to express to their own states' delegates in Atlantic City their views on civil rights in Mississippi."[46] But for Governor Brown and President Johnson, the Freedom delegation meant trouble. Both feared white backlash, Johnson in his race against the Republican nominee, Senator Barry Goldwater, Brown in his fight to save the Rumford Act.

Among those forced to take a stand were the California delegates to the convention. There was strong support for the Freedom Party in the delegation. Two of the delegates, Representatives Phillip Burton of San Francisco and Augustus Hawkins, along with another California congressman, Don Edwards of San Jose, had just returned from Mississippi, where they'd observed the voter registration campaign being conducted by the Student Nonviolent Coordinating Committee, CORE, and other groups. They had also visited Ruleville, Mrs. Hamer's home, where Edwards's son Len was a voter registration worker and had stayed during the summer at Hamer's home. Burton, in fact, spoke at a rally at Ruleville.[47]

Unruh, who was serving as a delegate, also supported the Freedom Party. After a year spent, or wasted, on interminable party feuds, Unruh was thus thrust into a matter of great national importance. For him, it was an easy choice. His background had made him intimately familiar with the evils of racial segregation. Moreover, African Americans—Mervyn Dymally, Assemblyman Leon Ralph, both from South Los Angeles, and others—were an important part of his Southern California political operation. In the 1961 legislative session, he'd created the seats that made possible the election of two more African American legislators to the assembly. In the intraparty fights over representation, he had always stood up for the idea of black districts being represented by blacks.

Pressure from President Johnson was intense as the president tried desperately to prevent a floor fight over seating of the Mississippi delegation. "The White House feared a floor fight that would embarrass the party and the president and intensify a backlash that could cost the Democrats all over the country," the historian Robert Dallek notes.[48] Johnson had another reason to focus on the California delegation. He was afraid Unruh might support Attorney General Robert Kennedy for the vice presidency.[49]

Despite the efforts of Johnson and Brown, a substantial number of California delegates arriving in Atlantic City were ready to endorse the seating of the Freedom Democratic Party delegation instead of the all-white group. Mrs. Hamer's powerful appearance before the Credentials Committee added to the determination of the Freedom delegation supporters. She told how she had been beaten after a meeting. State highway patrol officers had had two black prisoners beat her with blackjacks. "All of it is on account of we want to register, to become first class citizens, and if the Freedom Democratic Party is not seated now, I question America. Is this America . . . the home of the brave where we have to sleep with our telephones off the hooks because our lives be threatened daily, because we want to live as decent human beings in America?" Johnson was so afraid of her televised testimony that he suddenly preempted it with a news conference. But the networks ran Hamer on Saturday night in prime time, and telegrams and telephone calls began hitting the White House and the convention in support of the Freedom delegation.[50]

The White House proposed a compromise. The Freedom Democratic Party delegation would receive two seats on the floor as at-large delegates. The rest of the delegates would be considered honored guests. Members of the regular delegation would pledge loyalty to the party's nominee, and in the future all convention delegations would have to be chosen without regard to race, color, creed, or national origin. Pat Brown, who had joined other governors at the White House for dinner with the president on Saturday night, favored the compromise.[51] So did black leaders such as Roy

Wilkins, executive secretary of the NAACP, and Aaron Henry, head of the Freedom Delegation, who was to be one of the two delegates seated. Andrew Young, then a top aide to Dr. Martin Luther King Jr., said that assuring President Johnson's election was the most important matter before the convention. "We felt that the most important thing for the civil rights movement was to get Lyndon Johnson elected," he said. "I think the Lyndon Johnson landslide made it possible to get the civil rights bill passed."[52]

At the meeting of the California delegation, Phil Burton moved to support the Freedom delegation and vote against the Johnson compromise. Discussion was heated.

Winslow Christian, one of Governor Brown's top aides, saw Unruh, who was known to be against the compromise, working the back of the room. Christian alerted a Johnson aide, who tried to stop Unruh. Roger Kent, a top party official, remembered the Johnson assistant telling Unruh: "You don't seem to realize that what you're talking about is contrary to the wishes of the president, and you have got to make it clear before this vote is taken that you want these people to vote in favor of the compromise." Unruh apparently didn't stop, but asked for a ten-minute recess. Kent said, "I said to Brown . . . 'What the hell, we've been through what was agreed. We've had three speeches on each side. They're waiting in the hall. Call the roll.'"[53]

Backers of the White House compromise won 114–49.[54] Carmen Warschaw, Unruh's ally and the Democratic Southern California chair, said she, Unruh, and other state party leaders, along with Congressman Hawkins and Assemblyman Rumford, "believed we should follow our consciences and the overwhelming expression voiced by delegates to California's state convention a week before and work for the seating of the Mississippi Freedom delegation. When a majority of the [California] delegation voted to support a plan giving only two votes to the Freedom delegation, we moved to make the vote of the delegation unanimous, and it was on this note of harmony that the caucus was concluded."

The November election was to confirm Unruh's doubts about the Rumford Act. It was too extreme for white voters. But, as he warned Democratic activists in a racially mixed district near his own, "The alternative to this [Rumford] act is to force our minority population into the streets, into acts of violence, into taking their frustrations out in other ways instead of allowing them the right to buy a house wherever they are economically able to buy one."[55] Proposition 14 was approved overwhelmingly, nullifying the Rumford Act, until the U.S. Supreme Court, a year later, in turn nullified the proposition.

The issue drove Democrats to vote Republican, allowing George Murphy to defeat Salinger for the Senate. Salinger was also hurt by the ceaseless Unruh-Brown feud. Despite his years in the White House and his experience as a journalist, Salinger was a novice campaigner, and the discord prevented him from putting together an effective campaign team that might have saved him.

Unruh's own base narrowed in the election. The Democratic share of votes for state assembly seats declined, as it had in the previous two elections. President Johnson carried California by a landslide, but he ran stronger in every other big state except Florida. Although the Republican Goldwater lost to Johnson, the beginnings of the conservative movement he inspired paid off for his party. Political scientists Anderson and Lee conclude that "a reaffirmation of the latent potential of the minority party [the Republicans] was clearly evident."[56]

Unruh was one of the few leaders who understood the big picture. He knew the meaning of the Democrats' loss of their blue-collar base in the Proposition 14 contest. No other Democratic leader was better equipped to foresee the tragic outcome—the white backlash that would help fuel the Watts riots the following year. With his plain but compelling speaking style, still tinged with a bit of the Southwest, and his moderate philosophy, Unruh would have been his party's best spokesman to win the disaffected blue-collar and middle-class vote.

More than others, he understood how to navigate a dangerous road and could have been a strong and moderating voice in the difficult days ahead. He was hobbled, however, by his preoccupation with fights, big and small, and his need to win every contest. His priorities were wrong and his vision, skewed. As a result, the smartest member of the Democratic team took himself out of the fight.

TEN

Dirty Dealings and High Idealism

MUCH OF WHAT HAPPENED in Jesse Unruh's California State Assembly went unnoticed by the public. The press, disinclined to dig beneath the surface, was uninterested in the complexities of legislative life, and newspapers of that era refused to print stories about lawmakers' drinking and carousing. The fraternity house atmosphere of the lockout—so telling a commentary on the 1960s legislature—never made it into the newspapers, nor did much of the serious work done in the Unruh legislature. As a result, the popular view of Unruh as a political leader, while based on reality, was little more than a political cartoon.

Part of this can be explained by the momentous events that were occurring during the Unruh speakership, beginning with the civil rights movement and the assassination of President John F. Kennedy. My own experiences probably reflect the impact of these events. During the 1960s, I was covering the powerful forces that were sweeping the country, particularly those originating in California. Later, I would try to make sense of the history I had witnessed. But at the time, scrambling for news did not allow much time for thought, and I found it impossible to dig deep into the intricate world of California legislation, much less its relationship to national issues.

Such is the way of daily journalism, and, as a result, actions with lasting impact often do not get the attention they deserve. Only now is it possible to see how Unruh separated the world of power politics necessary to his survival from the idealistic world of policy that he hoped would be his legacy. Unruh drew a clear distinction between helping society's neglected and dealing with a big campaign contributor. "I always knew how Jess would vote," his friend Marvin Holen said. "It never failed. If economic interests were competing, he would go with his friends. If it was the underdog versus the overdog, or however you would put that, he was always with the underdog."[1]

Two stories from the period illustrate the contradictions. One shows Unruh at his toughest, the cynical political boss, Big Daddy in action. The other shows him as a creative policy maker, working with legislative colleagues and staff members.

Unruh's toughness came into play in an incident involving Harry Farrell, the Capitol correspondent for the *San Jose Mercury News*. It was 1963, and Farrell was reporting and writing an exposé of Unruh's fund-raising operation. Farrell was one of the first of a new generation of aggressive reporters slowly transforming journalism from sleepy acceptance of the status quo into the inquiring force that would shape public policy during the Vietnam War and Watergate. His paper circulated in the suburbs south of San Francisco Bay, and the owners, the Ridder family, were profiting from the area's transformation from farmland to subdivisions, and eventually from an agricultural economy to one based on new technology. Orchards would disappear as the area became Silicon Valley, and the *Mercury News* would grow, covering the technological revolution with sophistication and thoroughness. But in 1963, the paper immersed itself in the most local kind of coverage, and Farrell confined his Capitol reporting pretty much to the activities of legislators in his paper's circulation area. Oil was not on his beat.

Oil was high on Unruh's agenda, however, as it had been since he entered the legislature. It was, and is, a valuable commodity in the legislative marketplace, and Unruh was right in the middle of the maneuvering between its opposing sides. He had observed how the major oil companies, divided into factions, contributed to legislators who supported them. His sociability and late hours on the Sacramento nightlife trail put him close to the most powerful lawmakers, including those long involved in oil politics.

Such social skills had helped build a relationship with the conservative senate president, Hugh M. Burns. When Unruh's Democratic assembly colleague, the more straitlaced Allen Miller, found himself out of his depth while managing the 1957 session's biggest oil bill, he turned to Unruh for help. Miller had been appointed chairman of the committee handling oil legislation. His immediate task was to rewrite a giveaway bill allowing oil companies, especially the major ones, to pay the state comparatively low royalties for developing oil fields in the tidelands off the California coast. Miller introduced legislation increasing the state's royalties and regulatory powers and assumed he could persuade the assembly to pass the bill.

But he could foresee trouble in the senate, where the major oil companies were in control. Miller was aware of his own inadequacies. "I didn't pal around at night with these guys, drinking and carousing and all that business," he said. But Unruh, said Miller, had become "a good old real politician—God bless him." Miller recalled Unruh telling him, " 'No legislation is any good until it's passed. And there are two houses, Allen. There's two houses you got to pay attention to. You just can't give them a good argument here and get it out of the Assembly and forget about it. You can't do things like that up here.' Oh, he learned the rules, personal rules of getting legislation passed and dealing with people, wheeling and dealing that was away ahead of me."

Unruh told Miller that he would talk to Burns about the oil legislation. "Hughie and I already have some pretty good plans," Unruh said. "Let me go over and talk to Hughie about it and see what gives." A few days later, Unruh told Miller, "Allen, Hughie's on our side in this thing." The bill passed the senate and became law. "It skidded over there because of Jesse Unruh and Hughie Burns," Miller said. "It's as simple as that."[2]

So it made sense a few years later that when the local grandees who ran the city of Long Beach needed help with an oil bill of their own, they, too, turned to Unruh.

With inland fields becoming depleted, the oil industry's attention had focused increasingly on the offshore oil fields, especially one in the tidelands off Long Beach, the largest oil field in California.[3]

The harbor city of Long Beach, connected to the heart of Los Angeles by a commuter rail line and a few 25-mile-long boulevards, had developed a culture and political life of its own. The city was so favored by immigrants from the Midwest that it was known as "Iowa by the Sea." When the Depression struck, one of the immigrants, Dr. Francis Townsend, a physician, was moved by the sight of impoverished oldsters. He sent a letter to the Long Beach newspaper proposing a plan: give $200 a month to every American citizen sixty years of age or older, provided they spent the money within the United States. While the Townsend plan never made it into law, the idea caught on around the country and may well have prodded Franklin D. Roosevelt to propose Social Security, a far more limited version of the scheme.

Some of the era's impact on Long Beach was eased with the discovery of oil in the Wilmington field under Long Beach Harbor, with the city benefiting from royalties from oil leases. Years of drilling in the underwater field, however, caused parts of Long Beach literally to sink into the sea. The elevation of the Long Beach Naval Shipyard, at the center of the subsidence zone, dropped two feet in a single year. Elsewhere in Long Beach, streets buckled, and city hall shifted three feet.[4] But by injecting water into the field and changing drilling practices, the subsidence was stopped, and Long

Beach actually began to rise again. It was now possible to extend oil drilling into an undeveloped portion of the field, East Wilmington, thought to contain a billion barrels of oil.[5]

Although the tidelands were owned by the state, a 1911 law gave Long Beach control of them—and of the oil revenues that resulted from drilling. Driving a hard bargain with the oil companies, Long Beach took 85 percent of the revenue, using the money to finance a major expansion of its port. But a 1955 state supreme court decision gave the state half of the revenue, and some legislators demanded more.

With the city awash in oil revenue, Herman Ridder, the publisher of the *Long Beach Independent and Press Telegram,* and the paper's general manager, Sam Cameron, the two most powerful men in Long Beach, had big plans for development of their city and the resulting growth of their newspaper. They feared that development would be hurt if hostile legislators succeeded in reducing the city's share of oil royalties. The personable Cameron cultivated Unruh, making friends with him and his family. In addition, Unruh became a partner with Ridder, Cameron, and other prominent Long Beach figures in the ownership of a luxury apartment house on the shore, Pacific Holiday Towers.[6]

Hank Ridder's brother, Joe, ran the *San Jose Mercury News,* which was Harry Farrell's employer, a circumstance that may have seemed unimportant to the Long Beach crowd early in the game. Neither Cameron nor Ridder counted on Harry Farrell's skill and perseverance as he made his rounds, checking up on the doings of San Jose area legislators. Nor would the two—preoccupied with power politics, oil, and newspaper revenues—have understood the importance of the tidbits Farrell was gathering, how they would add up to a big story once Farrell put them all together. To the vast majority of publishers and their top executives, such reporters were wage slaves, occasionally of value but not really important to the fate of a business that happened to be a newspaper.

One of the stops on Farrell's beat was the basement of the Capitol, where records of campaign contributions were stored in the secretary of state's office. There, he compiled the amounts of contributions to San Jose area legislators and reported them in the paper. It happened that one of Farrell's readers was State Controller Alan Cranston, Unruh's old political enemy, who came from the town of Los Altos, in the *Mercury News*'s circulation area. As the detail-oriented Cranston combed through the tiny agate type in which the *Mercury News* listed the contributions, one item attracted his attention. He talked to Farrell, but not in his own controller's office on the first floor of the Capitol, which he feared was bugged. Instead, he took Farrell for a walk in Capitol Park.[7] He pointed out the name of a contributor listed in the story, that of Unruh's friend Marvin L. Holen, the legislative aide who had written the Unruh Civil Rights Act. Holen, as it turned out, helped distribute political funds for Unruh. Check it out, Cranston said. Farrell returned to the basement of the Capitol and pored through all the campaign records and then followed up the paper trail with interviews.

It was a sharp departure from the usual Capitol style of reporting in those days. Stories in 1963 skimmed the surface, and reporters were seldom given the time—or had the ambition—to dig into the process. But Farrell's editors were interested. They ordered him to work full-time on the project. It began running on May 5, 1963, in the combined *Mercury-News* Sunday paper. "Strange Bedfellows in a Political Jungle" was the headline, with a kicker above it, "Money Power Politics." An unsmiling, forbidding picture accompanied the story on page one with the caption "Jesse Unruh . . . The Money Man." The series continued for the next few days in the afternoon paper, the *San Jose News.*

Farrell reported on how he often found the name Holen. "Sometimes the full name was spelled out, sometimes just M. Holen or M. L. Holen is listed," Farrell wrote. "His shadowy name emerges as that of a campaign time Santa Claus, who bestows fat checks on candidates from Eureka to San Diego." Farrell reported that in addition to giving contributions in his own name, Holen also gave money on behalf of the California Committee for Better Legislation.[8]

Farrell looked for more information about the committee with no success, until "[t]he answer came to me in a way I never could have predicted." The trail led directly to the Ridder family, owners of the newspaper that employed Farrell. Twenty years later, Farrell recalled these events in his memoir,[9] which remains a chilling revelation of the underside of journalism and politics.

While Farrell was working on the series, the general manager of the Long Beach paper—Farrell does not identify him in his memoir, but when we talked years later, he said it was Sam Cameron—dropped by the Capitol office Farrell shared with the correspondent of the *Long Beach Independent and Press Telegram,* Jim McCauley. Farrell thought Cameron was paying a courtesy call on McCauley. Cameron invited the reporters to a Capitol cafeteria for coffee. "After some opening pleasantries, I learned that the general manager was not there to see Jim at all; it was me he was after. He laid his facts on the table. I had unwittingly stirred up a hornet's nest in the Long

Beach newspaper office because . . . [the] 'California Committee for Better Legislation' was a front for the Long Beach tidelands oil lobby, and Hank Ridder was its biggest contributor. In effect, I was investigating my own publisher's brother."

Each year, bills were introduced giving Long Beach oil royalties to the state. "By contributing liberally to Unruh's slush fund, the Long Beach interests counted on derailing any such legislation," Farrell wrote. "That in effect was what the general manager of the *Independent and Press Telegram* told me over coffee. I think he assumed that this disclosure, coming from a top executive of the Ridder organization, would halt me in my tracks, dissuading me from further exploration of the embarrassing terrain I had stumbled into. I listened courteously, trying to hide my feeling of having been hit in the stomach with a brick."

Farrell called his editor and said he had found where the body was buried—the true identity of the California Committee for Better Legislation. "That's great," the editor said. "No, it's not," said Farrell. "The body is named Ridder." But his San Jose bosses allowed him to continue working on the story. The two brothers disagreed politically, with Joe Ridder from San Jose still fuming over damaging stories the Long Beach paper had run about Richard Nixon. "So on my series he saw a chance to get even with his brother on that score," said Farrell. Before long, however, Farrell found out that Unruh and the Long Beach Ridders were pressuring the San Jose paper to kill the rest of the series. He learned that the San Jose and Long Beach Ridders were planning to meet with Unruh for dinner at a San Francisco hotel. Farrell, not invited to the dinner, waited in Sacramento, contemplating his future.

"My first word of what transpired there came the next morning, not from my home office but from Jess himself," Farrell wrote. "I encountered him in midmorning in the third floor corridor of the Capitol. Great bags under his eyes told me that the showdown dinner had been a traumatic one, contentious and lasting into the early morning hours, with alcohol flowing freely.

" 'Well, Jess,' I asked, 'who won last night, you or I?'

" 'Hell, Harry,' the speaker replied, 'it was about a Mexican standoff.' "

Farrell said he gathered that "the Ridders had gotten from Unruh a strong message that unless he emerged from the episode with his aura of statesmanship intact, they could jolly well look elsewhere for protection of their $2 billion oil pool." The series continued, but the headlines were toned down and the stories ran beneath the fold, still on page one but in a much less prominent position. And Farrell was ordered to change his final article "specifically to exonerate Speaker Unruh of wrongdoing and repair any damage I had done to his image." After the series ran, he said, someone had asked him if he had not prostituted himself with the last story. "'Well,' I said, thinking about the $2 billion oil pool under the Long Beach harbor, 'if I had to be a whore, at least I got a good price.'" He did not get the price for himself, of course. The beneficiaries were the city of Long Beach and its business community, most notably the newspaper.[10]

Farrell continued in a long and outstanding career with the *Mercury News,* reporting on Unruh among his other assignments. Unruh showed no hard feelings. He had taken care of Long Beach, protecting its share of the oil revenues. To him, the series had been part of Farrell's job, and it was Unruh's obligation to stop him.

Holen dropped out of fund-raising as it became more intense. In a few years, the Unruh fund-raising operation expanded into a complex of front groups, such as the California Committee for Better Government, various Democratic Legislative Dinner Committees, and the JMU Trust, bearing his initials. All of them were under the supervision of Unruh's friend Manning Post, who had come west riding the rails and become one of California's biggest auto dealers. The loose campaign-contribution-reporting laws of the time and the desire for secrecy by Unruh and Post kept the details of the funds hidden from view. But Post's papers fell into the possession of a family friend, Robert Hertzberg, who, years later, himself became a speaker of the state assembly. After Post's death, Hertzberg turned the papers over to me. In Post's neat handwriting, they show the workings of the Unruh system—how the big donors funneled their money through him. One note also seems to show Post's conflicting feelings about his friend: "Alcoholic," it reads, "psychopathic, demagogic, brilliant, loyal, strong, weak, grasping." There is no name on the note but it echoes what Post had told friends about Unruh in moments of anger.[11]

Unruh was a thorough cynic when it came to deal making. I saw this cynicism while standing next to him during an assembly hearing on his Long Beach oil bill. It was the millionaires versus the billionaires. Each side came to the table with their pockets figuratively filled with legislators' pledges of votes. I was covering the meeting for the Associated Press, but in my spare time, I was the Capitol correspondent for a small liberal magazine called *Frontier.* I enjoyed writing for *Frontier,* blasting the Sacramento lobbyists and the utilities, racetracks, liquor interests, and oil companies that employed them. Unruh turned to me and, obviously thinking of the impassioned liberal-reform spirit of *Frontier,* said in a needling tone: "Tell me, Bill, what's the liberal side of this issue?" There was none, as he well knew. It was just business.

An entirely different Unruh listened sympathetically when he met with a group of parents of retarded children in 1965. He had received a letter from a mother who said that her son "was considered unteachable by the school. A private psychiatrist felt the only alternative would be a private school for insane children."[12]

He could not have found a more daunting or politically unrewarding challenge. In the mid 1960s, the mentally ill and retarded were society's rejects, shunted away to a distant institution where they would be out of sight and, for the majority of the population and the political leadership, out of mind. Occasionally, there were journalistic exposés of poor conditions in mental hospitals. The title of a postwar book and film, *The Snake Pit,* became a symbol of such institutions. The 1948 movie stars Olivia de Havilland as a young woman institutionalized in one of the era's facilities. De Havilland's character, Virginia Stuart Cunningham, recovers with the help of a sympathetic psychiatrist and electroshock treatments and returns to her loving husband, Robert. Just before she leaves the hospital, the patients gather for a party, and, in one of the film's most moving moments, the camera pans over them as they sing the old hymn "Going Home." Some of the words express an undercurrent then scarcely heard in the mental health field:

> Mother's there 'spectin' me,
> Father's waitin' too;
> Lots o' folk gather'd there,
> All the friends I knew.

The words caught the feelings of many mentally ill and retarded patients and their families. Why couldn't these patients go home and be treated near family and friends instead of at distant, crowded state mental hospitals? The hospitals for the mentally retarded and ill were in communities far from major population centers, the inmates tucked away in unpleasant and unfamiliar surroundings, in facilities often so poorly run that conditions could push patients over the edge. Such confinement was considered the best way to treat the mentally ill. It also relieved society from being threatened or simply annoyed by them. There was no alternative to the overcrowded institutions for those without money to pay for expensive private care. The

California Department of Mental Hygiene operated nine hospitals for the mentally ill, as well as three for the retarded. More than 30,000 mentally ill were confined to the hospitals, along with 13,000 mentally retarded. In addition, there was a waiting list of 3,500 mentally retarded.

The patients were poor or working class, defined by their inability to afford private care. The limited amount of research done on the patients provided only sketchy information. Those in state mental hospitals tended to be the most difficult to treat, or the poorest, lacking money or ability to fight involuntary commitment. Few were in business, the professions, or white-collar jobs.[13]

What prompted the parents to visit Unruh was a proposal by Governor Brown's Department of Mental Hygiene to deal with overcrowding and the waiting list in the hospitals for the retarded by expanding the hospitals by 3,000 beds. This was exactly opposite of the close-to-home care sought by the parents. The parents' stories of children being shipped off to crowded institutions triggered Unruh's sense of outrage.

For parents of children in the institutions, daily life was lonely. They were separated from their children and had nobody to talk to about it, as some of them had told Carolyn Fowle, a University of the Pacific scholar. One parent said:

> It's so far to Porterville [state hospital] . . . we can't go very often . . . and I feel so guilty . . . sometimes it's so long in between that S. doesn't recognize me. . . . We didn't want S. to go to Porterville, but we couldn't take the expense. We didn't always live this way; before this all happened we had a good home and five rooms of furniture. Just one year cost us over $5,000; I finally had to take bankruptcy . . . there's no hesitation for me on what I'd like to see—community, 24-hour care. We would like to see S. more often. The trip is really hard on us. We're older. Our car is older. There's so much traffic on Highway 99. If it were only 40 to 50 miles, we could go for a Sunday or bring him home for a weekend.

Another parent, with a child on the waiting list, said: "A lot of times, I just wish I had someone to talk to. . . . I'd like to ask about Porterville. Do they ever come home again? People talk about you if you keep the child, and they say you're sacrificing the other children. And then the other people think you're awful if you put the child away, so you don't know what to do."[14]

The lack of care close to home was only part of the problem. Patients, particularly those exhibiting symptoms of mental illness, senility, or simply behavior contrary to society's norms, were hustled into mental hospitals after perfunctory legal hearings, or no hearings at all.

Inside the institutions, they were treated like prison inmates. They were required to wear shabby uniforms. They could not have personal possessions, such as toilet articles or even small amounts of money for purchases at the canteen. Storage space was denied them, as were materials to write and send letters. Authorities opened their letters. Phone calls were limited.

Treatments could be cruel, and inmates could not refuse them. The electroshock administered to Virginia Cunningham in *The Snake Pit* still can be a brutal experience, causing permanent memory loss. The electroshock treatment forced on the patient McMurphy, played by Jack Nicholson, in the 1975 film *One Flew Over the Cuckoo's Nest* conveys the horror of the experience. Countless patients were also subjected to lobotomies, a procedure for cutting nerves in the frontal lobes of a brain. Egas Moniz, who pioneered the operation, won the Nobel Prize for it in 1949, but in the 1950s, lobotomies were largely abandoned because so many patients worsened, some degenerating into a vegetative state.[15]

In California, about 20,000 inmates of state mental hospitals and prisons were sterilized from 1909 through 1964, in the largest such program in the nation. California's laws gave broad power to the superintendents of state institutions to sterilize inmates, with little or no consideration of their civil rights. Officials administering the policy said they were acting to protect society—and the afflicted themselves—from the procreation of mentally ill and retarded children.

When the parents of the mentally retarded children spoke to Unruh, and he decided to examine their problems, it drew him into the complexities of the issue. It was an opportune time, for Unruh was also engaged in building up the legislative staff. The mental health controversy provided the new aides with an important issue, which also permitted them to offer an alternative to the executive branch's programs.

"The level of staffing in the assembly is relatively new to California and all but unique among state legislatures in America," Unruh later wrote. "For this reason, the assembly may be considered something of an experiment in modern federalism. . . . Legislative studies of important issues can draw upon the information and viewpoints of all the vested interests in the community. It is possible for one of our studies to become a central forum for examining and debating a problem. The legislative study can be 'where the action is,' and if properly conducted can gather the most influential opinions and information from academic and other communities to produce a definitive analysis."[16]

Complicating Unruh's efforts was his feud with Governor Brown, which continued to grow. The Brown administration believed that Unruh's staff was just trying to grab power. The fights within the Democratic Party had created an irreparable breach between Unruh and Brown. The division extended beyond political power, for Unruh came to believe that he knew how to run state government better than Brown did. To Unruh, the Brown administration was hidebound and unequal to the task of solving California's most complex problems, such as care of the mentally disabled. He and his legislative allies and aides expressed this attitude bluntly and frequently in private, and increasingly in public. This attitude further antagonized Brown and his team, and they fought back. The speaker knew that once his staff started questioning Department of Mental Hygiene policies, the Brown administration would resist mightily.

Unruh needed someone who was smarter and tougher than anyone on the administration side. He decided on Assemblyman Jerome Waldie, who was already an impassioned advocate for handicapped children. Unruh and Waldie had reconciled after their chilly parting at the end of the lockup. For Waldie, helping the afflicted and their families was a challenge worthy of the era. Like Unruh and others of the GI Bill generation, he believed government should use its vast powers to help people. That was the lesson he took from World War II and from his parents, who had scraped out a living during the Depression. For Waldie, Unruh, and other liberals in power during the 1950s and 1960s, big government was a good thing, not a concept to be scorned.

Waldie's interest had been piqued when a constituent, father of a mentally handicapped son, talked to him about how he and other parents had no place to seek help. "He said, 'I would like you to come over and visit,'" said Waldie. "He sounded so decent and sincere, so I went over. This call became momentous. . . . This area had the most lasting impact for good of anything I did in politics. He got me into this, two or three visits with him."[17]

Unruh asked Waldie to head a special subcommittee to look into the children's situation. "I never got the sense Jess was involved for political profit," Waldie said. "I think he wanted something done."[18] Waldie was to be the subcommittee's chairman. Unruh suggested another member, Assemblyman Nicholas Petris, a liberal Democrat from Oakland who had earned a reputation as a serious legislator from his work on taxes and other difficult issues. Waldie and Unruh agreed on the third member, Frank Lanterman, a Republican. All three were noteworthy for their lack of participation in the assembly's fraternity boy antics. They were serious and independent men, respectful of Unruh, but each guided by a strong moral and intellectual compass. Lanterman, as it turned out, was Unruh's most perceptive choice.

Lanterman represented the La Canada area, an affluent suburb in the foothills east of Los Angeles and Pasadena. The foothill subdivisions, with their rambling ranch-style homes, sheltered some of Southern California's most militant conservatives, including a number of members of the extreme right-wing John Birch Society. But there were moderate Republicans, too, and Lanterman represented them with a skill and dedication that pleased all the factions. He could seem grumpy, but he was warmhearted, a quality that proved crucial in the months ahead. "Frank was a very emotional guy, who occasionally had trouble holding back tears," said Karsten Vieg, one of the subcommittee's staff members. "Lanterman really listened. . . . Some of these things had a disproportionate impact on Frank, strong emotion trumped intellectual arguments for Frank."[19]

Waldie, Petris, and Lanterman began a campaign to change state policy in respect to care of both the mentally retarded and the mentally ill. They began with the mentally retarded. In Sacramento, parents had organized a sheltered workshop for the retarded, an early alternative to institutional care. They applied for a United Way grant, and Arthur Bolton, the young assistant director of an agency that approved such aid, was assigned to review the application. "I got interested in the issue and the problems and difficulties these families faced," he said. "They had no place to go, there was very little expertise. Doctors recommended they put them [their children] into institutions; [they] said, '[There is] nothing we can do for this child,' and there were no services in the community, so the state institution was the traditional answer."[20]

Although Bolton was new to the field, he had become enough of an expert to be invited to President John F. Kennedy's newly formed panel on retardation. Kennedy, whose sister was retarded, had brought the much-avoided subject into the national spotlight. "We, as a nation, have for too long postponed an intensive search for solutions to the problems of the mentally retarded," he said in 1963. "This neglect must end."[21]

Bolton's work with the parents had attracted the attention of Unruh's top aide, Larry Margolis, who was the spark plug behind staff expansion. "I had really been hired by the speaker's office, and Waldie had not worked with staff before," said Bolton. "Waldie was a very bright man and didn't feel he needed any staff hanging around." Waldie said he wanted to hold hearings. Bolton suggested that the subcommittee first prepare for them. "We sent a questionnaire to every family on the waiting list, all 3,000 of them, asking them, 'What is it that you want?' We were demonstrating what an independent legislative study could be."[22]

After the subcommittee began its work, Unruh kept his eye on it without interfering. "He initiated the whole thing by creating the subcommittee and getting Art [Bolton]," Waldie said. "From then on he left it pretty much up to us. Lanterman, Petris, and I had a total understanding that what we recommended he would back. He started it, [but] he did not take an active day-to-day role."[23]

On May 15, 1965, Unruh gave his views in a speech to the major parents' group, the California Council for Retarded Children. In the speech, he laid out the problem clearly and advocated a solution that was unusual coming from a Democrat of that era—cease relying exclusively on government and provide care through a combination of government and private resources. It was an example of how he differed from the standard liberal orthodoxy of the time and its strong reliance on government.

He was also scornful of mass-marketing techniques appealing to the public's sense of pity. The first Jerry Lewis telethon for handicapped children was a year away when Unruh spoke, but the idea of such an approach, even then finding its way onto television, offended him. "In the middle ages it was common for the lame and sick to expose their broken bodies on the street," he said.

And even today, the telethon to raise money to serve the handicapped child is a sad comment on the state of our present culture. The video parade of crippled children is little more than a Madison Avenue version of medieval beggary.

Since the 1930s, social responsibility has been translated into public service at public expense in public agencies. The practical effect has been to establish public hospitals and welfare agencies which separate the poor from the rest of us. . . . The same sterile approach has blocked our efforts at solving the problems of the mentally retarded. Since 1850, we have been stuffing the retarded into large state hospitals far removed from their families and communities. The price of a low I.Q. is a lifetime of idleness on a drab hospital ward. We have been fooled and fooled again into believing that just a little more money, more drugs, or more psychiatrists would make the hospital system a fine answer to the problem.[24]

The subcommittee's first job was to reduce the waiting list for the state hospitals for the mentally retarded and to change the system that led to it. What the parents wanted was care and advice close to home. Backed by solid information obtained from hearings, the answers to the 3,000 questionnaires, and other information, Waldie's subcommittee proposed creation of two pilot regional centers in San Francisco and Los Angeles, the forerunners of twenty-one such centers around the state. On the last night of the 1965 session, the legislature approved the creation of the two regional centers. Bolton ran into Unruh's office and announced the news. Unruh replied with a mixture of pride that his team had succeeded and a realistic understanding of what would happen once the bureaucrats took over. "Sit down," he told Bolton. "I assure you they will screw it up faster than you can unscrew it."[25]

Fortunately, Unruh's pessimism was misplaced. The pilot centers worked. They evolved into a statewide system in which 8,000 small facilities, financed by state and federal funds, provided work, recreation, transportation, independent living, education, and other programs for about 200,000. Still being helped by these programs are those with cerebral palsy, epilepsy, and autism, as well as mental retardation.

"It was a good model for what could be done," said Bolton. With that accomplished, the subcommittee turned its attention to the mentally ill.[26]

The problem of the mentally ill was much more difficult. In fact, it has proved insoluble. The same issues that confronted Unruh and his staff linger a half century later. There was little disagreement over the proposition that it was better to treat people close to home than in large state hospitals—assuming there were enough of those facilities. But there were deep disagreements over a definition of mental illness. Did the mentally ill include those who wandered the neighborhood ill clad and carrying on loud conversations with themselves, but posing no apparent harm? Should annoying or repulsive behavior be grounds for open-ended involuntary commitment to a state mental hospital? And what about the people who had been violent in the past or could turn dangerously aggressive in the future?[27]

Waldie focused on the commitment procedures. They offended his strong sense of civil liberties. In addition, the subcommittee and its staff also saw that making commitment more difficult would cut off the flow of patients to the mental hospitals, permitting them to be closed or reduced in size. At least in theory, community treatment centers would take over.[28]

"We saw that if we could lodge a huge boulder in the center of that overused road to the mental hospital, the patients would have to be sent somewhere else, to more appropriate facilities. The system would have to move off dead center," Bolton said.[29]

As he sought information in the field and during subcommittee hearings, Waldie was not overbearing but coldly direct in his examination of witnesses. They could not dodge his questions. He wondered why psychiatric examinations were not conducted in private at crowded San Francisco General Hospital. "The examination I saw conducted—there were three or four patients listening in and watching and observing the one being examined," he said.[30] He was appalled by the short time allocated to hearings—five to ten minutes in Los Angeles County. Under a strong interrogation, the public defender in charge of representing the mentally ill replied: "I am not sure where to start answering these questions." Waldie told him: "It's not fair to say 'questions,' they are accusations, and what I suspect I am asking you to do is defend them."[31] This tough, almost prosecutorial approach, backed up by thorough staff work, was exactly what Unruh had in mind when he created the assembly staff.

Two years later, when the staff and the legislators began to write a reform bill, Ronald Reagan had been inaugurated as governor, bringing with him an administration determined to reduce the size of government. Reagan's interest in mental health was budgetary. "His aspirations were to give California a new sense of direction and to limit the growth of state government, objectives that anticipated the domestic goals of his presidency," Reagan's biographer Lou Cannon writes.[32] Moreover, some of his right-wing supporters distrusted psychiatrists and state mental institutions.

Meanwhile, Unruh's strong team was breaking up. Waldie had left the assembly for the U.S. Congress. Petris had moved on to the state senate, where, as a freshman, he had considerably less influence than in the assembly. And the Reagan administration had tossed out the liberal agenda that had dominated the California Capitol since 1959.

It was at this point that Unruh's appointment of the Republican Lanterman to the subcommittee paid off. Reagan's prime target was the state mental hospitals, where he proposed to eliminate 3,700 jobs, a move that generated immense controversy. Lanterman was furious. Eugene Bardach of the University of California, who followed the course of the legislation and wrote about it in an enlightening book, *The Skill Factor in Politics,* observes:

"Not only were they [the cuts] indecent in his view, they were also unrealistic."[33] The legislature decided to cut only 2,600.[34]

Aware of Lanterman's influence, Reagan joined Unruh in supporting the Lanterman and Petris bill, creating stringent standards for commitment, and it passed 77–1, with two abstentions. As usual, the senate was an obstacle, just as it had been to other measures backed by the speaker, including his civil rights bill in 1959 and the Rumford Act in 1963.[35] The measure was sent to the "graveyard committee," Governmental Efficiency, where the civil rights bill and the Rumford bill had almost died. One of the committee members was Senator Alan Short, who didn't like the Lanterman and Petris bill. Short was one of the authors of the Short-Doyle program, which had set up locally controlled community health facilities years before. Clearly, he felt that this was his turf and resented the Unruh crowd moving in with a new idea. But Short needed support from the assembly for a bill of his own increasing state funding for the community facilities from 50 percent to 90 percent, which was awaiting a hearing in the assembly budget committee.

Lanterman, vice chairman of the budget committee, called in Bolton. "He decided we would sit on Short's bill because they were not treating us kindly over in the senate," Bolton said. It was a pure Unruh-style maneuver, and Bolton figured the speaker had his hand in it. "He was involved in everything. And all of the staff, no matter which committee we worked for, we all knew that we worked for the speaker.

"Lanterman said, 'Arthur I want you to go over to the senate and I want you to inform [Short] his bill isn't going anywhere as long as our bill isn't going anywhere. . . .' So I go over and see Short, and Short says, 'Come on in, have some Scotch.' He was a drinker. 'What can I do for you, boy?' he said. I said, 'You need to know your bill is in trouble.'"

He offered Short a deal—the assembly would approve his finance bill if the senate would relent on the assembly's mental health measure.[36] In fact, the two bills would be combined, and Short would become an author of what became known as the Lanterman-Petris-Short law. Short reluctantly agreed. A few hours before the end of the session, the bill was passed by both houses and Reagan signed it into law.

The Lanterman-Petris-Short Act took away judges' power to order indefinite commitment to mental hospitals. Comprehensive evaluation was mandated and a fourteen-day limit placed on involuntary detention and treatment, except for ninety days for the potentially dangerous. Courts could appoint conservators for those incapable of taking care of themselves.

Unfortunately, the law did not deliver what it promised. The drafters had assumed that community health facilities would spring up after the state mental hospital system was dismantled. But neither Reagan nor his successor, Democrat Edmund G. "Jerry" Brown Jr., shared that vision. State allocations to the local clinics proved inadequate to the immensity of the task, a situation made worse when Proposition 13 reduced local property tax revenue, making it difficult for the counties to pay for their share. "Neither local governments nor private services would provide sufficient community services," Sherry Bebitch Jeffe, a former assembly staffer, observed in 1987. "That is where Lanterman-Petris-Short truly failed." In addition, Reagan, as president, reduced federal funds for mental health.[37]

By 2003, an increasing number of county jails and hospitals were thrust into the role of unwilling caregivers for Californians suffering from mental illness, and the state ranked fourteenth in per capita spending for mental health.[38] Mentally ill homeless people had become a common sight on the streets of California cities.

That year, the trend was reversed when voters approved Proposition 63, which levied an additional income tax on those earning $1 million or more a year. This would at last allow the state and the counties to begin to implement the vision of the Lanterman-Petris-Short Act.

The act remains an uncompleted part of the Unruh legacy, but an important one. It also offers a fascinating contrast to the speaker's behavior in trying to suppress Harry Farrell's stories about Long Beach fund-raising. In that episode, the speaker's tactics were as crude as the oil under Long Beach Harbor. But when it came to mental health legislation, it was a completely different story. Unruh harnessed every facet of the legislative process to change public policy in an attempt to help society's neglected. He listened sympathetically to troubled families and understood how the legislature could help them. He delegated the job to altruistic but tough colleagues, among them the conservative Republican Lanterman. He provided them with an intelligent and imaginative staff. He persuaded a governor inherently suspicious of him to sign the measure. It was a perfect example of Unruh at his high-minded best.

ELEVEN

A Full-Time Legislature

IN POLITICS, AS IN THE rest of life, admirable deeds are often accomplished for motives that are not especially high-minded. In Jesse Unruh's career, that was never clearer than in 1966 when, against all odds, he persuaded the voters of California to give legislators a pay raise and to make the part-time legislature full-time.

The year is best remembered in California as that of Ronald Reagan. Casting himself as a citizen politician, Reagan captured the votes and hearts of many California voters with his compelling speaking style and a message that exploited the fears of a state battered by racial riots and student protests. As the Reagan campaign steamrollered any chance of a third term for Governor Pat Brown, it greatly overshadowed Unruh's plan for the legislature, contained in Proposition 1-A, which appeared on the same November ballot as the governor's race. But, even though it received much less publicity, Unruh's ballot measure won by a larger margin than did Reagan, and it had an impact on California that was almost as great as Reagan's conservative revolution.

Unruh had long wanted to raise the status of the legislature and make it into a policy-making body equal to the executive branch. Just as important—and undoubtedly of more immediate personal concern—was the matter of his paycheck.

"Most vexatious to me was when I was a candidate for speaker [in 1959–60], the second most powerful job in the political hierarchy in California, I was running around the state soliciting votes for the speakership [from legislators] in a borrowed car because my used car at that point was simply not in good enough condition to drive from Los Angeles to San Francisco and other far reaches of the state," he said.[1] One person who supplied him with a car was his friend the auto dealer Manning Post, who became one of his biggest fund-raisers. It was an Edsel that Post couldn't sell.

"He didn't have a suit," Post said. "I took him down to my tailor and I got him a half a dozen sport jackets and suits"[2]

"Compared to the governor who in those days was making $35,000 a year, compared to mayors and city councilmen who were making many times that, compared to elected officials at almost any other level of government, the legislature was miserably underpaid which made them suspect and made them really, really dependent on their outside income," Unruh said, although he was exaggerating the pay of most mayors and council members. "This made them more dependent upon the members of the third house— the lobbyists, who were always around willing to pick up the tab."[3]

In need of money, Unruh started a business in 1962, although he knew it would take him to the edge of ethical limits. "I made arrangements to set up an economic research consulting firm and got a couple of clients, quite clearly clients I had constituted a conflict of interest with," he said. "The president of the parent company [with] which I had an ongoing under-standing was also deeply involved in the retailers association [a trade group that was a lobbying power in Sacramento]. While never asking me directly for legislative help, I always knew his concerns and as such I cannot hon-estly say that I was as objective about their aims and purposes as I might have been had I not been partly reliant on him for my income."[4] Unruh called his firm Western Economics Research Corp., incorporated "to serve as a general management and business consulting firm."[5]

By July 1963, the firm's activities had attracted the attention of a friend of Unruh's, the attorney general of the United States, Robert F. Kennedy. Unknown to Unruh, who later supported RFK for president, Kennedy summoned an assistant FBI director and asked, in the words of an FBI re-port, for

a limited discreet investigation of Unruh to substantiate existence of West-ern Research Bureau [sic] and identify the principals behind it. Attorney general asked that we determine what long distance telephone calls Jesse Unruh, well known California politician, made from his own telephones as well as from Western Research Bureau. Attorney general interested in de-termining whether there is any substance to an allegation received by the department that Unruh is engaged in lobbying activities on behalf of large oil companies as well as other business firms with officials of the federal government.[6]

FBI agents chased down Western Economics Research records in the California secretary of state's office and obtained information on Unruh's telephone calls, but they turned up nothing to back up the allegation. In August, the bureau reported to Kennedy that "no information was obtained indicating Mr. Unruh is engaged in lobbying activities . . . no further [action] is contemplated in this matter in the absence of a specific request from you."[7]

Despite his discomfort with the potential conflict of interest inherent in the Western Economics Research client list, Unruh kept on with the enterprise. In 1966, he investigated the possibility of his political allies the Ridders, owners of the Long Beach newspaper, buying a paper in Eureka. He flew to that city, in the far northwestern corner of the state, met with the owner of the local paper, and sent a letter to Sam Cameron, his friend and general manager of the Long Beach newspaper. The Eureka newspaper owner, Don O'Kane, "told me he would give the . . . offer every consideration because of his regard for me," Unruh wrote Cameron. While the sale never materialized, his sounding out of O'Kane shows how Unruh mixed private business with his public office.[8]

In 1965, he told *Los Angeles Times* reporters that Western Economics Research was the source of more than half of his income. His compensation from the state was $500 a month, plus money for mileage, living expenses, and per diem payments for attending legislative hearings outside Sacramento, all of it adding up to more than $10,000 a year. In addition, he was provided with a car leased by the state and an oil company credit card. He also said he owned stock in eleven companies, all acquired at market price. The *Los Angeles Times* reported that his holdings included savings and loan stock and that his wife also owned stock in a savings and loan company. With his income and assets, Unruh was able to buy a home in Inglewood, a small city on the western edge of his district, in 1961 for $50,000, largely financed with a $35,000 loan from the Great Western Savings and Loan Association, the state's second-largest savings and loan.[9]

In 1965, Unruh was doing rather well in terms of his personal finances. He bought a share in an avocado ranch in rural San Diego County, a deal offered to him by Virginia's father, Ray Lemon. "Total price is $100,000— a little over $156 per acre. We also want about $10,000 for roads and water, both of which would add a lot to the price of the property," Lemon wrote. "We have the down payment available and several who will want in. There is only about 40 to 45 percent open and it is not begging yet, even with time this short."[10]

Of more lasting significance to California than the issue of Unruh's and other legislators' paychecks was the transformation in state policy that was part of his proposal for a full-time legislature. Since his early days in Sacramento, Unruh had felt that the governor had too much control over the legislature. While the lawmakers could consider whatever issues they chose during their regular sessions, held for six months in odd-numbered years, the governor had command of the legislative agenda at other times. In even-numbered years, the legislature met to act on the governor's budget. He could add to its agenda by the device of calling a "special session" to consider a specific issue. These sessions would usually run at the same time as the budget session.

"The governor had pretty much control and of course, he liked it that way," Unruh said.[11] As Unruh envisioned it, full-time legislators, controlling their own agenda and assisted by talented staff members, would help the legislature "to raise its decision-making ability, to scrutinize, to originate, and yes, to innovate, . . . to ask the right questions and grope with more insight for better settlements."[12]

Changing the status quo would take all of Unruh's cunning and political skill. A major obstacle was the constitution of the state of California, an 80,000-word document, which spelled out the running of the legislature, including the lawmakers' pay, and could only be changed by popular vote. A state ballot measure was thus needed to raise legislative salaries. Unruh decided to remove the pay provision from the constitution, permitting legislators to set their own salaries. He knew the voters would never support such a move, but there was a way around this—bury the salary provision in a long-planned revision of the state constitution.

A Constitutional Revision Commission had been at work since 1962 on a rewrite of the unmanageable document, drastically shortening the constitution and putting the remainder in clear language. Unruh had supported the creation of the commission and thought highly of its chairman, Superior Court judge Bruce Sumner, who had been a Republican assemblyman. Unruh had collaborated with the commission and had met with newspaper editors, academics, and other opinion leaders promoting its recommendations on constitutional reform. Naturally, one of the recommendations was for lawmakers to have authority over their own salaries. The recommendations of the commission were so logical, so badly needed, and so well intentioned that Unruh hoped few would notice that a legislative pay raise was tucked away among them.

Governor Pat Brown was also an obstacle. It would be up to the governor to add the Constitutional Revision Commission's recommendations to the legislature's agenda in the 1966 budget session so that they could be approved to appear on the ballot. "The Brown administration was adamantly opposed to doing anything that might aggrandize Jesse Unruh," Unruh said. "But they also felt they needed Jesse Unruh's help for Pat Brown's reelection in 1966." Still smoldering over what he considered the governor's broken promise to support him for governor, Unruh had refused to endorse Brown's reelection bid. With the two so far apart, Unruh turned to coercion. Brown needed legislation passed to help him forestall a tax increase until after the November election, and Unruh held up the governor's bill until Brown agreed to include the constitutional revision on the 1966 legislative agenda. The legislature put the constitutional reform measure on the November 1966 ballot.[13]

Yet another obstacle was Brown's appointee, the state attorney general, Tom Lynch, a veteran Democratic politician, formerly San Francisco district attorney, and an old friend of the governor's. A ballot measure needs a title, which serves as its headline on the ballot, and a bad title could have turned off voters and sent the proposal down to defeat. Titles are written by the attorney general's office, which labeled Unruh's constitutional reform proposal a measure to raise legislative salaries. "That would have sunk the proposition all by itself," Unruh said later, and he immediately telephoned Lynch. He recalled:

> I think I was about as tough with Tom Lynch as I've ever been with anybody in my political career. I called him up and I said, "You know you can let this stand if you want to. I know your civil servants wrote it; you didn't, but if you let it stand, let me just tell you, you're not going to get anything out of this legislature as long as I'm around here or as long as [assembly Republican leader] Bob Monagan is around here or as long as [Senate President] Hugh Burns is around here. . . . Well, Lynch is a fine gentleman, and they reworked [the language] and came out with a much better, more neutral thing.[14]

Unruh put considerable effort into a campaign to win the support of the skeptical media. He visited almost every newspaper in the state. He made concessions to mistrustful editors. He offered to limit mileage payments and the per diem allowance and deny legislators who were lawyers the right to practice before powerful state agencies that depended on the legislature for financial support. "We wanted $25,000 a year salary but the newspapers weren't prepared to go that high. . . . The bigger newspapers agreed to let us go to $16,000 as long as we would give up the other things."[15] But the result was solid newspaper support of the campaign in an era when newspaper opinion really counted.

Finally, Unruh recruited the two rivals for governor, Pat Brown and Ronald Reagan, to endorse the measure. Knowing Reagan would be reluctant to support anything that Brown backed, "I got through the backdoor, and through some of my Republican friends I got Reagan to endorse Proposition 1-A before Pat Brown endorsed it," Unruh said. Brown went along. "We got Reagan and Pat to become cochairmen," Unruh said."[16]

Their pictures were on campaign material produced by Whitaker & Baxter, a company Unruh had chosen carefully. It had been founded by Clem Whitaker and his wife, Leone Baxter, who, in the process, had created the modern political campaign. In the early 1930s, Whitaker, a former newspaper reporter, and Baxter, who had been general manager of a small city chamber of commerce, saw an entrepreneurial opportunity in the Progressives' early twentieth-century passion for reform, as embodied in voter initiatives and disdain for political parties. Whitaker and Baxter were masters of what was then a primitive art, publicity in the new mass media age of broadcasting and movies, as well as traditional newspapers. They groomed their candidates' appearances, shaped their messages, and designed initiative campaigns with simple, powerful, and often misleading slogans. Political campaigns around the nation—even around the world—now swarm with such consultants, but Whitaker and Baxter were the first to sell a campaign as if they were selling cigarettes or soap.

"They flourished because they filled a need," Gladwin Hill observes. "The important electoral device of the initiative was becoming a far bigger affair than the simple citizen-petition operation the Progressive reformers had envisioned. Many of the issues were multi-million dollar matters. . . . It was sensible to have such outlays handled with professional skill."[17]

The firm, by 1966 in the hands of Clem Whitaker Jr. and his partners, generally handled the campaigns of Republican candidates and issues promoted by major businesses. "They had what we needed which was the ties to the business community," Unruh said.[18] The firm understood the need to play down the legislative salary issue. "This strategy . . . was to single out no particular feature of the revision package for special attention but to present the package for executive, legislative, and judicial reform as a whole and to dwell heavily on the measure's bipartisan backing," Whitaker and his associates said in a report to Unruh and the other legislative leaders. In the Whitaker & Baxter tradition, the campaign had a single simple slogan: "Update the State! Brown-Reagan, Business-Labor All Say Yes on 1-A."[19]

With Whitaker & Baxter's connections, and his own relationship with Sacramento lobbyists, Unruh was able to raise the money he needed. "We had the big shots in the third house [the lobbyists] in, and we simply set them down and said to them, 'Lobbyist X you represent the banks. Now we expect you to raise $50,000 for this proposition and to have it into this campaign by the first of September. Lobbyist Z, we expect you to raise $75,000 from your clients, the oil companies.' . . . That's the way we did it." Money in hand, Unruh and Monagan, the assembly Republican leader, traveled around the state, speaking side by side to business and labor groups. "So eventually, we had almost a totally united front . . . and that is pretty much how all of that got passed," Unruh said.[20]

The measure changed California government, but not in the way that Unruh intended. In the 1980s, Unruh sat down with pen and legal pad and reflected on what he had wrought. "The California Legislature: Reforms of the '60s; are they working?" he questioned.

His answer was yes, in some ways. "The legislature is much more open and accessible than it was prior to the changes," he said. "No one would want to return to the old system." He also believed that the approval of Proposition 1-A had led to an expansion of the staff he had been building and gave the legislature "access to independent expertise which it did not have prior to the reform."[21]

The staff was, as one of its members, Sherry Bebitch Jeffe later wrote, composed of young and bright women and men "inventing a whole new legislative system. . . . Policymaking flourished. The legislature and its staff were building programs and institutions from the ground up. Those were heady times."[22]

But making the legislature a full-time job had an unforeseen effect. The job increasingly became much more valuable. In 2006, state legislators earned $110,880 a year, plus about $20,000 in expense money and a car. Not as much as is paid to a partner in a big law firm or corporate executive, perhaps. But for someone addicted to the political life, the job of a California lawmaker offers both comfortable pay and power. And the pay is higher for the assembly speaker, senate president, and floor leaders.

By 1983, Jerry Gillam and Carl Ingram reported in the *Los Angeles Times*, the full-time legislature had become "a corps of professional politicians, many of whom work year-round gathering contributions for their next election. The never-ending task of raising more and more money, especially from those who come before the legislature, has become almost an end in itself, particularly in the assembly. It has raised troubling questions about the independence of lawmakers from those who bankroll campaigns."[23] And the staff, so prized by Unruh, had turned into a cadre of campaign workers for legislative bosses. Jeffe lamented "a dangerous shift in the function of legislative staff from being the professional arm of the legislature to a taxpayer-funded political muscle."[24]

The nature of campaigns had changed since Unruh's days as speaker. There was no longer much call for volunteers to perform simple tasks like stuffing envelopes. Demographic and political data on neighborhoods were sorted with complex computer programs, and campaign mailings were designed for specific groups and had to be tailored to the appropriate addresses. In one mailing, the candidate would be shown talking seriously to rabbis. In another, he would be praying in a barrio church. Still another would show him in a gay pride parade. It was expensive to design, write, and mail this material—and costly to hire the consultant who supervised every step of the operation. Within a few years of the approval of Proposition 1-A, these expensive communications had become the common medium for spreading the message in state legislative races. Candidates rarely walked door to door, and volunteer campaign participation declined. Voter turnout on election day diminished along with it. Unruh noted:

> The overwhelming change which took place between then and now happened outside the legislature and overtook the legislature—the enormous cost of running for office. In a way, you could say the reforms of the '60s could have been entirely successful but the entire ship of state was swamped by the rising tide of campaign costs. Raising money for election campaigns has become the number one priority. Everything else has become subservient to that single goal. The remark, "Money is the mother's milk of politics," which I quoted but did not invent, could be restated in terms that it is the mother's milk, the meat and potatoes and the dessert and frosting of politics now.
>
> Whatever changes we would have made in the operation of the legislature in the '60s would have been overtaken by this single phenomenon.[25]

Unruh felt his reforms for legislative independence should have been viewed as a three-legged stool: a professional staff to provide advice and expertise; an adequate salary for legislators; and public financing of campaigns, freeing lawmakers from the need for campaign contributions. He didn't know whether public financing would eliminate this, "but I think it would be a significant palliative."[26]

Meanwhile, public discontent with the legislature grew. Why, after voting overwhelmingly to make the legislature full-time, did the public then turn against it? One reason stands out—rising taxes, which slowly turned discontent into outrage. The year that saw the election of Ronald Reagan as governor and the establishment of the full-time legislature also saw the beginning of one of the most significant movements in California history, the property tax revolt. Between 1966 and 1978, property taxes soared, and the well-paid full-time legislature did nothing about it.

By 1966, property taxes were already rising fast, especially on homes. In a few years, Californians on fixed incomes began to fear they would not be able to pay future tax increases and would lose their homes. Well-publicized proposals to limit property taxes failed in the legislature, despite the efforts of Unruh, his assembly allies, and Governors Brown and Reagan. In the 1970s, taxes increased even more. David Doerr, one of Unruh's smart young consultants, who became a leading California tax authority, notes: "From October of 1972 to October of 1977, home prices in the seven Southern California counties more than doubled." Rising property taxes and the stalemate on the issue in Sacramento focused public attention on the legislature.

Finally, under the leadership of the most famous of the antitax crusaders, Howard Jarvis, the tax revolt engulfed the state. In 1978, California voters approved Proposition 13, which reduced property taxes by 50 percent and imposed ironclad property tax limits, depriving state and local governments of needed revenue and crippling government at every level.[27]

Adding to public discontent with the legislature was the exposure in the 1980s of corruption in the Capitol. An FBI sting operation resulted in the arrest and conviction of several legislators on bribery charges.[28] Finally, in 1990, voters staged their ultimate rebellion against the legislature, approving an initiative limiting assembly members to three two-year terms and senators to two four-year terms. It was designed to restore the days of the citizen politician who served in the legislature for a time and then returned home to the community. Instead, assembly and senate members began to consider themselves career politicians, and their overriding concern became remaining in an elected office. True, the old days of lawmakers trolling Sacramento bars for pigeons to take them to dinner had pretty much gone. But those nights on the town were replaced by something worse—nightly events to raise money for new races after their current terms expired. Lobbyists dashed from one event to another, perhaps thinking longingly of the more peaceful era when all they had had to do was buy dinner or supply a prostitute or two.

Imposition of term limits by angry voters turned the legislature Unruh had created into a body of short-timers, a fund-raising machine no longer capable of producing the policy initiatives, the plans for the future, that he had envisioned.

TWELVE

Unruh, Robert Kennedy, and the Anti-War Movement

THE YEAR 1968 WAS A difficult one for Unruh as it was for the nation. A huge change was taking place in American politics. The Democratic Party that year was dominated by "the fracturing of the relationship between conventional liberals and left-liberal to radical protest movements," social scientist and historian Robert Cohen observes.[1] Democrats disagreed with one another on such basic issues as the Vietnam War, racial conflict, and student rebellions like the Free Speech Movement at the University of California's Berkeley campus. The flight of blue-collar Democrats, which Unruh had foreseen during the 1963 and 1964 fight over the Rumford housing bill, had already deprived the party of what had been its base since the New Deal. Spearheading the GOP's ascendancy, Ronald Reagan was elected governor of California in 1966, and Richard M. Nixon became U.S. president in 1968.

Until 1967, Unruh had tried to straddle the great divide between growing radical protest movements and traditional liberals. As a conventional liberal and a centrist, he opposed radicals during the events that divided the liberal community through much of the 1960s. By 1967, the Vietnam War was growing more intense, as was opposition to it, and California was at the center of the debate. "Because of the state's location on America's Pacific shore, its concentration of military installations and industrial capacity and its role in the development of protest politics, countercultural activities and grass-roots conservatism, California was particularly affected by the war," Marcia A. Eymann writes. "Events in California, transmitted nightly on the evening news, profoundly affected the rest of the nation. The state's experience was both a microcosm and magnification of the national experience."[2] Unruh was not initially part of the anti-war movement. "I don't know that he was for the [Vietnam] war, but [he felt] this is the president; this is our foreign policy, . . . and they must know what they're doing," Frank Burns recalled.[3]

Although the dissenters feared crossing President Lyndon B. Johnson, opposition was also slowly, cautiously growing in Washington, D.C. One of the increasingly committed critics of the war was U.S. senator Robert F. Kennedy, who favored a halt in American bombing of North Vietnam and a beginning of negotiations. On March 2, Kennedy gave a speech in the Senate asking the Johnson administration to stop the bombing and begin talks within a week. "Can anyone believe this nation, with all its fantastic power and resources, will be endangered by a wise and magnanimous action toward a small and difficult adversary?" he asked.[4]

President Johnson's resistance to this suggestion was fierce, and the war still commanded the support of most Americans. The historian Arthur Schlesinger Jr., who had been special assistant to the president in John Kennedy's administration and was close to Robert Kennedy, recalled a dinner with the latter during this period: "Before I drove away, he said, 'How can we possibly survive four more years of Lyndon Johnson? Five more years of a crazy man?' But he could not see what he could do to prevent it."[5]

Unruh's doubts were also about Johnson himself rather than about the Vietnam War as such, but he slowly and cautiously followed Kennedy in opposition to it. By early 1967, Unruh had begun thinking of the possibility of RFK running for president. "By that time, there was a considerable disenchantment with the Johnson administration—not a breach but a feeling that things weren't going well, and that something needed to be done," Frank Burns said. "I would say early in '67, we started to make contact with Senator Kennedy concerning his coming out here [to California] to broaden his base." In March, after Kennedy's speech to the Senate, Unruh and Burns flew east to meet with him on St. Patrick's Day. A snowstorm delayed Unruh for four hours, but the three men finally got together at the Bull & Bear steakhouse at the Waldorf Astoria in Manhattan. "He walked over there and we talked for quite a while about his . . . doing a dinner for the legislators and getting plugged in with other elements of the party that he really didn't have much of a base with," Burns said. "At that time he agreed in principle that he'd like to do this and suggested that a follow-up take place with his staff."[6]

Unruh did not question the war itself until the night of June 23, 1967. Grassroots organization against the war had increased as the number of troops in Vietnam approached 400,000, and the draft reached into college campuses and the middle class. Activity was particularly intense in California. On that June night, opponents of the war mobilized for a protest against the president, who was speaking at a $1,000-a-couple Democratic

Party fund-raiser at the Century Plaza Hotel in Los Angeles. The hotel was a perfect place for the beleaguered president to speak. It was the centerpiece of a huge Century City office and entertainment development on the site of the old Twentieth Century–Fox studio back lot, just west of Beverly Hills. With most of the development uncompleted, the hotel stood alone, surrounded by vacant fields. The president could be whisked from his helicopter through a heavily guarded back entrance of the hotel.

But the site was also a perfect place for a demonstration. A huge field, now occupied by office buildings, fronted the hotel. It was big enough for the 10,000 protesters who had gathered at a nearby city park, having walked there in the afternoon and early evening. There were college students and the elderly, as well as conventionally dressed middle-aged men and women and young couples wheeling children in carriages or strollers. They seemed solidly middle class. As one of the reporters covering the demonstration for the Associated Press, I wandered among them, struck by their earnest nature and peaceful demeanor. I checked in with the Los Angeles police and chatted with a few of the officers. They were ready for trouble, although I didn't see how it could come from this crowd.

Unruh and Burns arrived at the hotel early in the evening and went to a hotel room that had been reserved for them. They looked down at the gathering crowd. "These were people who really believed," Burns recalled, "and they weren't a bunch of beatniks or crazies . . . you might dismiss. This was middle America out there. And that made a real impression on Jess. I guess it was just the first time we had talked seriously about it, about where it was all going, and it wasn't going well."[7]

As I watched the scene unfold, a line of about 1,000 policemen stationed themselves between the hotel and the demonstrators. The hotel had obtained an injunction against the demonstrators. The demonstrators massed in front of the building, and the police ordered them to leave.[8] The crowd was growing unwieldy, and people were so agitated that getting away was almost impossible, especially for those who had brought small children.

The situation was tense. Realizing that the police might try to break up the crowd, I was appalled that demonstrators had brought their children along. Suddenly, the police charged, beating some of the demonstrators and poking others with batons, and the crowd retreated. I moved along behind the police. Someone in the crowd threw a dirt clod. I ducked, and it hit the chest of a reporter behind me, Tom Brokaw, who was covering the demonstration for the Los Angeles NBC station. I turned and apologized.

After the dinner, Unruh and Burns returned to their room and looked down at the police and the scattered demonstrators who remained. Burns recalled a few years later:

> I would say that was the beginning of Jess's changing positions. . . . We were up in a high hotel room overlooking the plaza itself where all the people were—and all this turmoil, . . . I can't tell you exactly who said what but the conversation went . . . to the effect that the president can't keep going this way. He's going to lose the election . . . Jess started thinking that the people who were against the war were right, that this was an unwinnable and bad war.[9]

But Unruh was too cautious to share his doubts with the public—too aware, perhaps, that the majority of Californians, having recently voted Reagan into office, had little sympathy for the Century Plaza demonstrators. A week later, Unruh appeared at the "Hughie-Jesse Show" press conference with Senator Burns, who was still the Capitol's foremost red baiter. "I think it is a disgrace when the president of the United States can't come to California and come in the front door of a hotel without the threat of violence," Unruh said. "These people are doing great violence to the traditional respect the people of the United States have for the president. I agree with their right to protest . . . but as far as I am concerned, the Los Angeles police did a good job. There is no evidence the police were out of line in maintaining law and order." Hypocritically, he criticized the press for reporting what he and Burns had seen for themselves.[10]

In private, Unruh played a different game. By now, he definitely wanted Kennedy to enter the California presidential primary in June 1968, against a slate of delegates favoring President Johnson. Kennedy had agreed to come to California to speak, as Unruh had requested, and in August 1967, he addressed the speaker's legislative fund-raising dinner in San Francisco. Wallace Turner, reporting for the *New York Times,* wrote that the event was "a resounding personal triumph for Unruh." Kennedy's appearance "was seen as strengthening Mr. Unruh's hand among California Democrats, for the implication was that whatever national political plans Senator Kennedy has will include Mr. Unruh."[11]

Robert Kennedy still hesitated to challenge the president directly, and the anti-war movement crystallized around another Democratic senator, Eugene McCarthy of Minnesota. Political insiders did not take McCarthy particularly seriously when he entered the race. But his words resonated with war opponents outside the traditional Democratic structure. On November 30, 1967, he announced he was entering the California presidential primary, as well as those in Oregon, Wisconsin, and Nebraska. "I am concerned that the administration seems to have set no limit to the price which it is willing to pay for a military victory," he said.[12]

The new presidential challenger was not Unruh's kind of politician. McCarthy was too cool, too cerebral, too disdainful of conventional politics. In short, he was too much like the liberals of the California Democratic Council. The Kennedys were Unruh's style, and Robert Kennedy was his candidate. Unruh said McCarthy's campaign "showed no promise of getting off the ground whatsoever."[13]

Meanwhile, Unruh was getting pressure from another direction. He was asked to join with President Johnson's supporters in California. They were preparing a pro-Johnson delegation to the national convention, which would be nominally pledged to a "favorite son" candidate, the only remaining Democratic statewide officeholder, Attorney General Thomas Lynch. This device would spare the president the trouble, and the risk, of campaigning in the California presidential primary. In an act of considerable defiance of the president, Unruh declined to join the Lynch delegation.

On December 12, 1967, Unruh flew east with Burns for a meeting at the Eagleton Institute at Rutgers University in New Jersey, where Unruh was teaching as politician in residence. When they checked into the Americana Hotel in Manhattan, they found that RFK had left a message for Unruh to call him. Unruh recalled later:

I had not talked to Senator Kennedy at this point for quite a bit of time and I thought it was somewhat strange that he would be calling me. I talked to Bob for quite some time, rather lightheartedly, and finally deduced that what had prompted the call was his knowledge that I was not participating in the formation of the Johnson delegation. We joked for a while about it. He asked me what I was going to do and I told him that I was going to do nothing for a while. Then I said, "Why don't you run?" That was the first time I really had any inkling that he was even thinking about it. But I think even that early, he was very seriously considering it, at least the stirrings were within him, urging him to run. I remember also commenting on what a poor showing Senator McCarthy was making. He was getting very little press, very little notice at all. And I talked to him about this. I said, "My God, couldn't you get a better stalking horse?" and he said, "Yeah, how about Teddy?" When I hung up the telephone, I remember turning to Frank Burns, who had been sitting in the room with me while I was talking and saying, "By God, he's really thinking about running." Frank, who had been listening only to my end of the conversation, nodded his head in agreement. We then discussed that for a little while and sort of dismissed it although, I think, both of us filed it away in our minds.[14]

Before Christmas 1967, Frank Mankiewicz, by then a trusted Kennedy adviser, called Unruh. He said the senator would be in Sun Valley, Idaho, with his family for Christmas, but intended to fly to California afterward, and he "wanted to see me [Unruh] and me alone." On Christmas Eve, said Unruh, "I was feeling full of good cheer and rather happy about the world in general. I called his [Kennedy's] place in Sun Valley. This was rather early in the evening, I think maybe Mountain Standard Time, perhaps 10 o'clock or 10:30. I got Ethel, who was still up. [She] told me the senator had spent the entire day or entire afternoon skiing and that as a result he was already in bed. I was sort of amused by it but accepted it, and we went to bed later on ourselves."

After Christmas, Kennedy and Unruh made a date for drinks and dinner in Los Angeles. To ensure secrecy, Jack Crose, Unruh's top aide, booked a hotel suite under his name. Everyone wanted the meeting secret. Unruh, Crose, and Burns met in the suite with Kennedy and Peter Edelman, the senator's aide. "We kidded for a little while about various things, lightheartedly and good naturedly. . . . His [Kennedy's] private sense of humor, with me at any rate, was always highly developed," Unruh later recalled. "At one point, Kennedy asked me point-blank, 'What would you do if I do something?' I said, kiddingly, 'I don't know, what do you want to be when you grow up?' He said without a moment's hesitation, 'I want to be what my brother was.'" Unruh left the meeting with the impression that Kennedy was "at least thinking strongly" of running for president. A week later, Unruh urged Kennedy to run and pledged his support.[15]

Kennedy was torn. "Only one professional—Unruh of California—was urging him on; and this, Kennedy recognized, was for Unruh's reasons as much as Kennedy's," Arthur Schlesinger Jr. writes.[16] President Kennedy's speechwriter Ted Sorensen makes the same point, that Unruh's position was "good for Jess but it wasn't good for Bobby."[17] Most of the big financial contributors in California had sided with Governor Brown in his feud with Unruh and would not forgive him for his halfhearted support of the governor against Reagan. They would never support him for governor in 1970 unless Robert Kennedy were elected president and insisted that they finance an Unruh campaign. Unruh's future depended on Kennedy.

On January 20, Unruh, accompanied by Burns and Jack Crose, took the red-eye east for a meeting at the Kennedy home in Virginia, Hickory Hill, just outside of Washington, arriving there early in the morning. "Someone was beginning to cook breakfast," Unruh recalled. "The house was filled with smoke from the fireplace or something. I had to open the windows in my bedroom before I could sleep. The smoke was so dense and heavy. The dogs were lying all over the hallway. One of the boys was awake and banging around pretty noisily. But I was quite sleepy, and I took only a couple of minutes until I was sound asleep."[18]

When he awoke, Ethel Kennedy was cooking brunch, a big meal with bloody Marys, served outside despite chilly weather. The dogs were jumping around, barking. The children were playing in the backyard with their governess. Two of the children returned to the house and unfurled a banner with a caricature of the senator and the words "Bobby For President in 68." The music from *Camelot* was playing over the house sound system, Unruh recalled later.[19] Burns remembered it as being from the 1965 Broadway musical *Man of La Mancha*. In any case, whether it was "Camelot" or "The Impossible Dream," the music evidently captured the spirit of the enterprise. "The people for Bob running were Ethel and the kids, and Jess," said Burns. Sorensen argued strongly against a candidacy. Ethel Kennedy responded, "Why, Ted! And after all those high-flown phrases you wrote for President Kennedy." Burns said, "She really chopped him off right at the ankles . . . it made me wince."[20]

The meeting broke up without a decision. Unruh, Crose, and Burns flew to New York, pretending they were on a business trip there, in a ploy to hide their visit to Hickory Hill. "We had no hesitancy in supporting Bob if he decided to run, but we did not want to be in a position of having it said that he [Unruh] urged him to run and then he didn't run, thereby further alienating the Johnson people and at the same time indicating our influence on Bob was not very great," Unruh said.[21] But at the airport, their cover was blown. Pat Brown, by then a former governor who had to stand in line, was behind them in the queue for the plane. Unruh didn't lie. Unruh knew Brown was too canny to accept any cover story about a business trip east. Despite their feud, the two veteran politicians understood that the conventions of politics required them to go through the motions of friendship. They talked about Unruh's meeting with Kennedy. "There was disagreement between us as to whether the senator would run," Unruh remembered.[22]

Unruh had been put in a corner by Kennedy's indecision. A few days after the Hickory Hill meeting, Kennedy's brother-in-law and adviser Stephen Smith called Unruh to tell him that the senator was not running.

Smith offered several reasons for Kennedy's decision, but the one that stuck in Burns's mind was that "he was terribly concerned about the fact that the people that marched with him—that the retaliation against him could destroy all of their careers. It was going to be a hideously unpleasant sort of battle. The power of the presidency was so great . . . that even to ask people to support him was to ask them essentially to commit suicide, political suicide."

Unruh's position was perilous. The financial powers supporting the president would never support Unruh for governor if he turned against Johnson. These were powerful people, and they would have their revenge. Aware of Johnson's growing weakness, and of Unruh's concerns for his own future, the Johnson supporters continued to pressure Unruh to join the pro-Johnson nominating convention delegation headed by California attorney general Lynch. "There was this constant attempt to box Jess into where he had to go aboard [the pro-Johnson delegation] or he would be considered a party wrecker again, which was a charge Jess was very sensitive to because it had been leveled so many times," Burns said. "We were getting sort of an emissary-a-day type of approach, and from people that were close to Jess in one way or another."[23]

While Robert Kennedy pondered his future, the American position in Vietnam took an unexpected turn for the worse. North Vietnamese troops attacked Ke Sahn, a Marine base near the demilitarized zone between North and South Vietnam. Lyndon Johnson was so worried about the attack that he had a sand-table map of the area put up in the Situation Room at the White House. He would go there at night in his bathrobe and, reports of the day's activities in hand, study the battleground.[24]

Johnson was picking bombing targets himself, afraid that American bombs would trigger a wider war. He agonized over his choices. "In the dark at night, I would lay awake picturing my boys flying around North Vietnam, asking myself an endless series of questions," Johnson said. "What if one of the targets you picked today triggers off Russia or China? What happens then?" Sometimes, lying in bed, he pictured a plane crashing. "I knew one of my boys must have been killed that night. I jumped out of bed, put on my robe, took my flashlight and went into the Situation Room."[25]

On January 30, almost 70,000 Viet Cong and North Vietnamese troops launched an offensive throughout South Vietnam during Tet, the observance of the New Year. More than 100 cities and towns were attacked, including the old imperial capital of Hue, which was occupied for twenty-five days. The Viet Cong penetrated the U.S. Embassy compound in Saigon and attacked the Saigon airport. Although the Communists suffered heavy losses, the Tet offensive, coming at a time of increasing American concern about the casualties and cost of the war, was a defeat for President Johnson, whose recitation of Communist losses was "irrelevant when it came to convincing the American people that the Vietnam War was worth the cost the way it was going," Robert Donovan observed.[26]

On the day the Tet offensive began, John Criswell, one of the president's top political aides, met in Washington with Burns, who was there on his own legal business, as well as to gather intelligence for Unruh. Criswell pressed Burns on Unruh's intentions in the 1968 presidential race and invited both Burns and Unruh to meet with the president in the White House. Unruh was headed east for a meeting in New York with John Kraft, a pollster who had taken a survey of Kennedy's chances in California.

The poll results were favorable to Kennedy. Kraft found that Kennedy would carry California in a three-way race (Kennedy, Johnson, and McCarthy) with 45 to 48 percent of the vote.[27] "Jess called Bob down in Florida," Burns said. "Got him off the tennis courts, gave him the results and his [Kennedy's] comment was, 'You son of a bitch! Why did you have to tell me that?'" The poll results also were encouraging for Unruh if he chose to run for the U.S. Senate. It showed that the state's incumbent Republican senator, Thomas Kuchel, would be defeated in a Republican primary by an ultraconservative, Max Rafferty, the state superintendent of public instruction. And Unruh would beat Rafferty in November.

The day after the session with Kraft, Unruh and Burns met at the White House with President Johnson, Criswell, and the president's friend Arthur Krim, a major film industry executive and Democratic fund-raiser. Krim was an important part of the nationwide network of Democratic big donors, which included San Francisco's most powerful developer, Walter Shorenstein; Lew Wasserman, the head of MCA; and influential insiders and go-betweens, such as Eugene Wyman in Los Angeles. Without their support, it would be all but impossible for Unruh to raise the money needed to run for governor in 1970.

"The proposition was very clear," said Burns. It was join the Johnson team, run for Senate with the president's backing, or else. The threat was never stated, but Unruh understood the meaning of Krim's presence.

The men drank bourbon and chatted. Johnson was constantly interrupted with telephone reports on the worsening situation in Vietnam. At one point, he said the American forces had found General Vo Nguyen Giap, the North Vietnamese defense minister, and that U.S. planes were "going to blow him out of his world." Then, as Burns recalled it, Johnson said Unruh ought to consider running for the Senate, and, motioning toward Krim, said he had many friends who would support Unruh. "Then Johnson said, 'Jess let's take a little walk in the Rose Garden,' and off they went for a walk [that] lasted two hours." In the Rose Garden, Johnson pressed Unruh even harder to run for the Senate, telling him that his natural place was in the legislative arena and that in a decade, he'd be majority leader, the post once occupied by Johnson. When they returned, the men exchanged pleasantries, and Unruh and Burns left.

"Let's take a walk," Unruh said to Burns. They talked about Johnson's offer of help for the Senate campaign, and about the president himself. Both men were appalled at Johnson's phone calls and his obsession with the small details of the war. "It was frightening," said Burns. "It was pretty much a snap decision. We would go with Kennedy."

Krim and Criswell persisted on behalf of Johnson. Each called Burns. Again, they pledged to rally the big Democratic donors behind Unruh if he ran for the Senate—to, as Burns put it, "take Hillcrest Country Club and turn it around." Hillcrest, near Beverly Hills, was the country club favored by LA's richest Jews, started by them when they were denied membership in the city's anti-Semitic clubs. In Los Angeles, Hillcrest and checkbook Democrats were synonymous. Unruh needed Hillcrest.

By now, Unruh, still shaken by his glimpse of President Johnson directing bombing raids from the White House, was wholeheartedly against the war and for the defeat of the president. So were an increasingly large number of Americans. On February 23, 1968, the *Wall Street Journal* wrote: "The American people should be getting ready to accept, if they haven't already, the prospect that the whole Vietnam effort may be doomed, that it may be falling apart beneath our feet." Four days later, Walter Cronkite, returning from a trip to Vietnam, told his viewers that it "is increasingly clear to this reporter that the only rational way out, then, is to negotiate, not as victors but as honorable people who lived up to their pledge and did the best they could."[28]

On March 2, Unruh decided against a Senate campaign, despite his earlier interest. He wanted to be part of the campaign to elect Robert Kennedy president rather than put his efforts into the Senate race. "Jess was really so involved in the presidential thing that most of the discussion about running for the Senate kind of took place in [a] back water," Burns said. Most important, Unruh wanted to be governor. His decision was made at a meeting with the pollster Kraft on a second survey. The numbers were even more favorable for Kennedy's winning the California presidential primary. But there was no time to waste. The deadline for filing papers with the state for presidential delegations in the primary was March 6. On March 4, Kennedy called Unruh and said, "Okay, get me on the ballot. But don't get caught at it."[29]

Kennedy's instructions reflected his own indecision at the time about whether he should challenge President Johnson. Kennedy consulted friends endlessly, receiving conflicting advice. But, with just two days left before the deadline for filing the nominating papers necessary to form the 172-person delegation to run in the primary, Unruh could not wait. He needed experienced, respected people to sign the papers. But because of Kennedy's insistence on secrecy, they could not be known Unruh allies. Unruh's friendship with Kennedy would have blown the senator's cover. Unruh needed a front. There was no shortage of choices. A group of young Democratic leaders were lined up, but their car broke down on the way to Sacramento to file the papers.

"Everybody was really getting frantic," Burns said. "Jess is trying to stay out of sight. So he's calling me to find out what I know about what's going on."[30] Another group, part of a national "draft Kennedy" movement—amateurs unrecognized and scorned by the senator's professional team—were also preparing to file nominating papers. With the young Democratic leaders out of the picture, and the deadline just a few hours away, Unruh's aide Crose turned to the amateurs. He found three women in the draft organization and personally took them to the secretary of state's office, where friends of his processed the papers just in time.[31]

Kennedy was still endlessly consulting with others, but he seemed to know exactly where he was going. On March 5, as Unruh was scrambling to get the nominating papers prepared and filed, Ted Kennedy told Fred Dutton, part of Robert Kennedy's team, "Bob's just about made up his mind to run. The thing now is to make sense of it."[32] A few days later, RFK flew to California to be with César Chávez when the United Farm Workers Union leader ended a fast. His reception in the small Central Valley town of Delano, union headquarters, was warm, even loving, although somewhat frantic. Flying back east from Delano, Kennedy said, "Yes. I'm going to do it. If I can, I've got to try to figure out a way to get Gene McCarthy out of it; but if I can't, I'm going to do it anyway."[33]

On Monday, March 11, Unruh called Burns: Kennedy had telephoned him. "He told him he was going to run for sure," Burns said.[34] The campaign was on, and California would determine whether Kennedy could win the nomination. It would also decide Unruh's future. A day later, McCarthy ran strongly against Johnson in the New Hampshire primary, a clear demonstration of the president's weakness. It would be Kennedy versus McCarthy in California.

The California Kennedy campaign was thrown together, a disorganized mixture of Kennedy people from the East Coast, the Unruh Californians, and some anti-Unruh liberal outsiders, whose vision of politics revolved around peace marches and the United Farm Workers Union. But McCarthy had first claim on the anti-war Democrats, particularly the students.

As is the case with all political campaigns, the Kennedy drive operated at two levels, one in public and the other behind a protective screen designed to keep the messy internal operations of politics out of sight. Kennedy's eastern insiders fought with the Californians. "It is now 4 A.M. of my third consecutive night of sleeplessness caused by concern over the failure to move the campaign," an anguished Northern California official, Ray King, wrote Unruh's aide Art Seltzer. "Unfortunately, the inability to function properly is directly related to the interference of our candidate's associates, who seem to know California's needs and requirements better than we do."[35]

A day later, Bill Thomas, the Northern California campaign press secretary, wrote to Southern California headquarters, "The campaign peaked during the first week and has been going downhill ever since." To make things worse, Thomas was shorthanded. "I suppose I could run the teletype with one hand, the beeper system with the other, type news releases with my right foot, hold envelopes to be licked with my left foot and seal them with my tongue," he wrote.[36]

But it didn't matter. Events and the supercharged atmosphere of that spring were more important than whether Kennedy's campaign teams bonded.

As a reporter, I was assigned to cover RFK's campaign in California. It was an exhausting trek around the state, a blur of speeches and Sunday masses. There were motorcades from one spot to another, each packed with crowds so large and emotional that they conveyed a sense of history, exhilaration, and fear that the whole thing would get out of hand.

Adding to the emotion were the political tensions pulling the nation apart—the issues of the war and race. On March 31, the growing opposition to the war and McCarthy's showing in New Hampshire forced President Johnson to tell the nation, "I shall not seek, and I will not accept, the nomination of my party for another term as your president." Then on April 3, Martin Luther King Jr. was murdered in Memphis, Tennessee.

In opposing the war the year before, King had linked race to the war. The war, he said, had ended the federal government's efforts to improve the lives of poor Americans. And the draft had unfairly drawn upon the poor— blacks, Latinos, and poor whites—while providing an escape to the more affluent through educational deferments. Speeches combining these two is- sues heated up the atmosphere even more. In such an overcharged time, Johnson's withdrawal and King's assassination, coming one after the other, devastated the nation.

But things were to get even worse. In the days after King's assassination, riots and racial disturbances rocked Washington, D.C., and other cities across the nation. The total effect of these events was to give Americans the feeling that their country was out of control. Robert Kennedy's speeches, like Martin Luther King's, connected the war with poverty and racism. Kennedy's manner of speaking, full of coiled emotion, stirred deep feelings. He was a man on the edge, courting danger, even death, as he dove into crowds or, as I saw him one day, riding with an aide on the trunk of his cam- paign convertible crossing the San Francisco–Oakland Bay Bridge. Even when engaged in an act as simple as joining his sisters in taking Holy Com- munion in a small barrio church, his actions, words, and manner were re- minders of tragedy, of his brother's assassination.

In San Jose, a San Jose State College senior, Jeff Mullins, drove a con- vertible taking Kennedy from one campaign appearance to another. In an account written for his college paper, the *Spartan Daily*, Mullins described an atmosphere of near hysteria. With Kennedy and Unruh in the backseat, a crowd of 500 swarmed around the car at the airport. The crowd started to pull at Kennedy, and Unruh called to a big young assemblyman, John Vas- concellos. "They're trying to keep him, John," said Unruh. "We need some muscle." Vasconcellos climbed into the backseat. He, Unruh, and two oth- ers wrapped their arms around Kennedy's legs and waist. "Mullins, move, Mullins," shouted the advance man Jim Tolan, signaling the college student to start driving.

A young woman, squeezed by the crowd against the slowly moving car, reached toward Kennedy. He briefly clasped her hand. "My hands have be- come slightly shredded today," Kennedy said after the convertible had cleared the crowd.

His car was enveloped again in the evening when 10,000—7,000 more than expected—packed a downtown San Jose park for his speech. He went into the crowd, emerging ten minutes later, climbing onto the podium. "Jesse," Kennedy said as they drove back to the hotel, "I thought you said we were going to take a nice peaceful walk through the park after dinner."[37]

Kennedy's fatalistic disregard for his own personal safety was a haunting feature of the campaign. It continued through the final days, the senator exhausting himself. He beat McCarthy in their one televised debate. Finally, on June 3, he embarked on what the reporter Jules Witcover called "another of those incredible days that marked the Robert Kennedy campaign as among the most emotional and exhausting in the annals of presidential elections." In San Francisco's Chinatown, Robert and Ethel Kennedy were standing on the backseat of the convertible, watched by crowds three and four deep, when three sharp claps were heard. "Ethel jumped down and sat on the seat hunched over, but the candidate remained standing, waving and shaking outstretched hands, as if bracing himself," Witcover wrote. The sounds were from firecrackers.[38]

On election day, Unruh "wasn't terribly sure we were going to win. So," he said in an oral history, "I visited a few friends that day. I went out late in the afternoon to the Hollywood Park race track, and every place I went, in spite of the fact that the sophisticates were telling us we were down, . . . the working people including the gatekeepers at Hollywood Park told me, 'Aw, don't worry about it. Bobby's in.'"

The gatekeepers called it right. Kennedy defeated McCarthy. The Kennedy party had taken over the Ambassador Hotel, a rambling brown stucco pile of a building surrounded by lawns, cottages, a large health club, and a swimming pool. Although its 1920s grandeur had faded, the hotel was still a favorite political hangout. At 11:30 P.M., Burns and some of the others decided enough returns were in for Kennedy to proclaim victory. Burns made his way through the crowd to an elevator to Kennedy's floor. Unruh told him they had decided to wait. Instead, Unruh, Virginia, Crose, and two or three others went to the Embassy Room, where Kennedy was to speak. Unruh talked to the crowd, and, in an aside to Burns, told him to fetch Kennedy. But Kennedy was already there.[39] He spoke to the crowd, both humorously and seriously. Now that the primary was over, he said, he hoped for a "dialogue—or a debate, I hope—between the vice president [Hubert H. Humphrey, who had not entered the California primary] and perhaps myself on what direction" the country should take. "My thanks to all of you, and on to Chicago, and let's win there."

Kennedy had promised to meet with reporters after his speech. The crowd in the ballroom was thick, and time was short. Aides directed him through the kitchen. Unruh was among those following. In the kitchen, a Palestinian immigrant, Sirhan Sirhan, waited with a .22 caliber pistol. Kennedy's only security, a former FBI agent, Bill Barry, had become separated from him. Unruh had fallen behind in the crowd. Burns, who was standing next to Senator Kennedy, recalled:

> I was standing right next to him. You see Bob wasn't supposed to go that way . . . he was supposed to come off the podium and go . . . down to the lower ballroom where [there was] another big crowd. Instead the guy from the hotel took him right by and turned to the right into the kitchen, and I ran to stop him, and I had run just a step past him and turned around, and he was shaking hands with the guys [kitchen workers]. And I said, "Say Bob, got to go the other way" . . . then Sirhan started shooting, and I went to Sirhan's gun and grabbed ahold of him, and we wrestled around and everybody turned into a big pileup and in the course of it I remember getting one clear view. . . . There was Kennedy laying straight flat, right on the floor, I thought "dead." I remember thinking that. But at that time all I was concerned about was getting Sirhan and keeping him alive. I'm the voice screaming on the tape, "Don't kill him." Because they were bending him around, you know, and they couldn't get the gun out of his hands and it was just a bad scene. I got a little burn across the cheek [from] the bullet going by.[40]

Burns said he remembered Barry "coming up and plunging into the knot of people, yelling for a rope so that we could tie him up. I remember taking off my belt and handing it to Barry and bending down to grab the assassin's legs so as to get him off his feet." Five others were wounded, including Paul Schrade, a young United Auto Workers union official.

By then, several people were holding Sirhan down, including Roosevelt Grier, a former National Football League star lineman, who had campaigned for the senator. Burns recalled:

> About that time, Jess Unruh jumped up onto the top of the table and leaned over Sirhan and started yelling that he should be kept alive because he should stand trial. Unruh was pulling people off Sirhan and yelling for the police . . . Unruh then jumped off the table and told the officers to get the suspect out of there before he was killed. I led the officers into the Colonial Room through the doors from the kitchen and then out . . . into the lobby. . . . I led them out the stairway and out the main entrance. There was a police car parked there with its right front door open. There was quite a crowd of people, and when they saw us coming out with the suspect, they

started screaming and surging forward. The officers pushed the suspect in the back seat and Unruh jumped in the front seat and yelled for the officers to get out of there. At this time, I was struggling with some people, who were trying to get to the prisoner, so I shoved the door shut and the police car took off.[41]

In the patrol car, Sirhan said, "I did it for my country." Unruh asked Sirhan, "Why him?" Sirhan's reply was enigmatic. "It's too late," he said.[42]

Virginia Unruh was nearing the kitchen when she heard the shots. Thinking Unruh had been shot, she pushed her way into the room. When she saw he was not wounded, she left the kitchen, only to be hit in the head by a television camera. Standing in the doorway to the kitchen, she would not let the cameraman through.[43] The former PE teacher remained a formidable woman.

Dr. Marvin Esher, a physician who happened to be in the Embassy Room celebrating Kennedy's victory, answered the call for a doctor.[44] He said he found Kennedy in cardiac arrest, semi-comatose, and in critical condition. An ambulance took him to Central Receiving Hospital, a few miles from the hotel. He was transferred to nearby Good Samaritan Hospital, where he died two days later.

At the time of the shooting, I was in the AP office in downtown Los Angeles. I had just written a new lead saying Kennedy had won the primary. My boss wondered if enough votes had been counted to back up my story. As we discussed the matter, Bob Thomas, the AP reporter at the Ambassador, called with the first word the senator had been shot. I was sent to the hotel.

Knowing cabs were scarce in Los Angeles, I ran to a nearby hotel and found one. I told the cabbie to drive to the Ambassador, located a few miles west on Wilshire Boulevard, and make it fast. As we raced west on deserted Wilshire Boulevard, I saw an ambulance speeding the other way. I took a chance. "Follow that ambulance," I said. The driver executed a U-turn and trailed the ambulance. It was the right one, heading to Central Receiving Hospital. As I left the cab, after giving the driver a generous tip, I saw Senator Kennedy being taken into the hospital. For the next two days, I was either outside Central Receiving Hospital, or Good Samaritan Hospital, where the senator had been transferred, or working in the AP office, focused only on doing my job.

After Kennedy's body was taken east, I flew back to Sacramento, where we lived, and where I usually worked in the Capitol bureau. Only on the plane ride home did I finally allow myself to think about all I had seen. No longer on a journalist's autopilot, giving in to emotion, I was overwhelmed by a sense of disappointment and cynicism, the feeling that politics didn't matter, an opinion that has never quite left me.

With Sirhan in police custody, Unruh left the Rampart police station and returned to his suite. Sherry Bebitch Jeffe, who was in charge of the Students for Kennedy operation, recalled:

> He was shattered. He looked white. And I was so out of it, I was nuts, I was screaming and yelling. . . . I yelled, "I can't stand it here any more. I'm leaving tonight, I'm going to London. I'm never coming back." Unruh looked me straight in the eye and said, "There are no problems in London? There is no segregation in London? There is no crime in London? You can't run away." I guess I just came back to reality and started looking after some of my students who were coming up and were totally whacked.

Virginia was already in the suite. "She was cool," Jeffe said. In fact, Unruh's wife had been calm and strong enough to help the big Roosevelt Grier up to the suite. She "put him on the bed. Rosey had just fallen apart, fallen apart," said Jeffe.

Unruh had a drink. Everyone in the suite was as stunned as he was. The enormity of the event was beyond their comprehension. After a time, the suite emptied, except for the Unruhs, Sherry Bebitch, and her soon-to-be fiancé, Douglas Jeffe, a young Democratic political aide. About 4 A.M., Unruh and his wife went to bed. Two hours later, the hotel manager knocked on the door. He asked everyone to leave. The Kennedy family was arriving that morning, and Jacqueline Kennedy was to stay in the suite. The Unruhs drove home to Inglewood, and Bebitch and Jeffe headed to her apartment, stopping on the way at a drugstore to buy something to help Sherry sleep.[45]

In a day or two, Unruh returned to Sacramento. His friend Jaci DeFord saw him there. She remembered:

> He was devastated. . . . He kept going through again what had happened and how it had happened; he had this need to go through the whole thing. It was as though if he could go through it in slow motion he could see somehow how he could have prevented it. And he would keep going through it, through his part of it, what Rosey Grier did, and what he did and how they manhandled the guy and Bobby lying there . . . just the total waste of it was more than he could handle.

We sat and drank and listened to country-and-western music. That was his way. Whenever he was really sad, the music would come on. It was as though . . . the music expressed the sadness and sometimes he would sing along with it.[46]

For the rest of the year, Unruh alternated between bursts of activity and sitting and drinking in his Sacramento apartment. But he at last understood his obligations to his followers and to himself. In the next year, his campaign for governor would begin. He had defied the president and the state's richest Democrats. Now he was alone as he faced the challenge of uniting a Democratic Party shattered by the events of 1968 and still divided over race and the war. Could Jess Unruh, himself a divisive figure, rebuild the old coalition in the face of such great obstacles?

THIRTEEN

Unruh versus Reagan

THE 1970 GUBERNATORIAL CONTEST between Unruh and Ronald Reagan is little more than a footnote in the broad history of postwar California. The popular incumbent governor Reagan, on the path that eventually took him to the White House, defeated Unruh as expected and remained the central figure in California political life for the next four years. No story, in the view of journalists at the time.

But, in fact, there was a significant story: Unruh waged a tenacious, if unsuccessful, fight for the broad center that the Democratic Party had lost to Reagan when he was first elected in 1966, and to Richard Nixon in the 1968 presidential election. Inspired by his own unique background, and moved by the cataclysmic events that had so recently shaken the nation, Unruh diverged from the liberal Democratic orthodoxy of the day. Campaigning for Kennedy had crystallized Unruh's political philosophy. He saw how the senator had tried to bring together African Americans, Latinos, and working-class whites. As Kennedy's friend Arthur Schlesinger Jr. explained it, "His [Kennedy's] aim was to reconstitute the Roosevelt coalition . . . through his own intense and effective communication with the excluded groups in American society and through their own direct participation in the political process. . . . His appeal to . . . both Negro and backlash districts demonstrated the power of this strategy to unify disparate groups."[1]

Unruh decided against another term in the assembly and began preparing for the 1970 election. He remained the same centrist who had favored Truman over Wallace in 1948, supported the Cold War, fought the liberal California Democratic Council, and feared that the Rumford Act in 1963 would touch off a white backlash. Like John and Robert Kennedy, he was a pragmatist. He had an intensely practical view based on his life, his experiences in the Capitol, and his years representing an urban district with a racially mixed Democratic constituency of poor and working-class people.

From those vantage points, Unruh saw a post–New Deal California—and America—that had been lifted up economically but divided socially. The Depression, the war, and the charismatic leadership of Franklin D. Roosevelt had united impoverished white working people, of whom Unruh himself was one, with blacks, Latinos, Jews, and other societal outcasts. But postwar prosperity had ended that brief moment of unity when white workingmen and -women, now comfortable, resisted the demands of those left behind. Unruh wanted to bring them together—as much as practical politics, human nature, and prejudice would permit.

Unruh was ahead of his time. By the mid 1980s, enough Democrats would see things as Unruh had to form the influential centrist Democratic Leadership Council, which became a platform for the moderate young governor of Arkansas, Bill Clinton. Clinton, like Unruh, came from a southern state impoverished by the Depression, where blacks and whites had known great poverty. When Clinton was elected president, this philosophy became dominant in the Democratic Party.

The task facing Unruh as a candidate for governor was immense. Big-money Democrats denied him funds, just as they had threatened to do in 1968. They were scornful of his chances of winning and bitter over his opposition to the Vietnam War and his support for Kennedy. And they wanted revenge for his feud with Governor Brown. Even more important was the fact that Reagan was on the popular side of issues that reached deeply into the nation's soul.

In the forty months between Robert Kennedy's assassination and the 1970 election for governor, the powerful social currents that had swept through the divided country continued to shape politics in a way that achieved little for Unruh and other Democrats. The Vietnam War still raged, as did the protests and the poisonous debate that accompanied it. The King assassination and the subsequent rioting in black neighborhoods exacerbated racial divisions. Capitalizing on the unrest, George Wallace, the segregationist governor of Alabama, campaigned in blue-collar areas in the Midwest and through the so-called solid South in 1968, magnifying racial tension in that year's presidential election.

Nor was there any relief the following year. At Berkeley, the radical Third World Liberation Front staged disruptive demonstrations, hoping to draw Reagan into a fight.[2] Front members hurled firebombs at several targets and made threats against faculty members and students.[3] Demonstrations in 1969 over a large plot of land near the Berkeley campus known as People's Park brought in the National Guard and law enforcement, which led to the fatal shooting of a student.[4] In 1970, students burned down a Bank of America branch in a community adjacent to the University of California at Santa Barbara.[5] The National Guard at Kent State University in Ohio shot four students to death and wounded several others.[6] During the the National Chicano Moratorium March against the war, an LA County sheriff's deputy shot and killed a respected journalist, Ruben Salazar, in East Los Angeles.[7]

After Robert Kennedy's murder, Unruh sought to navigate these tumultuous currents.

At the Democratic National Convention in August 1968 in Chicago, two months after RFK's death, Unruh headed the California Kennedy delegation. Many of the delegates were shattered rebels without a candidate, left with only their opposition to the Vietnam War and to President Johnson. But with Kennedy dead after having beaten McCarthy in California, the steam seemed to have gone out of the anti-war insurgency. Vice President Humphrey, with support from LBJ loyalists, the big unions, and major Democratic contributors, tightened his grip on the nomination. Unruh's goal was to keep the California delegates together, rather than let them disintegrate into the kind of feuds that so often afflicted the state's Democratic politics. Leading such a group was a new and demanding experience for a man accustomed to being in control. But he understood that success would be a huge boost to his chances for governor. "He was running for governor, and he needed everybody's help, and he was going to have to reach out to all these movers and shakers," Sherry Bebitch Jeffe recalled.[8]

McCarthy supporters asked him to swing the delegation to their man. One request particularly moved him. It was a letter from a 17-year-old, Vicki Gregerson of Oceanside, who seemed to be the kind of young person he admired, not a hippie, flower child, or rebel against the political system. "All through my high school years and now in my college years I have seen my generation become soft and lazy, over-permissive, too drug-oriented, apathetic, rebellious, lawless, and uncaring," she wrote. "I ask you to remember Robert Kennedy's definition of leadership—that which inspires the people to exercise their best qualities. Senator McCarthy has already shown such ability and I don't believe Hubert Humphrey can offer inspirational leadership. I fear that like LBJ they [sic] can only inspire the people to exercise their worst qualities."[9]

Unruh replied, "In all my years of public office I have received very few letters which are as clearly stated and vocal as yours. I do not say this to flatter you but rather to encourage you to continue your political activity—regardless of what might happen in Chicago."[10]

But Unruh remained uncommitted. "It matters little to get on the winner's bandwagon early before the August convention if that candidate lacks freedom to take the new direction that the people of this country demand," he said in a statement to the delegation. "It matters little to be an early supporter of the victor in November if that man perpetuates the alienation and division among our people which now threatens to destroy us."[11]

Despite his grief and shock after Robert Kennedy's death, Unruh did his best to organize the delegation. He put details of convention planning in the hands of Steven E. Smith, who had managed Senator Kennedy's Southern California campaign. In August, they took their seats in chartered jets and headed to Chicago. Despite Kennedy's assassination, the mood on the plane was upbeat. These were political activists, and most of them loved to party. Sherry Bebitch and Douglas Jeffe were soon to be married, and the passengers scrambled for invitations to the wedding. Linda Unruh, Unruh's daughter, would be the junior bridesmaid, and Unruh had agreed to give away the bride if Sherry's father couldn't make it out to California. Upon landing, chartered buses took the crew to the old, rundown LaSalle Hotel. It had been advertised as newly redecorated, but delegates could see no sign of such improvement.

These concerns melted into insignificance in the face of what confronted the California delegation in Chicago. The delegates were under intense pressure to support McCarthy. But as they arrived, they learned that Unruh was trying to persuade the surviving Kennedy brother, Senator Edward M. Kennedy, to accept a draft. Unruh had breakfast with Mayor Richard Daley of Chicago, the boss of the Illinois delegation. Daley didn't think much of Humphrey as a candidate and wanted to keep the convention open in hopes that Ted Kennedy would run.[12] But the senator decided against it, and Daley swung his support to Humphrey. After an Illinois delegation meeting, he stepped to the microphones and announced that Humphrey had won overwhelmingly over McCarthy and Senator George McGovern of South Dakota. Young Kennedy supporters shouted, "We want Teddy," but the mayor growled, "We will not be stampeded by the booing and shouting." Then he turned his back and stalked away.[13]

Determined to put down any dissent in his city, Daley sent his 11,900-man police force, supplemented by thousands of Illinois National Guard troops and federal soldiers,[14] to keep order among the hordes of young men and women who had come to Chicago to protest the war and the certain nomination of Humphrey. The mayor, rather than Humphrey, became the central figure of the convention, and the assaults by police on the demonstrators dominated the news more than anything that happened inside the convention hall. When some of Sherry Bebitch's Students for Kennedy returned bloodied from Grant Park, scene of the biggest battles, she told Unruh that she was going to the park.

He insisted she take his delegate pass as protection.[15] The young men and women in Grant Park considered a California delegate's badge a pass into their beleaguered club. After an anti-war platform plank was defeated the night of Humphrey's nomination, the California protesters had worn black crepe armbands and marched around the convention hall with protesters from New York and other states, singing "The Battle Hymn of the Republic." The California and New York delegations, seated next to each other, had smuggled in a banner reading "We Shall Overcome" and unfurled it on the convention floor.

With no candidate at the convention, Unruh spent some of his time outlining his views on the party's future. Speaking to the platform committee, he criticized aspects of post–New Deal Democratic philosophy that he felt were dividing society. The nation, he said, had outgrown the heavy hand of Washington it had once needed to guide it through the Depression and the war.

He had seen the War on Poverty under Lyndon Johnson turn into a political battleground between Washington, state capitals, and city halls, and he criticized the national system of welfare for the poor. "If anyone doubts that inequitable laws do exist in this nation where all men are supposed to be equal before the law, I would refer him to that vast body of statutes, regulations and interoffice memos known as the welfare system, or more properly the medieval 'poor laws' of our affluent society," he said.[16]

When Humphrey won the nomination, Unruh returned to California and his intermittent periods of brooding and politics. He continued his criticisms of the Johnson-Humphrey administration. On October 7, in a speech to Democrats in a Northern California seaside community, he went even further. "The promises made in the name of the Great Society have turned into a virtual nightmare of racial tensions, dispirited youth, rising crime and a mushrooming federal bureaucracy," he said. "The War on Poverty, as one example, has neither justified its enormous cost nor filled the very real needs of the people it was supposed to benefit. Dollars continue to be poured into welfare programs in the same old way—robbing the recipient of his dignity at the same time that it empties the pocketbooks of the middle class."[17] As the election neared, Unruh did give his nominal support to Humphrey, but important Humphrey supporters felt it was too late and too little.

In an essay the following year, Unruh wrote, "The tendency [of the Democratic Party] to concentrate on the very pressing problems of our minorities can lead to greater alienation of the majority." Expanding on his views in an interview, he said, "That is the principal thing that has happened to the Democratic Party. People have so identified it with minority problems they think we've forgotten everybody else. We have such intense identity with the poor and the black we've almost become a minority party. It isn't politically salable, what we've been doing. We've temporarily lost credence."[18]

Unruh's most nuanced criticism of Democratic orthodoxy was in an article for the liberal magazine *The Nation* on February 17, 1969. Writing for a national audience of liberals, he spared no portion of the party's establishment, including organized labor, or at least its largest component, the AFL-CIO. Labor, he said, had failed to improve minority employment, "the principal canker in our central cities. The labor movement could be expected to lead the attack on the problem but it has not. . . . It can be convincingly argued that the policies of the National Association of Manufacturers regarding minority employment are often more progressive than those of the AFL-CIO."[19]

Unruh's comments before the 1968 election hurt Humphrey. The race between Humphrey and Nixon was closer than had been expected. California went for Nixon, and Unruh's foes in the Democratic Party blamed him for not campaigning hard enough for Humphrey. In this election tide, Republicans captured the state assembly, and Unruh lost his speakership.

"He was shell-shocked," said Douglas Jeffe. "We weren't expecting it." Unruh blamed himself for not taking charge of the assembly elections, as he had done in the past. The memory of Kennedy's assassination haunted him. "I think we lost our Democratic majority that year," Unruh said in remarks to the Steelworkers Union, "because most of what I did that summer was to sit around and cry and drink—and I didn't cry much," he said.[20] Robert T. Monagan, who became speaker after the GOP took over the state assembly, thought Unruh had lost his focus. "He was starting to figure 'Where am I going to go?'" Monagan said. "He wanted to start running for governor."[21]

But there was more to it. Republicans had been gaining seats through the decade as California became more conservative. "All of a sudden the tide turned, the attitudes, the political attitudes in California changed," Monagan said. Using new methods of computer analysis to track the political and demographic changes, the Republicans targeted districts where they thought they could win. And the Democrats lost good candidates and brainpower as some of the better members in the assembly moved on to the U.S. Congress.

For Unruh, losing his prized job as speaker was painful. "I was well aware when I was speaker that it would be very difficult to move from the speakership to the governorship," he said. "But I just couldn't quite cut the umbilical cord as far as the speakership was concerned. . . . So the net result was that I didn't leave the speakership when I should have, and all of a sudden it left me."[22] But the loss also gave him the freedom to campaign for governor. As speaker, Unruh's priorities were passing his legislative program, improving the assembly's operations, and holding onto his majority. Running for governor, he had to focus on the broad problems of California. It was a different ball game.

As the campaign for governor began, Unruh and his advisers pondered the question of how he could present himself as an alternative to the popular Reagan. His message of centrist moderation, while scorned by the Democratic Left, made sense in middle-of-the-road California. Unruh and his advisers agreed that he had to bring the Democrats together, as had been Robert Kennedy's goal.

Recognizing that Unruh was no Kennedy, Frank Burns urged him to run as the rough-and-tough blue-collar guy he had always been. Fred Dutton, a Kennedy adviser, agreed. Dutton had been the tactical mastermind of Pat Brown's first successful campaign for governor, and Unruh had served with him then as Southern California director. They had worked together in the first years of Brown's administration,

Dutton told Unruh his best chance of an upset victory was to run as "a respectable but gutty and colorful populist concerned with the needs, and exploitation, of ordinary working people. . . . This approach is consistent with your own personality as much of the public already sees it, is compatible with your own origins, is consonant with your legislative accomplishments."[23]

Dutton said Unruh must make a strength of his weakness—the Big Daddy image, as well as his reputation for bullying, deals, and the compromises he had made to attain his policy goals. "If you are going to go the populist route, you will have to be flamboyant, slashing, specific," even if it required disavowing deals Unruh had made in the past with the special interests in the legislature. That approach was necessary, Dutton wrote, for Unruh to "break away from Reagan much of the working-class vote that is traditionally part of the Democratic base."[24]

Unruh's campaign manager, John Van de Kamp, also saw it that way. "What you wanted to do with Jess was sort of show his common man background, where he came from and what he was trying to do for real people. That was the only way to beat Reagan. Reagan was sort of [in] this ivory tower with his business friends," he said.[25]

Unruh himself was not confident enough to accept the role. "Everyone was trying to advise Jess on what to do," said Van de Kamp, who was hired to manage the campaign in the fall of 1969. "Everyone told him he had to be television-ready." Unruh was determined to slim down even more, and limited his intake to a meal a day. "The problem we had as campaign managers," Van de Kamp said, "was to really humanize him in some way so people did not look at him as this big fat man who was a boss."[26]

At the same time, Unruh decided to place himself in the hands of an orthodontist, who straightened his teeth. The structure of his front teeth had caused him to lisp slightly. "It was terrible in terms of putting him on the air," said Phillip Schott, who left the assembly staff to work on the Unruh campaign and eventually replaced Van de Kamp as campaign manager. "It was very painful, distractingly painful."[27] At the suggestion of his advertising adviser, Michael Kaye, Unruh also changed to a more conservative wardrobe.

His main opponent in the Democratic primary, to be held in June 1970, was the mayor of San Francisco, Joseph Alioto. Alioto, a successful attorney before he went into politics, was a charming, extremely intelligent man whose appreciation of fine wine, food, and music reflected the sophistication of his city. In 1968, he had stood steadfastly with Humphrey and was just as loyal to the Johnson-Humphrey philosophy as Unruh was skeptical. But in September 1969, *Look* published an article linking Alioto to the Mafia. Alioto sued the magazine for libel and eventually won, but too late for the 1970 campaign for governor. The bad publicity caused him to withdraw in January, leaving Mayor Sam Yorty of Los Angeles, a perennial losing candidate for higher office (he ran for president in 1972) as Unruh's only opponent in the June primary.[28]

Alioto's departure did not bring the Humphrey Democrats over to Unruh. I saw the depth of their resistance when I visited the law offices of Eugene L. Wyman during this period. He was a former Democratic national committeeman and, at the time, the Democrat to see in Southern California for raising campaign contributions. He was a pleasant, friendly man. I'd interviewed him many times and sensed that he was intelligent, analytical, and unforgiving in a fight, a perfect combination for a high-stakes lawyer and political power. Like so many of his kind, Wyman had covered his walls with pictures showing his influence. I was struck by one of him and Lyndon Johnson. LBJ, sitting on a rocking chair, his eyes narrowed, his mouth grim, was listening to Wyman. It was a great, unstated advertisement in the days when lawyers were not permitted to advertise: Let the man who advises presidents advise you.

He told me, "The question that is really floating around the people who raise and give money is, 'Can a person in good conscience give full support to a candidate when that candidate has not given full support to the party?'" The answer obviously was no, and with great satisfaction, he explained to me, in a chilling dissertation on the power of big contributors, how this would paralyze the Unruh campaign. "A long time ago Jess was the one who said, 'Money is the mother's milk of politics.' If the fund-raisers and givers do not participate, it simply means Jess will run out of milk. He will not be able to maintain an effective campaign."

The impact was painfully clear to Chloe Pollock, a Democratic fund-raiser who was a close friend of Unruh's. A potential contributor, she reported, had told her:

> Wyman is his biggest and oldest client—although he personally is all for Jess, and always has been, really he absolutely cannot move on ANYTHING as long as Wyman opposes [it]. . . . Several of my [i.e., Pollock's] people can't use names because of business affiliations—I am getting quite a bit of flak, both from those permitting use of names and those not, that he [Unruh] absolutely should not [run] in 1970. Apathy reigns supreme—they've already thrown in the towel. This election [is] going to be a real Mother!![29]

The campaign got off to a slow and uncertain start, with money a constant worry. One adviser tried to make something positive out of Unruh's lack of contributors: he should run as an anti-money candidate, accept no contribution of more than $1,000, and forgo "all use of paid TV or radio spots as well as billboards."[30]

Another problem was Unruh's discomfort with his campaign manager. Van de Kamp was a member of a prominent and affluent Los Angeles bakery and restaurant family, who was later elected district attorney of Los Angeles County. He had run a strong but losing race for Congress, and although he was pretty much a novice, he was given the job of directing the campaign. Surrounding him was a committee of volunteer, part-time advisers—generally successful, youngish attorneys, who were smart but had never run a statewide campaign. Fred Dutton was the most experienced, but he was practicing law in Washington. The first meeting of the advisory group was what might be expected from a group dominated by lawyers, talky, disputatious, and unfocused. "Unfortunate," is how one participant described it.[31]

Not only did the Unruh team face a popular opponent, but Reagan had a sophisticated and experienced group of managers, equipped with the newest techniques money could buy. This was the dawn of the age of advanced technology in politics, and experts could instantly analyze demographics, quickly produce the results of political polls, predict with some accuracy how a district was likely to vote, and accomplish other marvels that personal computers would make commonplace by the end of the century.

Stuart Spencer and Bill Roberts, Reagan's campaign managers, and their associates in the firm of Decision Making Information conducted daily polling for Reagan's campaign, an innovative idea in 1970. Then, for a more precise breakdown, census data on individual households—ages, ethnicity, income, number of appliances and motor vehicles, and much more—were compiled by precinct, along with party registration, voter turnout, and other political information. Such was the state of the art in the pre–personal computer era that the data were sent by phone wire to a Univac 1108 computer in Phoenix, Arizona. This kind of information had long been available, but until Decision Making Information and a few other pioneers figured it out, there was no way to sort the data in a manageable way.[32]

During an interview at that time, Spencer told me that political writers knew nothing about how campaigns actually ran. His comment goaded me into learning the system at least well enough to write a story describing it to readers of the *Los Angeles Times*. I was intrigued by the idea of bringing order to a political system that had traditionally been run by instinct. With these new skills, I was able to gain a precise understanding of neighborhoods I had previously examined with random interviews. Others were also fascinated by the prospects of the new technology. Bob Levine, an Unruh volunteer, wrote Van de Kamp early in 1970 calling for more research. "Who are the people who voted for Reagan and voted for Humphrey two years later?" he asked.[33]

But answering these questions, as Spencer and Roberts were doing, was expensive. With the most of the Democratic fat cats continuing their boycott of the Unruh campaign, money for such research was not available. The atmosphere among Democrats was poisonous. For example, when the Unruh campaign staff asked for a desk in the office of the Northern California Democratic organization, Roger Boas, the anti-Unruh state chairman, demanded $250 a month rent, payable in advance. "Bullshit," the new campaign chairman, Phillip Schott, wrote to the treasurer, Manning Post. "And if they should send us a bill put it in the paper shredder."

Unruh and Van de Kamp were very different kinds of people. "I always liked him on a personal level," said Van de Kamp. "He was a different person, you were never quite sure whether he liked you or not. He could be, I think, very warm to some people. I think with me—I came out of a different social class, or so he thought." Clearly, Unruh was uncomfortable around rich people. "I would take him to a fund-raiser, and I was trying to get him to schmooze with people who might give him money. He'd end up over in the corner talking to the only minority person there, black or Hispanic, or someone he felt more comfortable with. And so with me, there was a little reservation because of my last name and where he thought I came from." In April 1970, before the June primary election, "it was clear Jess wanted a comfort level that I could not provide him," Van de Kamp said. Schott, an Unruh protégé who had risen to the top of the assembly staff, replaced him.[34]

As the fall campaign began, Unruh and his team finally agreed on the image he should be striving for. He should run as the tough populist, presenting himself as a sharp contrast to the polished Reagan and his wealthy supporters. But they all recognized how difficult it would be to spread the message without money for television advertising.

One adviser proposed that, on the first day, Unruh take his campaign bus, loaded with reporters, to the home of Henry Salvatori, one of the conservative rich men who comprised the Reagan kitchen cabinet. Salvatori was an engineer who had made millions from drilling for oil. The idea was to show how people like Salvatori would benefit from the Reagan tax policy. The day would also serve to reintroduce Unruh to the public. A bus was hired, and on Labor Day, the press was assembled at the campaign headquarters on Wilshire Boulevard. Supporters were brought in, and Unruh spoke before the party boarded the bus.

Unfortunately, Unruh and his team mixed the message. Rather than embracing the rough and tough image that had made him famous, Unruh said Big Daddy "isn't here any more." In the unaccustomed manner of a repentant sinner, Unruh said he had learned how to "arm-twist, to compromise, to make deals, to get the last extra vote." It was a game, he said "and the people were entitled to something better than games."

The words didn't ring true. He was attacking the very reason for his accomplishments. But an inexperienced campaign staff had persuaded him on that important morning to present himself as a sleek new Unruh.

After that awkward introduction, Unruh and the reporters boarded the bus and rode a few miles to a middle-class, Democratic neighborhood, where they stopped at the home of the Blatts. There, in what became a trademark of the early campaign, an easel stood, holding flip cards. The flip cards were there because the campaign managers thought television news would not run stories unless they were visual. Unruh, now more the populist, flipped the cards and explained how the Blatts, who faced an $82 property tax increase, would not be helped by the Reagan proposal. Then the bus headed west toward Los Angeles's richest neighborhood, Bel Air, and the home of the Salvatoris. The developers of Bel Air had not planned for buses. In fact, Bel Air was designed for exclusion, with entrance gates and narrow streets that are hard to navigate. Despite the obstacles, the bus lumbered up to the Salvatori home.

The Salvatoris were a proud and domineering couple. Neighbors had alerted them to the arrival of the bus, and Grace Salvatori was waiting behind her closed iron gate. Soon her husband, wearing tennis clothes, joined her. He shook hands with Unruh through the gate but stepped outside when Unruh began to talk about property taxes. "Oh, you ass, you," Salvatori said. Standing at Unruh's elbow, he said, "You're a liar, Mr. Unruh." As the dialogue rose to the level of shouts, Grace Salvatori joined in. "We worked for the money to pay for it," she said. "This is what you call cheap politics."[35]

The scene put the Unruh campaign on national television. Van de Kamp, who was in Washington at the time, watched in dismay. "A disaster," he said. "It reinforced all the old notions about Jess. I saw Jess later, however, and we talked about it. He said 'That was great. We got . . . attention.' "[36]

Schott, Van de Kamp's successor as campaign manager, said, "Nobody thought Mrs. Salvatori would come down, that hadn't occurred to us. Nor had it occurred to us that we couldn't turn the buses around and get out of there. . . . It didn't take us long to realize that this was having repercussions, and my personal view of it is that we probably gained. . . . We got the attention of the media."[37]

The target area for a populist campaign was easy to determine, especially for Unruh. It was where he had first come as a young man from Texas to California, to the city of Hawthorne and others like it. This part of Los Angeles County had attracted many southwestern immigrants, especially during the Great Depression. Since then, life had changed in Hawthorne and the rest of the small suburban cities on the coastal plain southeast and southwest of Los Angeles. World War II had turned the area into an aircraft manufacturing center, and the Cold War expanded it even more. The impoverished southwesterners of the late 1930s were now the skilled craftsmen on plant floors, and their children were the engineers and scientists in the laboratories and offices upstairs.

The immigrants and their families, with their conservative religious and social values and populist economic instincts, remained just as politically important as they had been when they settled in Hawthorne, Downey, Norwalk, and other such LA suburbs. Their attitudes were shared by many Californians. A union official told me, "As Downey and Norwalk go, so will go most of the blue-collar workers of Southern California." It was a big enough population to swing elections, and its behavior was a tip-off to what Middle America was thinking. Would these voters, embraced by Reagan as his Forgotten Americans and by Nixon as his Silent Majority, swing back to the Democrats and to Unruh, the candidate whose roots were identical to theirs?

Covering the campaign, I was forever trying to think of new twists to interest readers. I had an idea. Unruh loved country-and-western music, and I enjoyed listening to a popular local country-and-western music station, KFOX, which called its listening area "KFOX Country." I drove to KFOX Country to check on how its inhabitants felt about Unruh. I went door to door in precincts that fit the demographic I was seeking, white and blue-collar. One afternoon, I walked into a bar to interview the patrons. I could not have been more inappropriately dressed in my tie and Brooks Brothers seersucker sport coat. I sat down and introduced myself to the woman tending bar. Then I ordered a beer and bought a round for the four or five others seated there. They all accepted their beers wordlessly. I asked the woman and the others what they thought of the election. "We don't talk much to strangers around here," she said, her voice resonating with the accent of the Southwest. Those were the only words spoken to me at the tavern.

Most people were more friendly in the three days I spent in KFOX Country. They nonetheless remained concerned about the issues that had attracted their Democratic neighborhoods to Reagan in 1966. "What worries me most is the riots the colored people are having and the kids who take dope and the riots these college kids are having about the war," said Margie Cannada, the Kentucky-born wife of a truck driver. Others said much the same. But on another day, I visited the state unemployment office in Norwalk. Five cars waited in the street, lined up to find space in the packed parking lot. Long lines of unemployed waited at each window. Requests for unemployment insurance were up 35 percent. "Every time we have a Republican in office, it seems there is a work slowdown," said Texas-born Charles Bradford, a laid-off welder waiting for benefits.[38]

That was in July. By the fall, unemployment was worse in California and the rest of the nation. The huge arms buildup for the Vietnam War had ended. The Defense Department payroll was reduced, and payrolls were also cut sharply in the aircraft and military equipment industries. In aircraft plants and other factories with defense contracts, workers on plant floors and engineers and scientists in the offices and laboratories upstairs lost their jobs. California, which received almost 20 percent of the nation's defense contracts, was hit hard. More than a third of the cutbacks were in the state.[39]

Suddenly, California was more receptive to Unruh as a populist. The poor economy changed the dynamics of the campaign. Unemployment became more important than dislike of student rebels. By now, Unruh had made his position clear on social unrest. He didn't like it either. At Berkeley, he told about 200 students in a rally near the campus on October 1: "The faculties and administration must assume responsibility for maintaining campus order. . . . All too often we have seen faculties display indifference to violence and refuse to take responsibility for doing something about it." He further said, "If all else fails we must not hesitate to call upon the police when their presence is needed to protect order and freedom." When a student asked, "Why have you changed to a hard-line tactic?" Unruh replied that he had always felt that way. "It's not a change," Unruh said. "It's just that the governor has been screaming so loud he's obscured everything else."[40]

As election day neared, Unruh found his voice. Polls showed him substantially behind Reagan, but after campaigning for a year, Unruh now moved with confidence and purpose. Crowds grew in size and enthusiasm. I was traveling with him during the last days of his campaign, and I could see that things had changed as he traveled back and forth between the population centers of Northern and Southern California and through the Central Valley. In Bakersfield, so southwestern and so important to country-and-western music that it was known as "Nashville West," 150 workingmen and -women crowded into his storefront headquarters. If Unruh could have afforded a better advance team and selected a better site, the crowd probably would have been larger, judging from the enthusiasm of those present.

"I am not going to sit here and say that it [unemployment] is a national problem and say there is nothing I can do about it," he said. "If we beat Ronald Reagan . . . Dick Nixon is going to hear us say we don't like a policy of deliberate unemployment, and he is going to have to change. But if he doesn't change, I will be in Washington every other day banging on the White House door trying to get for the people of California what they deserve."[41]

In the San Francisco Bay Area, the story was the same. With country-and-western music playing on his campaign bus, surrounded by friends and supporters, Unruh was in good humor and even seemed optimistic. About 2,000 gathered in Aquatic Park in San Francisco heard him say, "Unless we turn this election around as sure as I am standing here on this flatbed truck, unemployment will go up to 10 percent next spring."[42]

The Reagan camp saw the change. Stuart Spencer, Reagan's campaign manager, said:

> Toward the end, he got the theme going—the economy. Very populist. He had a great thematic thing going. What I could see from all the data coming in, all of a sudden, we're losing the goddamn . . . blue-collar Democrat [area] that we had won [in 1966] . . . because his [Unruh's theme] was hitting right home. They thought they were going to lose their jobs, and Jesse was giving them all sorts of reasons [to vote against Reagan]. That was the story. He stumbled out of the box, coasted for a while, finally got it together thematically and started making points.[43]

Reagan's polling showed the governor's lead over Unruh had dropped 7 percent in a week. The Reagan camp, after ignoring Unruh, attacked him. The *San Francisco Examiner* had published a story about Unruh's part ownership of the Pacific Towers in Long Beach, and citing that, Reagan called him a "hypocrite" and "dishonest." By election day, the polls showed Reagan pulling ahead again, leading by six to seven points. In the end, Reagan was reelected with a vote of 52.9 percent to 45.1 percent. He carried the Republican vote overwhelmingly and was supported by 20 percent of the Democrats.[44]

There was more to the story, as the *Los Angeles Times* political writer Richard Bergholz found in a postelection study of Los Angeles County precincts. Unruh had been on the right track. He was able to bring working-class voters back to the Democratic Party. In Bell Gardens, in the heart of blue-collar Los Angeles County, Unruh beat Reagan, who had carried the town four years before. Even in areas where Reagan won, the margin was narrow. In the San Fernando Valley, overwhelmingly in favor of

Reagan in 1966, Unruh ran well. Unemployment was high, and in that era of stay-at-home moms, Bergholz noted, "some of the wives have gone back to work as supermarket checkers to help meet the financial bind."[45] Moreover, where Brown had lost to Reagan by a million votes, Unruh cut the margin down to 500,000. And his well-organized get-out-the-vote campaign helped the Democrats regain control of the assembly.[46]

In politics, there is no glory in defeat. But there are lessons to be learned. From the beginning of his career, Unruh had understood the need to forge a political coalition out of the disparate elements of California's population. His public skills were lacking, his Big Daddy image too firmly ingrained, his enemies too rich and numerous. But his message and style, now long forgotten, pointed the way for Democrats who would later recapture, at least for a time, the forgotten Americans, the men and women in the broad American middle.

FOURTEEN

The Man with the Money

THE FINAL YEARS OF Unruh's life are, in many ways, the most interesting and revealing. In 1974, he was elected state treasurer, and during his twelve-year incumbency, he turned a weak office into a powerful one. Before Unruh took over, wrote Robert Fairbanks, a Capitol journalist, "the treasurer had about as much political clout as the director of a local mosquito abatement district."[1]

Unruh changed all that. He quickly mastered the players and rules of Wall Street and became a national power in the financial markets. He was the principal arbiter of how California invested billions of dollars in pension funds. He approved the issuance of billions of dollars in state-backed bonds that financed new homes, businesses, and hospitals. All these transactions required the participation of investment bankers and lawyers, and Unruh, for the most part, chose them. In the competition for his favor, they deluged him with campaign contributions and entertainment.

Before he settled into the treasurer's office, Unruh had drifted at a loss outside the mainstream of politics, excluded from the policy making, power plays, and intrigue that had been the center of his life. The last weeks of his campaign for governor had been difficult but fulfilling, with daily contact with growing crowds of working families. Once the campaign was over, he could find nothing to fill the void.

So when Ben Hoberman, the general manager of a Los Angeles talk radio station, KABC, called with an offer, Unruh accepted. Hoberman was recruiting celebrities to appear on the air, and he added Unruh to his stable as a talk show host, commentator, and reporter.[2]

After a press conference announcing Unruh's new post at KABC, he sat down with the news director, Leo McElroy. "OK, boss," Unruh said. "What do I do now?" McElroy, seated at his desk in his cubbyhole of an office, pulled a tape recorder from his drawer. "You know how to work one of these?" he asked. "No," replied Unruh, "but I can learn." McElroy had been worried about dealing with his famous new reporter, but at that point, "I knew we would be all right."

Unruh learned to write lead-ins to his interviews and transmit them to the station. In those pre–cell phone days, a radio reporter would find a pay phone and remove the mouthpiece. The wire from the tape recorder would be fastened to the wires inside the mouthpiece, using a clip. Like the other radio reporters, Unruh carried a wrench to remove the mouthpiece, fastened tight by the phone companies trying to discourage the stations' practice.

Unruh reported from the Republican and Democratic national conventions of 1972. The station used an Unruh report every half hour. "He really learned fast," said McElroy. "He filed great reports. He was marvelous. Never came off as anything but a good news guy. He really loved it."

But Unruh wasn't happy outside politics. Casting around for something that would put him back in the political arena, he made a disastrous choice. He decided to run for mayor of Los Angeles in 1973.

The mayor, Sam Yorty, was seeking a fourth term. His principal opponent was City Councilman Tom Bradley, an African American with a strong liberal following. Yorty had defeated him in the 1969 mayoral election with a racist campaign, successfully appealing to white middle-class voters who still remembered the 1965 Watts riots. Almost every day after that defeat, Bradley had campaigned among whites, blacks, and Latinos, building a multiracial coalition that proved hard to beat.

Looking back at his own strong showing in Los Angeles in the governor's race, Unruh thought he had a good chance against Yorty and Bradley. But he also knew he'd need Republican support in the nonpartisan election. For this reason, he asked Stuart Spencer and Bill Roberts, who had managed Reagan's successful campaign against him in 1970, to take charge of this new effort.

"The first question I asked him was why he was running for mayor," Spencer said. "He wanted to build up a base so he could run statewide. He thought he could do a good job. I did, too."

As the campaign moved on, Unruh struck Spencer as a weaker candidate than he had been in the gubernatorial campaign. "He didn't seem assertive," Spencer said. "He didn't seem like the Jesse Unruh of the last six weeks on the 1970 campaign. He didn't seem convinced that what he was doing was right. . . . Probably the greatest mistake he made was in terms of timing. The situation wasn't right for him."[3] Unruh figured he could overtake Bradley. But he finished third behind Bradley and Yorty in the primary, and Bradley went on to win the runoff election.

This launched another bleak period for Unruh. For one thing, he needed money to live on. He sought out a friend, Selden Ring, a wealthy land developer, and asked for help. "He went through a period where he had substantial financial difficulties, and he went to my father and my father agreed to lend him money," said Ring's son, Doug. "I don't know how much, and I don't know what he did with it. I am sure it was never paid back. And my father would never ask for it."[4]

Unruh never got over his defeat in his bid to become mayor of Los Angeles. Chris Edwards, who had begun her relationship with him about this time, said he was devastated. For years afterward, whenever I encountered him, and he had been drinking, he would berate me for the way I'd covered the mayoral campaign for the *Times*. He thought my articles had favored Bradley. My coverage, he would say, was responsible for his defeat. Years later, after a particularly long tirade at a Christmas party, Chris told him to forget it, that the election had been a long time ago. He paused and, after a moment's thought, agreed that much time had passed. The three of us had a pleasant time talking the rest of the evening.

In 1974, the year after Unruh's defeat in the mayoral election, the state treasurer, Ivy Baker Priest, announced she was ill and was not going to run again. Chris recalled, "She [Priest] lived in West LA, and I remember us going over there. And he went in to talk to her. And he came out and said I'm going to run."[5]

He was so well known and well regarded that he won easily. In a way, his victory was ironic. His dirt-poor Texas family had despised Wall Street, blaming it for their troubles during the Depression. Now Unruh was in a position to become both a collaborator with the Street's bankers and their foe, always looking for a chance to outwit them.

He took office at a time when America's financial situation was troubled. Inflation was at 12.3 percent; employment was stagnant, and high interest rates were making buying a house increasingly difficult for a working-class family. Unruh relished the chance to work at his new job and do it in comparative obscurity. His time as a radio reporter had not made him more friendly to journalists. Grover McKean remembers saying when he went to work as Unruh's chief assistant: "Jess, you don't want to hire me to change your image, because I don't think that's possible." Unruh replied: 'No, my idea of good press is none at all."[6]

Unruh saw his new job as an opportunity to accumulate power and use it to shape public policy. "We always talked about power," his friend Stuart Spencer recalled. "And we would get into these raging arguments about where the greatest power rested. Jesse always said, 'I don't care what goddamn office you've got. You can make it into a power position.'"[7]

"He told me he was going to stay in this office," McKean remembered. " 'I am not here to run for governor. I am going to make something of this job.' He wanted to get back into making public policy. He had run for mayor and had lost, and he wasn't enjoying private enterprise."[8]

Early in January, Unruh checked into the Mansion Inn, a few blocks from the Capitol. The next day, he was sworn into his new job and then hosted a reception at the Del Prado restaurant, a political hangout. He was letting people know he was back.

Longtime employees in the treasurer's office anxiously awaited their new boss's arrival. Until then, life for them had been routine. California's biggest bank, the Bank of America, and a few others bought bonds issued by the state and sold them to investors, a process called underwriting. Working with them were a handful of major law firms, doing the legal work necessary for such transactions. The agency's employees were paid less than those doing comparable work in other state offices. Unruh immediately broke the pattern. "Every time he was in the office, there was electricity," said Bruce Van Houton, who was working in the office when Unruh arrived.[9]

Unruh, in his first administrative job, quickly got to know his new employees. He and his daughter Linda played volleyball with the office crew. When fellow workers gave a baby shower for Van Houton and his wife, Unruh invited Mrs. Van Houton and the baby into his office. "He said how wonderful it was and how his only regret was that he spent so little time with his family," Van Houton said. Dan Dowell, another official in the office, and his wife were invited to a party at Unruh's apartment. "My wife got all dressed up, and Jess was there in a T-shirt and jeans," he said. Another time, Unruh sent Dowell to Los Angeles to attend a conference. Dowell went to every session and returned to the office in Sacramento with a report a half-inch thick. "What the hell is this?" said Unruh. "I didn't send you there to work, I sent you there to enjoy yourself." With that, he threw Dowell's report in the wastebasket.

When state-issued bonds had to be signed in New York to complete transactions, the new treasurer sometimes sent secretaries, telling them, "I want you to sign the bonds and have a good time." Yet he was not always benevolent to his employees, and he could be intimidating. "He'd invite you into his office and direct you to a nice leather couch, and you'd sink down, so you were looking up at him," said Bill Sherwood, another veteran of those days.[10]

Most important to the staff was the fact that he began to raise the pay and level of many of the jobs in the office. The civil service system made it difficult. He ordered McKean to find a way to "upgrade the positions of the competent people and eliminate the jobs of the incompetent." McKean hired a civil service system expert. Together, they came up with a plan that was approved by the State Personnel Board. Dan Dowell was one of those who benefited. "He was so pleased he called me at home to tell me," Dowell said.[11] Unruh enjoyed giving good news. "If somebody had to be let go, I'd do it, somebody had to be promoted he'd do it," McKean said.[12]

While organizing his office, Unruh began to build a power base in the Capitol. He began with the institution he knew best, the legislature.

Most of his old pals were gone, but he was a legend among the new, a forceful, friendly presence who charmed them over drinks and who was always ready to offer advice to newcomers. The nightlife scene Unruh enjoyed was still pretty much the same as it had been when he left. Frank Fat's Chinese restaurant near the Capitol was still popular with politicians, whose favorite meal there—usually preceded and followed by many drinks—was a big steak, washed down with wine, and cream pie for dessert.

Unruh invited small groups of legislators to hear a presentation on the treasurer's office. McKean said, "Then Jess and I would take them out to dinner, four or five at a time. We'd sit at a table, and we would continue the discussion," said McKean. "They were fascinated by the fact that he was interested in the [treasurer's] job. And a lot of them, when they were new, wanted to know everything, and it didn't hurt that he was a legend; they liked that. And a lot of them really liked him." Republicans, Democrats, he hung out with them all. Ross Johnson, an Orange County conservative Republican, became a good friend of Unruh's. Late in the evening, he joined Unruh at the Torch Club, a Capitol area bar for serious drinkers, and they sang along as the jukebox played country-and-western songs.

"He was like the king of the roost when we went out to dinner. Unruh never dined alone, that's for sure," McKean said. In addition, Unruh made it a point to attend legislative committee hearings relevant to his office. He frequently visited the assembly during sessions, roaming the floor, exercising the privilege given to a former member. "He loved that. He could come and go as he wanted. He used to say that was one of the great things about the job. He had access to the floor, but he didn't have to stay there," McKean said. Carefully, he built a base of supporters, new and old. "He attended legislative hearings, which other treasurers had never done before," said McKean. "He appeared on behalf of his own budget. He would treat legislators with the respect they thought they were entitled to. . . . Unruh appeared at their fund-raisers, and they loved that. He would attend some Republican fund-raisers, and that really raised some eyebrows."[13]

Unruh quickly put his influence to use to try to ease the financial plight of the working class, which had been the heart of the Unruh constituency in 1970.

Two years before he took office, a plan to do just that had been conceived by two young Stanford Law School graduates, Michael BeVier and Bob Klein. They had built housing for the poor, depending on federal funds to subsidize their projects. But in 1973, the Nixon administration cut off the funds, and "without them we were finished," BeVier said.[14]

Rather than accept defeat, BeVier and Klein took an unusual course. They embarked on a campaign to create a state agency that would make possible low-interest housing loans for lower-income Californians, an effort chronicled by BeVier in his 1979 book, *Politics Backstage: Inside the California Legislature*. With Ronald Reagan in the governor's office, enactment into law would be difficult. But they found an ally in the state senate, Democrat George Zenovich, who had been one of the Unruh crowd in the assembly. He was interested in the housing issue. Zenovich created a committee to study how the state could help low- and middle-income residents buy homes. Klein and BeVier were appointed consultants.

In writing the bill, the two young consultants proposed that California sell tax-exempt bonds to investors to finance housing construction. The investors would, in effect, loan money to the state. It was a good deal, because interest on these bonds was, and still is, tax-free. Such securities are known as revenue bonds. They are repaid from revenue from the project, such as rent.

Until the 1970s, California's savings and loan industry had successfully opposed such financing. Savings and loans had produced the financing and mortgages that powered the post–World War II housing boom in California. As businesses regulated by the state, savings and loan institutions were a major power in the Capitol. The savings and loans' wealth, their political acumen—and campaign contributions—gave them huge clout in the legislature and the governor's office, no matter whether Democrats or Republicans were in charge. They saw the state loans, with interest lower than the market rate, as unwelcome competition.

BeVier and Klein figured out a way to win the support of the hostile financial institutions. They proposed bringing them into the program. The state agency would sell the bonds and lend the proceeds to the savings and loans and other financial institutions. Prospective home buyers, who met the low and moderate income standards, would actually borrow the money from savings and loans. Because the pool of money came from the sale of the tax-exempt bonds, the financial institutions could make the loans at below-market rate, repay the state, and still make a profit.

It was not just a program for low-income buyers. When the two consultants visited the working-class Mission District in San Francisco and talked to an executive of Bay View Federal Savings and Loan, they saw how inflation and high mortgage rates had hit blue-collar families. "The rise in mortgage interest rates over the previous decade had driven completely out of the home buying market many families to whom Bay View would have made a mortgage loan five years before," BeVier said.[15]

Governor Reagan vetoed the plan after it passed the legislature, but in 1975, the political situation changed. A Democrat, Edmund G. "Jerry" Brown Jr., succeeded Reagan, and the climate now favored the housing plan. From his new perch in the treasurer's office, Unruh watched the revival of the bill with approval. The working-class people BeVier and Klein had seen in San Francisco were his folks, the ones who had voted for him for governor four years before.

Even so, he wanted to change important parts of the legislation. As with so many things he did in politics, Unruh's motives were mixed. From a policy standpoint, he wanted to make sure the plan was financially sound. A New York state housing agency had failed to repay investors in its bonds. "Its troubles, which received considerable publicity, made the legislators very nervous, and they began to look for assurance that a similar thing could not happen to a California housing agency," BeVier recounted. Unruh insisted on control of the bond sales. He wanted to protect the state's credit by limiting borrowing. But he also saw the scheme's potential to benefit himself. The financial houses and lawyers involved in the bond sales would become his campaign contributors.

BeVier and Klein objected. But Senator Zenovich advised them to give in to his friend Unruh. BeVier recalled: "He said you've got to give him what he wants. If he asks for something outrageous, come and talk to me, but if he said put something in the bill, put it in."[16]

Governor Jerry Brown's administration, recalling Unruh's fights with Pat Brown, didn't want to give him so much power, either. But one of Unruh's companions on the late-night rounds was Michael Elliott, a high-ranking

Brown administration official. As BeVier recalled it, Elliott got swept up by the Unruh mystique. BeVier, who sometimes joined them, remembered the Unruh of those late nights. "In a small group, he was very effective," BeVier said. "He talked very well, he talked in a down-to-earth, very practical kind of way. I liked that about the guy. I think it would make anyone like him."[17]

The governor signed the bill Unruh wanted. Over the next thirty years, the California Housing Finance Agency sold more than $13 billion in revenue bonds, financing mortgages for more than 135,000 people. Reviewing the program in 1986, Unruh said: "For the last three years, we think three out of every four single family residences have been built with tax-exempt financing . . . the only reason we have a housing industry today is because we were doing tax-exempt financing. Almost all of the multi-family housing was built with tax-exempt financing."[18]

Rising interest rates coursed through other parts of the economy, raising the cost of borrowing for such enterprises as hospitals, private educational institutions, and industries using new alternative energy sources. Faced with high interest rates on bank loans, private interests turned to the government for help. The legislature responded by creating revenue bond programs, with each one supervised by a governing authority. The lawmakers made Unruh chairman of seven of the nine ruling authorities. Eventually, Unruh served on twenty-nine government bodies with the power to approve bonds. He was also chairman of most of them.[19]

There were just a few members on each authority, and Unruh dominated them all, hiring the staffs that ran day-to-day operations. By 1983, the state was selling almost $3 billion in revenue bonds each year. For the private bankers and bond houses doing business in the state, Unruh was the man to see, the boss. "From my perspective, he's the most powerful man in the state," said one of them. "He's got his hand on the money."[20] The business journal *Institutional Investor* said he was perhaps "the most politically powerful public finance officer outside the U.S. Treasury."[21]

Unruh was especially important to the banks, brokerage houses, and attorneys who were involved in the underwriting process of buying bonds from the state and selling them to investors. The underwriter received 1.5 percent to 3 percent of the face value of the bond. And the person who had the biggest voice in selecting the underwriter was Unruh.[22] It made him the object of the financial community's generosity, both in entertaining him and giving him campaign contributions. By the end of his time as state treasurer, Unruh had accumulated $1.6 million in campaign contributions, the bulk of it from financial institutions.[23]

The growth of support from the financial community is clear in the reports of campaign contributions filed by Unruh with the office of the California secretary of state. When he first ran for treasurer in 1974, his contributions and expenses were minimal. He put $5,000 of his own money into the campaign as a loan. By the time the campaign was over, he had spent $12,699 and collected $22,975. The biggest contributions came from longtime California supporters such as the state teachers' union and the large organization representing the state's retailers.[24]

But over the years, his campaign contributions from financial houses increased as state bond sales went up. Grover McKean had left as chief deputy treasurer by this time, going into the investment business himself with the Shearson firm. His replacement, Michael Gagan, was part of the fundraising apparatus. "It was a pretty wide-open era," said Gagan. "Money was flowing everywhere. We'd have fund-raisers in New York, and I'd tell a bank, 'Shearson is contributing $5,000.' That's all they needed to know. Because they would have to contribute at least that much. So there was sort of this frenzy among the firms to match each other." By 1983, firms were matching each other with contributions of $10,000 or more. Two years later, firms were making contributions of $30,000. For Unruh and his staff there was the generous hospitality of bankers and law firms who wanted to take part in the bond sales. "There were Super Bowl tickets, Oscar night tickets, the country-and-western awards, that was Jess's favorite," Gagan said. When Unruh went to New York on bond sales trips, "He enjoyed that when the limo shows up at the airport, and there is a chilled bottle of Stoli [Stolichnaya vodka] in the back, and you'd go to the 21 for dinner. He liked that and took advantage of its being available."[25]

By the mid 1980s, Unruh's campaign contributions from financial firms were huge by the standards of the day. In 1985, for example, Dean Witter Reynolds and Smith Barney gave him $30,000 each; Paine Webber and Kidder Peabody each donated $20,000; Merrill Lynch and Prudential Bache came through with $15,000 each; and Salomon Brothers gave $19,700. In the last six months of that year, Unruh collected $513,592.[26]

His campaign contributions and gifts from bankers apparently attracted the attention of federal investigators engaged in a wide probe of corruption in the Capitol in the mid 1980s. Gagan recalled that a Republican senator arranged a meeting between Unruh and a man representing a bank. The man offered to loan the state $300 million in a bond deal and "made it very clear that was something in it for" Unruh.

Rather than finding the offer tempting, Unruh was suspicious, and he asked a friend in the state attorney general's office to check out the man with intelligence sources. Unruh's friend found out the man was a federal informant, Gagan said. "They had tried to set up a sting. But if you watched Jess through this process, you would know that he's not a good candidate for a bribe."

Perhaps his most remarkable achievement as treasurer was his founding role in the modern shareholders' rights movement, which opened the way for big public employee pension funds and other investors to contest corporate policies and eventually overturn corporate giants such as Michael Eisner of Disney.

By 1983, Unruh rightly considered himself an expert on Wall Street. He had met the best of the Street's powers and had mastered them, personally insisting on the best deal for the sale of the state's bonds. On his trips to New York, after dining and drinking at the investment bankers' expense, he would show up in their office in the morning, seat himself at a desk, and watch the progress of the sales of California bonds all through the day. And if he was not in New York for a sale, he assigned one of his assistants to personally watch the bond traders and report back to him frequently by phone.[27]

Unruh was a member of the board of California Public Employees' Retirement System, known as CalPERS, and the State Teachers' Retirement System (CalSTRS), which, between them, held $37 billion in public employee pension contributions. The money was invested in a way to bring a maximum return to the two funds. As he did with every other institution with which he was involved, Unruh dominated the running of the funds and kept a close eye on their investments.

Reading the morning paper one day in 1984, he saw that Texaco, the big oil company, had repurchased from the Bass Brothers, legendary Texas investors and corporate raiders, their 9.9 percent holdings in the company for $1.3 billion. The purchase, to stop a Bass Brothers raid, was $137 million more than the stock would have attracted on the open market. He called the CalPERS investment officer and asked how much Texaco stock the California pension system owned. The investment officer replied that California was one of Texaco's largest shareholders. Unruh figured that the Bass Brothers had been paid $55 a share, $20 more than the shares owned by stockholders like the California pension funds. And it was legal. "Like hell," said Unruh.[28]

The Bass Brothers were engaged in "greenmail," the practice of buying enough of a company's stock to threaten a hostile takeover and then selling it back at above the market value. The Bass Brothers were major players in a rapidly changing financial market characterized by such takeovers. It was an era personified by Michael Milken of Drexel Burnham Lambert, who, as the nation's greatest bond salesman, dominated and changed the capital market by selling high-risk, high-interest securities, known as "junk bonds," and using the money to finance a wave of assaults on old companies.

From his office in Beverly Hills, Milken created a financial machine that, Connie Bruck writes, "would transform the face of corporate America." Stodgy management was forced to restructure, cut costs, and close out-moded plants to meet the raiders' demands for short-term profit. As a result, labor contracts were renegotiated downward and jobs were eliminated.[29]

In 1984, the California pension funds lost $7.5 million in a greenmail assault on Walt Disney Productions by Saul Steinberg, who was financed by Drexel junk bonds. The California pension funds' loss was part of a $500 million drop—15 points—in the market value of Disney's shares after Steinberg was paid off.[30]

Greenmail offended Unruh's populist soul, and the offense was exacerbated by his distrust of the rich. Why should a corporate raider be rewarded for tactics that are very much like extortion? And why should management, trying to hold on, discriminate against other shareholders?

Shareholders had little power. They were not organized and could not affect management decisions. Real life was not like the 1956 movie *The Solid Gold Cadillac* in which a small shareholder, Laura Partridge, played by Judy Holliday, triumphs. In the movie, she organizes other small stockholders, overthrows the crooked managers of a giant international company, and returns the old president to power. Not even the public pension funds, with their huge blocs of stock, had the courage to resist the will of management.

Unruh saw the potential power of these funds if they could be organized. He contacted Harrison Goldin, New York City's comptroller, and public pension officials in Kansas, Illinois, Wisconsin, Massachusetts, Minnesota, and New Jersey. Then he met with Robert A. G. Monks, who was serving in President Reagan's administration as the chief official regulating private pension plans. Monks shared Unruh's views on greenmail. He wrote later:

Unruh and I met in Chicago on an August night when the temperature never got below 100 degrees. He described his notion of an association of institutional owners that would meet periodically to develop an ownership agenda and to provide a forum for learning about ownership issues. And so the very

Republican federal pension official and the very Democratic state treasurer agreed that the interests of fiduciary owners transcended partisan politics, and we worked together to promote those issues.[31]

That was the beginning of the Council of Institutional Investors, a group of pension managers who at the time controlled assets of nearly $200 billion. Shareholders had been active before, but mainly on social issues, such as protesting against companies doing business with the then apartheid South African government. Under Unruh's plan, pension fund managers pooled their power to influence corporate management policies. It was, Monk and his coauthor, Nell Minow, write in their 1991 book *Power and Accountability,* the beginning of "the modern shareholder activism movement," which grew in influence into the next century. "Unruh's greatest legacy was his articulation of ownership responsibility as something our nation desperately needed," Monk and Minow argue.[32]

"Once organized, shareholders became people instead of simply sheep," Unruh said.[33] Years of work by the council and other shareholder groups in the growing movement laid the groundwork for congressional passage of the Sarbanes Oxley Act, which tightened disclosure and accounting requirements following the Enron, Tyco International, and Worldcom scandals. "There was nothing else before that," said Gagan, Unruh's former chief deputy. "Wall Street had said, 'This is none of your business.'"

By 1986, Unruh had been diagnosed with the prostate cancer that would eventually kill him, and its symptoms were growing worse. He was on medication, and he often didn't feel well.

It was the same year that his fund-raising attracted the attention of a tenacious investigative reporter, Paul Jacobs of the *Los Angeles Times.* Jacobs wrote a two-part series about Unruh as treasurer. Jacobs said that he had found "wide praise for his [Unruh's] mastery of the functions of his office but concern by many about the way he has used his growing power to maintain himself in his office. . . . Embroiled in the competition for the state's burgeoning bond and investment business, officials of many of these firms believe that they have no choice but to make sizeable contributions to Unruh's campaign committee."

Jacobs tracked the campaign contributions made by the financial houses and attorneys involved in the state bond process. All of the big givers had major business with the treasurer's office. In addition, they were generous with gifts. Searching through Unruh's reports of gifts and outside income, Jacobs found, for example, that the E. F. Hutton firm gave Unruh the use of its guest apartment in Paris for six days. During that time, Hutton was involved in two state bond issues that provided large revenue to the firm. One firm flew Unruh and an aide to Marco Island in Florida for an investment conference. Two others gave him $3,600 in tickets to the 1985 Super Bowl. Summing up the donations, gifts, and speaking fees, Jacobs said they show "that again and again the treasurer's office and various boards that he [Unruh] influences have made decisions financially helpful to his benefactors."[34]

While Jacobs tracked Unruh's campaign contributions and contributors, Unruh was tracking Jacobs. On May 20, 1986, Jacobs arrived at Unruh's office to interview him. "I gave Jesse a briefing on some of the issues that you wanted to talk about," Christina Youngblood, Unruh's press secretary, said. "So now I think without further ado we'll let you go ahead and start." But before Jacobs asked his first question, Unruh had a few things to say:

> Let me tell you first of all that I know who all you've talked to. I know exactly what you've talked about; and I don't want to go back over ground that we've been over, so I'll pick and select those questions, and if I find one that I think you've been into with somebody else, I most likely will tell you that you've already asked people about that.
>
> And secondly, I don't propose to talk about campaign financing. Your paper has written on it many times, and as far as I'm concerned we've been down through the list, and as a consequence, I've said all I have to say on that. Okay? Which is essentially that I don't like the way the game is played, and until we get some other alternative method, the only alternative to not using the present method is to lose. In this success oriented society of ours, that is not an acceptable alternative.
>
> Then I would like this interview over in 30 minutes.

When the reporter asked about bonds, Unruh gave him a long, detailed, and circuitous answer that used up a substantial part of the half hour he had allowed for the interview. When Jacobs asked whether Unruh was influenced by contributions from a businessman who by then was serving a seven-year term in federal prison for political corruption, Unruh replied, "I don't consider that to be a proper question."

"Why not?" Jacobs asked.

"If you have a charge to make, go to the district attorney," Unruh said. "That's the kind of question I consider that to be."

Jacobs moved on to honorariums paid to Unruh for speeches. Finally, Unruh said:

Let me tell you something. You know what your whole interview so far has been. . . . Originally you started out [talking] with most everybody [those Jacobs had interviewed] saying "I'm doing a profile on Jesse Unruh." I normally have thought that profiles would include asking me questions about: "Gee, how have your earnings [for the state] been? Have you actually made any money for the state? Have you done anything that's helped the state out. . . ." You haven't asked one single solitary question about any positive accomplishments.

"I have a lot of information about your accomplishments, in fact," Jacobs said.

"I'll be interested to see [it]," Unruh replied. "It will be the first time that the *Los Angeles Times* has ever run it, if that's the case."[35]

Grover McKean said that Unruh, debilitated by medication for his cancer, was unfocused, too curt with Jacobs, unwilling to take the time to explain things. But the transcript of the interview given me by McKean makes it seem like the encounters I'd had with him many years before. He was the same cantankerous, argumentative, hostile Unruh I remembered, and he treated Jacobs with the same dismissive contempt he always showed toward the news media.

In October, he and Chris were married in a small wedding at their Marina del Rey home. By the end of 1986, his cancer had progressed even more. He was absent from the office much of the time, but was reelected to another term that year with no Republican running against him. In December, Bud Lembke reported in his *Political Pulse* newsletter that Unruh was "battling bone cancer with medication, finds travel . . . an ordeal, experiences slurred speech from the medication but so far has no impairment of his mental faculties."[36]

At his inaugural in January, Unruh boasted that the 5,589,633 votes he had received was a national record for a state officeholder. He seemed groggy at the ceremony. "There is no doubt he is heavily medicated," his old associate Joe Cerrell told a reporter. "He definitely is sedated. He's definitely in sort of a fog. He's also a little combative. He wants to hang in there. The will is there. I don't know if the body is up to it."[37] Still, he managed to go dancing with Chris that night. By the summer of 1987, he was bedridden, and he died on August 4 of that year.

Epilogue

On Sunday, August 9, 1987, almost 1,000 people crowded into Santa Monica United Methodist Church for Jesse Unruh's funeral. "As he walked with us, he fought for the least of us," said California attorney general John Van de Kamp, who had been the first manager of Unruh's campaign for governor. "He used his power and trust we gave him well. He understood the higher cause." Willie Brown, the California State Assembly Speaker, and the only person to hold the job longer than Unruh, said "the rest of us who hold that title are caretakers."[1] Willie Brown was no caretaker. He was raised in the same rural Texas poverty that produced Unruh and, as an African American, had even greater obstacles to overcome. He, too, collected campaign contributions and great power.

Like Unruh, Willie Brown never forgot the business of politics. After he and Frank Mankiewicz, Unruh's old friend, had spoken their eulogies and were seated next to each other, Brown brought up a matter pending between the two. A few days earlier, Mankiewicz, by then a prominent Washington public relations executive, had asked Brown for his advice on who to hire as a lobbyist for one of his clients. As the minister began to speak, Brown gave Mankiewicz his advice.

"Willie, I don't think we should be talking about a lobbying matter up here on the podium at a funeral," Mankiewicz protested.

"Jess would have wanted that way," Brown replied. "What better time? It's private."[2]

Of course Jess would have wanted it that way. What better time, when all eyes were elsewhere, to talk about steering business to a favored lobbyist? What better time to strike a blow against pomposity with a witty and cynical remark? But the gift of humor, which I admired greatly in Unruh and Brown, was all but out of style in politics by 1987. Campaigns and candidates were scripted, and the political journalists saw cynicism as a mistake rather than a virtue. As the *Los Angeles Times* said in an editorial on Unruh's death, "his bulldog face, the rough edges left over from growing up poor and a sardonic sense of humor, which he used to shield from view a wide streak of idealism, conspired against him as television searched for pretty faces."[3]

I can't imagine Unruh going through today's rituals of television politics, mouthing answers that are the product of polling, focus groups, marketing experts, and political hacks who know far less than he did. He fought the rituals when he ran for governor in 1970. The political television image business was then in its childhood. What would he have thought of the current style of political campaigning, a process that is both impersonal and intrusive?

Researching this book took me back to the beginnings of my career. My opinion of Unruh changed as I dug deep into his life and career, as did my views on politics and the media.

• • •

There was much to admire about him when I was scrambling for stories in the assembly for the Associated Press. I knew he was smart then, smarter and quicker than I was. I was impressed by his debating skill on the assembly floor and admired the way he grabbed power. But I didn't completely understand why he craved power or what he wanted to do with it.

Now I understand Jesse Unruh better. He pursued power and seized it to assist those whose lives had been like his own. He also craved power to gratify his ambition and his need to be the boss. He did so without much pity or patience for anyone who stood in his way. He loved a fight and was contemptuous of those who lacked the will or ability to fight back. Such a relentless and open drive offended practitioners of a politer politics and humiliated many who were not as smart and effective as he was.

His idea of the people who needed help came from the experiences of his youth—as a poor farm boy, a blue-collar worker, an enlisted man in the Navy, a GI Bill vet, and the financially struggling father of a young family. These experiences made Unruh distrust, even despise, wealth and privilege from the beginning. In those days, the rich liberals—sipping wine and arguing for the recognition of Communist China—enraged the hard-drinking Cold Warrior Unruh. But it wasn't just their policies. It was their attitude. They were soft. They didn't know life. They didn't know the pain of poverty. They were the privileged class.

His resentment of such people was never clearer than one day in 1968 when he spoke to students at UCLA. His subject was the rebellion against the war that was sweeping through campuses. By then Unruh had turned against the war and was backing Robert Kennedy for president. His concern, as he spoke to the students, was not their cause but the way their generation—so much more affluent and with brighter prospects than his—pursued it.

"I must confess," Unruh said, "to an immediate feeling of disgust at the sight of barefoot flower children, quite apart from their philosophical convictions or the form of their social criticism. What repels me, quite frankly, is the memory of my youth in Texas where four of us in the family had to share one pair of shoes—where to be barefoot in public was to be ashamed." He confessed also to "a momentary feeling of rage" when, watching a TV newsreel of a student protest at San Francisco State College, he saw the students smash a glass door.

"When I was a child," he said, "a broken window was not something to be dismissed and repaired. It was something you patched and lived with until the family could afford a new pane of glass. That meant that in winter that room would be cold and drafty and all but unlivable for a matter of weeks or months." He continued, "Our flower children of the thirties died in the hobo camps, the drafty barns, and the welfare lines, and those memories haunt and motivate us just as much as the fear of death in Vietnam obsesses you."[4]

Motivated by these experiences, Unruh became one of the creators of twentieth-century California. Many decades later, historians, political scientists, journalists, and old politicians looked back on the Unruh era—and the Pat Brown era—as a golden age of politics. The political climate of those days would have shocked twenty-first-century sentimentalists. Great things were done. Government worked. But just about every mile of water project, every freeway, every new university campus, every civil rights bill, every piece of legislation protecting consumers, women, and children was won by ferocious combat, deal by deal. Nothing was given unless something was given back in return.

This was a game Unruh understood. He accumulated power so he could make those deals and win those fights.

Much of his drive came from the anger of his youth, which never left him. At his worst, he would explode at convenient targets, as he did with Virginia in the first years of their marriage, and with friends and colleagues. Drinking exacerbated his temper. But mostly he channeled his emotions into a single-minded search for power, and the plotting, planning, maneuvering, and intimidation needed to attain it. Of course, anger was not enough. Many qualities go into the making of a powerful legislative leader, and Unruh's life story reveals them. Unlike presidents or governors, the power of whose offices is defined by law, legislative leaders rely on relationships held together by friendship, favors, and campaign contributions. Powerful politicians must be respected and liked, but also feared, by their followers. Like Unruh, they need insight into their colleagues' needs, ambitions, and fears. They need a sense of command. They must be one of the crowd but above it. And they must be smart and blessed with natural political instincts, which can't be taught.

Also important to Unruh's success was a quality that seems out of place in a man haunted by dark and angry memories of his youth—congeniality. He had a sociable nature, convivial in the dinners and drinking that were so important to the fabric of the legislature of his day. But he wasn't just another drunk at the bar. What raised him above the barroom were his ideas and his vision of what California could be.

Decades after his death, injustice is still being challenged and corrected under the Unruh Civil Rights Act; his consumer protections are still California law. All through the state, clinics and hospitals serving the poor still exist because Unruh, as state treasurer, made the financial houses in New York underwrite bond issues for them.

He was a politician in the finest sense of the word, and he knew how to use that talent to help people whose lives had been like his own. In the twenty-first century, California has changed greatly, as have the rules governing politics. Unruh certainly would have fought the term limits that hobble today's legislators—and might well have figured out a way to beat them. But whatever the rules, Unruh would have mastered them and, no doubt, would be running the show.

NOTES

PROLOGUE

1. Molly Ivins, "Caro's L.B.J. Opus about Real Sumbitch Is Really a Beauty," *New York Observer,* May 6, 2002.

2. California Secretary of State, Report of Registration, May 22, 2006, "Historical Registration Statistics for Close of Voter Registration Gubernatorial Primary Elections, www.ss.ca.gov/elections/ror/15day_06/hist_reg_stats.pdf (accessed Dec. 26, 2006).

3. David M. Kennedy, *Freedom from Fear: The American People in Depression and War, 1929–1945* (New York: Oxford University Press, 1999), pp. 856–58.

1. THE DEATH OF A BOSS

1. Randall Unruh, interview by the author, Los Angeles, Feb. 21, 2005; Chris Edwards Unruh and Carmen Warschaw, interviews by the author, Los Angeles, Jan. 15 and Mar. 16, 2002.

2. Marvin L. Holen, oral history interviews, conducted January 17 to February 26, 1990, by Carlos Vasquez, UCLA Oral History Program, for the California State Archives State Government Oral History Program.

3. Marvin Holen, interviews by the author, Los Angeles, 2001–5.

4. The preceding analysis is based on the author's experience as a journalist covering these events.

5. Leon D. Ralph, oral history interview, conducted 1990, by Arlene Lazarowitz, Oral History Program, History Department, California State University, Fullerton, for the California State Archives State Government Oral History Program, p. 11.

6. Chris Edwards Unruh, interview by the author, Los Angeles, Jan. 15, 2002.

7. Phillip Schott, interview by the author, Sacramento, Mar. 31, 2005.

8. Jeffrey Stanton, *Venice: Coney Island of the Pacific* (Los Angeles: Donahue, 1993).

9. Frank Burns, interviews by the author, Los Angeles, Nov. 2, 2001–Aug. 15, 2005.

10. Larry Margolis, oral history interview, conducted 1989, by Carole Hicks, Regional Oral History Office, University of California, Berkeley, for the California State Archives State Government Oral History Program, pp. 312–13.

11. Carmen Warschaw, interview by the author, Los Angeles, Mar. 16, 2002.

12. Frank Burns, interviews by the author.

13. Unruh living trust, in the possession of Linda Unruh.

14. Frank Burns, interviews by the author.

15. Chris Unruh, interview by the author.

16. Ann Walsh, interview by the author, San Diego, May 16, 2002.

17. Ibid.

18. Jaci DeFord, interview by the author, Big Sur, Calif., June 7, 2003.

19. John Quimby, interview by the author, Sacramento, Calif., Aug. 28, 2002.

20. Larry Margolis, interview by Hicks, 1989, pp. 51–52.

2. THE ROAD TO CALIFORNIA

1. Virginia Unruh, interviews by the author, Manhattan Beach, Calif., Jun. 4, 1998–June 9, 1999.

2. Paul Unruh, interviews by the author, Lakewood, Calif., Jan. 5, 2004–July 7, 2004.

3. Ibid.

4. Statistics, immigration patterns, and other material on the southwesterners are drawn from James N. Gregory, *American Exodus: The Dust Bowl Migration and Okie Culture in California* (New York: Oxford University Press, 1989).

5. See www.cityofhawthorne.com/about/history.asp (accessed Dec. 30, 2006).

6. See www.bellgardens.org/n_about.asp?view=history (accessed Dec. 30, 2006).

7. Gregory, *American Exodus,* p. 52, quoting from Charles B. Spaulding, "The Development of Organization and Disorganization in the Social Life of a Rapidly Growing Working Class Suburb within a Metropolitan District" (Ph.D. diss., University of California, Berkeley, 1939).

8. Gerald Haslam with Alexandra Haslam, *Workin' Man Blues: Country Music in California* (Berkeley: University of California Press, 1999), p. 117.

9. Gregory, *American Exodus,* p. 168.

10. Katherine Archibald, *Wartime Shipyard: A Study in Social Disunity* (Berkeley: University of California Press, 1947), pp. 64–65.

11. Paul Unruh, interview by the author, Lakewood, Calif., Jan. 5, 2004–July 7, 2004.

12. Texas State Historical Association and the General Libraries at the University of Texas, Austin, *The Handbook of Texas,* www.tsha.utexas.edu/handbook/online (accessed Dec. 30, 2006); Harold S. Bender and C. Henry Smith, *The Mennonites and Their Heritage* (Scottdale, Pa.: Herald Press, 1974); "The Schmidt Family History" (microfilm), Latter Day Saints Library, Los Angeles, www.familysearch.org/Eng/Library/FHLC/frameset_fhlc.asp (accessed Feb. 22, 2007); and Luberta Mc-

Collough, "Descendents of Benjamin C. Unruh," an unpublished family genealogy.

13. See "The Amish & the Plain People," www.800padutch.com/amish.html (accessed Oct. 22, 2006).

14. Paul Unruh, interview by the author.

15. See Newton, Kansas, Chamber of Commerce website, www.thenewtonchamber.org/content/view/27/79 (accessed Dec. 30, 2006).

16. James C. Juhnke, "Mob Violence and Kansas Mennonites in 1918," *Kansas Historical Quarterly* 43, no. 3 (Autumn 1977): 334–50, www.kancoll.org/khq/1977/77_3_juhnke.htm (accessed Feb. 19, 2007).

17. Ibid.

18. Lou Cannon, *Ronnie and Jessie: A Political Odyssey* (Garden City, N.Y.: Doubleday, 1969), pp. 10–11.

19. Paul Unruh, interview by the author.

20. Virginia Unruh, interview by the author. The following two paragraphs also quote and draw on the interviews with Virginia and Paul Unruh cited in the preceding notes.

21. Rebecca Sharpless, *Fertile Ground, Narrow Choices: Women on Texas Cotton Farms, 1900–1940* (Chapel Hill: University of North Carolina Press, 1999), p. 2. Background and details of women's role in farming are from this source.

22. Howard Green, telephone interview by the author, Sept. 8, 2002.

23. Paul Unruh, interview by the author.

24. Howard Green, interview by the author.

25. Cannon, *Ronnie and Jessie*, p. 12.

26. Howard Green, interview by the author.

27. Paul Unruh, interview by the author.

28. Cannon, *Ronnie and Jessie*, p. 13.

29. Paul Unruh, interview by the author.

3. THE GI BILL OF RIGHTS

1. Lou Cannon, *Ronnie and Jessie: A Political Odyssey* (Garden City, N.Y.: Doubleday, 1969), p. 13.

2. Virginia Unruh, interviews, June 4, 1998–July 9, 1999.

3. Ibid.

4. Vivian Ringer, undated interview with Rip Rense, www.riprense.com/Dailynewspageringer.htm (accessed Feb. 19, 2006).

5. Jesse Unruh, letter to Greg H. Kieselmann, assistant news editor of the *Daily Trojan,* who had asked Unruh about his political career, undated; box 4, folder 7, "Correspondence, chronological, Jan. 1967–Aug. 20," Unruh Papers, State Archives, California Secretary of State.

6. Jesse Unruh, *Daily Trojan,* Apr. 23, 1946, untitled clipping, Bob Wells collection.

7. Virginia Unruh, interviews by the author.

8. Robert Berdahl, speech at Erfurt University, Erfurt, Germany, May 23, 2000, http://cio.chance.Berkeley.edu/chancellor/sp.privatization.htm (accessed Feb. 19, 2007).

9. Anthony D. Lazarro, interview by the author, Glendale, Calif., Sept. 6, 2002.

10. Edsel Curry, interview by the author, Glendale, Calif., Oct. 8, 2002.

11. Bob Wells, interviews by the author, Los Angeles, June 4, 2003–July 16, 2004.

12. Michael J. Bennett, *When Dreams Came True: The GI Bill and the Making of Modern America* (Washington, D.C.: Brassey's, 1996), pp. 21–22. Material on the history of the GI Bill is taken from there and from other parts of this book.

13. Bob Wells, interviews by the author.

14. Virginia Unruh, interviews by the author.

15. Beatrice Canterbury Lavery, interview by the author, Los Angeles, Mar. 11, 2002.

16. Bob Wells, interviews by the author.

17. Virginia Unruh, interviews by the author.

18. Manuel P. Servin and Iris Higbie Wilson, *Southern California and Its University: A History of USC, 1880–1964* (Los Angeles: Ward Ritchie, 1969). Material that follows on the history of the University of Southern California is drawn from this book.

19. Bee Lavery, interview by the author.

20. *USC Alumni Review,* June 1947, pp. 23–25.

21. Joseph Cerrell, interview by the author, Los Angeles, Jun. 6, 2003.

22. Lavery, interview by the author.

23. Jesse Unruh, letter to Kieselmann.

24. Virginia Unruh, interviews by the author.

25. Art Buchwald, *Leaving Home* (New York: Putnam, 1993), pp. 204–5.

26. *Daily Trojan,* May 31, 1946.

27. Ibid., Oct. 4, 1946.

28. Ibid., Dec. 13, 1946.

29. Jesse Unruh, letter to Kieselmann.

30. Commemorative issue of *Stumper,* Summer 1991, Bob Wells collection.

31. Ibid.

32. Lavery, interview by the author.

33. Cannon, *Ronnie and Jessie,* p. 23.

34. Graham White and John Maze, *Henry Wallace: His Search for a New World Order* (Chapel Hill: University of North Carolina Press, 1995), p. 250.

35. *Daily Trojan,* May 20, 1947.

36. Virginia Unruh, interviews by the author.

37. Edsel Curry, interview by the author.

38. Jesse Unruh, letter to Kieselmann.

39. *Daily Trojan,* n.d., Bob Wells collection.

40. Jesse Unruh, letter to Kieselmann.

4. HAT IN THE RING

1. Marvin Holen, interview by the author, Los Angeles, Apr. 4, 2003.

2. Bob Wells, interview by the author.

3. Frank Mankiewicz, telephone interview by the author, Mar. 3, 2003.

4. Robert McNeil, paper for a political science course, Bancroft Library, University of California, Berkeley, May 12, 1953.

5. Vance Packard, *The Status Seekers* (New York: David McKay, 1959), p. 7.

6. William H. Whyte, *The Organization Man* (New York: Simon & Schuster, 1956; reprint, Philadelphia: University of Pennsylvania Press, 2002), p. 404.

7. David Riesman in collaboration with Reuel Denney and Nathan Glazer, *The Lonely Crowd: A Study of the Changing American Character* (New Haven: Yale University Press, 1950), p. 19.

8. Bob Wells, interview by the author.

9. Ibid.

10. USC Democratic Guild Treasurer's Report, June 21, 1951, Bob Wells collection.

11. Bob Wells, Jean Wells, and Dan McCarthy, letter to membership committee, Aug. 28, 1953, Bob Wells collection.

12. Paper from Bob Wells collection.

13. Undated USC Democratic Guild publication, Bob Wells collection.

14. Ibid.

15. *Stumper,* February 1952, Bob Wells collection.

16. Wells, interview by the author.

17. Helen Douglas, letter, June 9, 1950, Bob Wells collection.

18. Mankiewicz, telephone interview by the author.

19. Wells, interview by the author.

20. Jackson K. Putnam, "The Progressive Legacy in California," in *California Progressivism Revisited,* ed. William Deverell and Tom Sitton (Berkeley: University of California Press, 1994), p. 247.

21. Kevin Starr, *Inventing the Dream: California through the Progressive Era* (New York: Oxford University Press, 1985), p. 139.

22. Carey McWilliams, *California: The Great Exception* (New York: Current Books, 1949), p. 180.

23. Seth Maskel, "The Power of Outsiders: How Activists Brought Party Government to the California Legislature" (paper prepared for delivery at the second annual conference on state politics and policies, Milwaukee, May 24, 2002), pp. 16–20.

24. McWilliams, *California,* p. 208.

25. Background on the old-age political movement is from Frank A. Pinner, Paul Jacobs, and Phillip Selznick, *Old Age and Political Behavior: A Case Study* (Berkeley: University of California Press, 1959); and Jackson K. Putnam, *Old Age Politics in California: From Richardson to Reagan* (Stanford, Calif.: Stanford University Press, 1970).

26. Robert J. McNeill, "The McLain Organization in California Pension Politics" (paper for Political Science 259B, University of California, Berkeley, May 12, 1959), p. 19.

27. Unsigned, unattributed memorandum, Paul Jacobs's collection of material for *Old Age and Political Behavior,* Bancroft Library, University of California, Berkeley.

28. *California Pension Advocate,* February 1944, Bancroft Library, University of California, Berkeley.

29. Charles Perrow, memorandum to Paul Jacobs, Frank Pinner, and Philip Selznick for *Old Age and Political Behavior,* Apr. 13, 1954, Bancroft Library, University of California, Berkeley.

30. *National Welfare Advocate,* March 1945.

31. *Los Angeles Examiner,* Oct. 26, 1949.

32. Ibid.

33. Bob Wells, interview by the author, June 4, 2003.

34. Thomas M. Rees, oral history interview, conducted 1987, by Carlos Vasquez, UCLA Oral History Program, for the California State Archives State Government Oral History Program, pp. 77–78.

35. Joseph Cerrell, interview by the author, June 6, 2003.

36. Ibid.

37. Bob Wells, interview by the author.

38. Ibid.

5. THE EDUCATION OF A ROOKIE

1. Ali Modarres, *The Demographic Transformations of California in the Post-War Era: 1950–1970, Responsible Liberalism: Edmund G. "Pat" Brown and Reform Government in California, 1958–1967* (Los Angeles: Edmund G. "Pat" Brown Institute of Public Affairs, 2003), pp. 25–33; Carey McWilliams, *California: The Great Exception* (1949; reprint, Santa Barbara, Calif.: Peregrine Smith, 1976), pp. 8–37.

2. Jesse Unruh, interview by Sherry Bebitch Jeffe, June 4, 1972.

3. Elmer Rusco, "The Election of the Speaker in the California Assembly" (paper for Political Science 259B, University of California, Berkeley, 1955).

4. Explanation and interpretation of speaker's role are from the author's observations reporting on the legislature for the Associated Press, 1961–70, and on state government periodically for the *Los Angeles Times,* 1970–2001.

5. Herbert L. Phillips, *Big Wayward Girl: An Informal Political History of California* (Garden City, N.Y.: Doubleday, 1968), p. 172.

6. "Luther H. Lincoln: Young Turk to Speaker of the California Assembly, 1948–1958," an oral history conducted 1980 by Sarah Sharp, Berkeley, Regional Oral History Office, University of California, Berkeley, p. 25. Courtesy, The Bancroft Library.

7. This information is based on the author's knowledge of his hometown.

8. *San Francisco News,* Jan. 7–8, 1954, quoted in Rusco, "Election of the Speaker in the California Assembly."

9. Unruh campaign brochure, Joseph Wyatt collection, 1082, UCLA Special Collections Library, box 1, folder 7, "Preprimary Campaign Literature, 1954."

10. "Luther H. Lincoln: Young Turk to Speaker of the California Assembly," p. 5.

11. Unruh memoir, 1988, entitled "Memoirs Transcription." Sherry Bebitch Jeffe collection.

12. "Luther H. Lincoln: Young Turk to Speaker of the California Assembly," p. 73.

13. Lester Velie, "The Secret Boss of California," *Colliers,* Aug. 13, 1949; Arthur H. Samish and Bob Thomas, *The Secret Boss of California: The Life and High Times of Art Samish* (New York: Crown, 1971).

14. Samish and Thomas, *Secret Boss of California,* p. 8.

15. Unruh remarks for Assembly Committee of the Whole Session on Campaign Finance Reform, Grover McKean collection, n.d.

16. Unruh reminiscences from an undated typed transcript from the Sherry Bebitch Jeffe collection.

17. *Legislative Investigative Report,* submitted by H. R. Philbrick, Dec. 28, 1938, published in the *Senate Journal,* Apr. 4, 1939, p. 1118; Phillips, *Big Wayward Girl,* p. 96.

18. Ralph C. Dills, oral history interview, conducted 1989, by Carlos Vasquez, UCLA Oral History Program, for the California State Archives State Government Oral History Program, pp. 38–39, 103.

19. John E. Moss, oral history interview, conducted 1989, by Donald B. Seney, California State University, Sacramento, for the California State Archives State Government Oral History Program, p. 136

20. Gladwin Hill, *Dancing Bear: An Inside Look at California Politics* (Cleveland: World, 1968), p. 130.

21. Phillips, *Big Wayward Girl,* p. 120.

22. U.S. Interior Department Mineral Management Service, www.mms.gov/omm/pacific/index.htm (accessed Feb. 19, 2006).

23. William Rintoul, *Drilling through Time: 75 years with the California Department of Oil and Gas* (Sacramento: California Department of Conservation, Division of Oil and Gas, 1990), p. 107.

24. Robert Sollen, *An Ocean of Oil: A Century of Political Struggle over Petroleum off the California Coast* (Juneau, Alaska: Denali Press, 1998), p. 183.

25. Lou Cannon, *Ronnie and Jessie: A Political Odyssey* (Garden City, N.Y.: Doubleday, 1969), pp. 94–95.

26. *San Francisco Chronicle,* Nov. 9, 1954, quoted in Rusco, "Election of the Speaker in the California Assembly"; Thomas Caldecott, oral history, interviews conducted by James H. Rowland, June 5–June 29, 1979, Bancroft Library, University of California, Berkeley, pp. 48–49.

27. Allen Miller, oral history interview, conducted 1987, by Carlos Vasquez, UCLA Oral History Program, for the California State Archives State Government Oral History Program, pp. 14–24.

28. Ibid., p. 14

29. Thomas M. Rees, oral history interview, conducted 1987, by Carlos Vasquez, UCLA Oral History Program, for the California State Archives State Government Oral History Program, pp. 119, 120–21.

30. "This Is How Payola Works in Politics by Assemblyman X," as told to Lester Velie, *Reader's Digest,* August 1960, p. 48.

31. Jesse Unruh, interview by Sherry Bebitch Jeffe.

32. Ibid.

33. "Luther H. Lincoln: Young Turk to Speaker of the California Assembly," p. 27.

34. AP story, Jan. 3, 1955, as quoted by Elmer Rusco, "Election of the Speaker in the California Assembly."

35. Cannon, *Ronnie and Jesse,* p. 93.

36. Mary Lynne Velinga, "Glory Restored," *Sacramento Bee,* Jan. 7, 2007.

37. Jesse Unruh, interview by Sherry Bebitch Jeffe, and an undated Unruh manuscript, apparently the beginning of an effort to write his memoirs.

38. Ibid.

39. Virginia Unruh, interviews by the author.

40. Rees, interview by Vasquez, 1987, pp. 129–31.

41. Jesse Unruh, interview by Sherry Bebitch Jeffe for Political Science 425, "The Special History of California Reapportionment." In the author's possession.

42. Cannon, *Ronnie and Jessie,* p. 95.

43. Robert DeKruif, interview by the author, Pasadena, Jan. 14, 2004.

44. Bob Wells, interview by the author.

6. SEGREGRATION AND THE UNRUH CIVIL RIGHTS ACT

1. Josh Sides, *L.A. City Limits: African American Los Angeles from the Great Depression to the Present* (Berkeley: University of California Press, 2003), p. 131.

2. Leonard Pitt and Dale Pitt, *Los Angeles A to Z: An Encyclopedia of the City and County* (Berkeley: University of California Press, 1997), p. 472.

3. *Los Angeles Daily News,* June 9, 1943.

4. Rudolfo F. Acuna, *Anything but Mexican: Chicanos in Contemporary Los Angeles* (London: Verso, an imprint of New Left Books, 1996), p. 44.

5. Joseph Cerrell, interview by the author.

6. Paul Unruh, interview by the author.

7. Bob Wells, interview by the author.

8. Rob Leicester Wagner, *Red Ink, White Lies: The Rise and Fall of Los Angeles Newspapers, 1920–1962* (Upland, Calif.: Dragonfly Press, 2000).

9. Paul Weeks, e-mail to author, Aug. 16, 2004.

10. Joseph Wyatt collection, 1082, UCLA Special Collections, box 1, folder 7, "Preprimary Campaign Literature 1954."

11. James Q. Wilson, *The Amateur Democrat: Club Politics in Three Cities* (Chicago: University of Chicago Press, 1962), p. 278.

12. Ibid., p. 285.

13. Mervyn M. Dymally, oral history interview, conducted 1996, 1997, by Elston L. Carr, UCLA Oral History Program, for the California State Archives State Government Oral History Program, p. 1.

14. Ibid., p. 106.

15. *CIO Newsletter,* Feb. 16, 1956, box 2, folder 6, Joseph L. Wyatt collection, UCLA Special Collections Library.

16. Sides, *L.A. City Limits,* p. 64.

17. U.S. Bureau of the Census, *Census of Population: 1950. Census Tract Statistics: Los Angeles, California, and Adjacent Area* (Washington, D.C.: Government Printing Office, 1952).

18. Minutes of Los Angeles County Human Relations Committee (later Commission), Aug. 7, 1946, Library of the Los Angeles County Human Relations Commission.

19. Charlotta Bass, *Forty Years: Memoirs from the Pages of a Newspaper* (Los Angeles: Charlotta Bass, 1960), p. 107.

20. Charlotta Bass, "On the Sidewalk," *California Eagle,* Mar. 26, 1942, quoted in Marti Elizabeth Tippen, "Talking Back: How Publisher and Activist Charlotta Bass Challenged Inequality through the *California Eagle*" (M.A. thesis, California State University, Northridge, December 2001), p. 119.

21. Bob Wells, interview by the author.

22. Bass, *Forty Years,* p. 102.

23. Sides, *L.A. City Limits,* pp. 98–100.

24. Bass, *Forty Years,* p. 109.

25. *Los Angeles Sentinel,* Oct. 30, 1947.

26. *California Eagle,* Mar. 16, 1950.

27. *People's World,* Sept. 26, 1952.

28. *Los Angeles Daily News,* Mar. 24, 1952.

29. Los Angeles County Human Relations Committee, minutes, Jan. 7, 1953.

30. *People's World,* Oct. 10, 1952.

31. Los Angeles County Human Relations Committee, minutes, Aug. 14, 1944.

32. Marvin L. Holen, oral history interview, conducted 1990, by Carlos Vasquez, UCLA Oral History Program, for the California State Archives State Government Oral History Program, p. 106.

33. Ibid.

34. Ibid., p. 107

35. Ibid., p. 166.

36. Ibid., pp. 166–67.

37. *Sacramento Bee,* Dec. 19, 1999.

38. Holen, interview by Vasquez, pp. 121–22.

39. Ibid., p. 98.

40. Ibid., p. 174.

41. Public Law Research Institute, http://w3.uchastings.edu/plri/spring98/appacalifag.html (accessed Feb. 9, 2006).

42. U.S. Bureau of the Census, *Los Angeles, California, by Census Tracts and Blocks: 1960* (Washington, D.C.: Government Printing Office, 1960).

43. Leroy Hardy, interview by the author, Long Beach, Aug. 6, 2004.

7. FAIR HOUSING AND WHITE BACKLASH

1. Edward Bliss Jr., *Now the News: The Story of Broadcast Journalism* (New York: Columbia University Press, 1991), p. 321

2. Ibid.

3. T. George Harris, "California's New Politics: Big Daddy's Big Drive," *Look,* Sept 25, 1962, p. 80.

4. Taylor Branch, *Parting the Waters: America in the King Years, 1954–63* (New York: Simon & Schuster, 1988), pp. 804–5.

5. Josh Sides, *L.A. City Limits: African American Los Angeles from the Great Depression to the Present* (Berkeley: University of California Press, 2003), p. 163.

6. Becky M. Nicolaides, *My Blue Heaven: Life and Politics in the Working-Class Suburbs of Los Angeles, 1920–1965* (Chicago: University of Chicago Press, 2002), p. 294.

7. Harris, *Look,* Sept. 25, 1962, p. 80.

8. Jesse Unruh, undated speech, Madale Watson collection.

9. Ibid.

10. Jesse Unruh, speech to Department of Social Studies, California State University, Los Angeles (then Los Angeles State College), Dec. 11, 1963, box 11, folder 10, Unruh Papers, California State Archives.

11. Branch, *Parting the Waters,* pp. 362–67.

12. Ibid., p. 824.

13. Thomas V. Casstevens, in *The Politics of Fair-housing Legislation: State and Local Case Studies,* ed. Lynn W. Eley and Casstevens (San Francisco: Chandler, 1968), p. 243.

14. "William Byron Rumford, Legislator for Fair Employment, Fair Housing and Public Health," oral histories conducted 1970 and 1973 by Joyce A. Henderson, Amelia Fry, and Edward France, Regional Oral History Office, University of California, Berkeley, p. 9. Courtesy, The Bancroft Library.

15. John Quimby, interview by the author, Nov. 18, 2004.

16. Augustus F. Hawkins, oral history interview, conducted 1988, by Carlos Vasquez, UCLA Oral History Program, for the California State Archives State Government Oral History Program, p. 95.

17. Ibid., p. 88.

18. Allen Miller, oral history interview, conducted 1987, by Carlos Vasquez, UCLA Oral History Program, for the California State Archives State Government Oral History Program, p. 61.

19. *Los Angeles Times,* Feb. 14, 1963.

20. Casstevens, in *Politics of Fair-housing Legislation,* p. 213.

21. Ibid., p. 247.

22. Ibid., pp. 187–88.

23. *Los Angeles Times,* Feb. 26, 1963.

24. Loren Miller, letter to Jesse Unruh, Feb. 26, 1963, box 8, file 44, "Rumford Fair Housing Act, 1963–64," Unruh Papers, California State Archives.

25. Gov. Edmund G. Brown [Sr.], press conference, Feb. 26, 1963, "Governor—Press Conferences, 1961–63," box 7, file 23, Unruh Papers, California State Archives.

26. Gov. Edmund G. Brown [Sr.], press conference, Mar. 5, 1963, ibid.

27. Opinion Research of Long Beach, public opinion survey concerning the civil rights issue in Berkeley, March 1963, Unruh Papers, California State Archives, Correspondence, Surveys, LP 236:345.

28. Casstevens, in *Politics of Fair-housing Legislation,* pp. 247–48.

29. Ibid., p. 231.

30. William Byron Rumford, interview by Henderson, Fry, and France, Sept. 13, 1971, p. 9.

31. Ibid., p. 7.

32. *Los Angeles Times,* Apr. 26, 1963.

33. John Quimby, interview by the author, Nov. 18, 2004.

34. Joseph Gunterman, interview by the author, Sacramento, Nov. 18, 2004.

35. George Skelton, *Los Angeles Times,* Dec. 2, 1993.

36. *Los Angeles Times,* Apr. 5, 1963.

37. Joseph Gunterman, interview by the author.

38. Don Bradley, an oral history conducted 1984 by Amelia Fry, Regional Oral History Office, University of California, Berkeley, p. 38. Courtesy, The Bancroft Library.

39. Ibid., p. 63.

40. John Quimby, interview by the author.

41. *Sacramento Bee,* Jun. 13, 1963.

42. *Los Angeles Times,* May 31, 1963.

43. William Byron Rumford, interview by Henderson, Fry, and France, Sept. 13, 1971, p. 97.

44. *Sacramento Bee,* June 12, 1963.

45. Ibid., June 14, 1963.

46. Ibid., June 15, 1963.

47. Paul B. Fay Jr., *The Pleasure of His Company* (New York: Harper & Row, 1966).

48. *Los Angeles Times,* June 12, 1963.

49. William Byron Rumford, interview by Henderson et al., Sept. 13, 1971, p. 97.

50. Joseph Gunterman, interview by the author.

51. *Sacramento Bee,* June 22, 1963.

52. Joseph Gunterman interview by the author.

8. ANIMAL HOUSE

1. Herbert L. Phillips, *Sacramento Bee,* June 28, 1963.

2. Ibid.

3. David R. Doerr, *California's Tax Machine: A History of Taxing and Spending in the Golden State* (Sacramento: California Taxpayers Association, 2000), p. 61.

4. James R. Mills, *A Disorderly House: The Brown-Unruh Years in Sacramento* (Berkeley, Calif.: Heyday Books, 1987), p. 64.

5. Peggy Lamson, with a foreword by Maureen B. Neuberger, *Few Are Chosen* (Boston: Houghton Mifflin, 1968), p. xii.

6. Ruth Rosen, "What's Going On?" in *California and the Vietnam Era,* ed. Marcia A. Eymann and Charles Wollenberg (Berkeley: University of California Press and the Oakland Museum of California, 2004), pp. 83–84.

7. Beth Reingold, *Representing Women: Sex, Gender and Legislative Behavior in Arizona and California* (Chapel Hill: University of North Carolina Press, 2000), p. 75.

8. Unruh may have been quoting Molly Ivins: "As they say around the Texas Legislature, if you can't drink their whiskey, screw their women, take their money, and vote against 'em anyway, you don't belong in office" (www.brainyquote .com/quotes/authors/m/molly_ivins.html [accessed Oct. 23, 2006]).

9. Jeane J. Kirkpatrick, *Political Woman* (New York: Basic Books, 1974), p. 106.

10. Donald G. Herzberg and Jess Unruh, *Essays on the State Legislative Process* (New York: Holt, Rinehart & Winston, 1970), p. 21.

11. Lee Nichols, interview by the author, San Francisco, Apr. 4, 2005.

12. Bill Boyarsky, *Ronald Reagan: His Life and Rise to the Presidency* (New York: Random House, 1981), pp. 179–80.

13. John Quimby, interview by the author.

14. Jaci DeFord, interview by the author.

15. Yvonne Brathwaite Burke, interview by the author, Los Angeles, June 10, 2004.

16. Ibid.

17. Ibid.

18. See chapter 7, n. 10.

19. It was called a special session because it was in addition to the usual regular session, just finished, and the budget session, held in even-numbered years to consider state spending. In a special session, the governor dictated the agenda, and no other matters could be considered.

20. *Los Angeles Times,* July 13, 1963.

21. Assessment of Rattigan is based on the author's observations while covering him for the Associated Press.

22. Craig Cotura, untitled honors thesis, 1973, in Lou Cannon collection, p. 104.

23. Herzberg and Unruh, *Essays on the State Legislative Process,* p. 29

24. Robert T. Monagan, interview by the author.

25. Ibid.

26. Ibid.

27. Unruh interview for Political Science 425, *The Special History of Reapportionment,* Oct. 6, 1983 (done for Sherry Bebich Jeffe's class, tape obtained from Ann Crigler at the Unruh Institute of Politics, USC).

28. Robert T. Monagan, interview by the author.

29. Cotura, thesis, p. 99.

30. Houston I. Flournoy, oral history, n.d., marked "re: lockup"; also box 11, file 31, "Legislators, 1959–69," Jesse Unruh Papers, California State Archives; also author's telephone interview with Flournoy, December 2004.

31. Doerr, *California's Tax Machine.*

32. Mills, *Disorderly House,* p. 106.

33. Jesse M. Unruh interview on the lockup, n.d., Sherry Bebitch Jeffe collection.

34. Flournoy, cited n. 30 above.

35. Mills, *Disorderly House,* p. 106.

36. Ibid., p. 109.

37. The sergeant can arrest them, but usually they are in their offices, the house lounge, or, occasionally, a nearby bar. On occasion, the sergeant has flown to distant parts of the state to retrieve members for an important vote. Once, the senate was on call for three days before an absent member was found to cast an aye vote on an important day. In 1939, the assembly was in session for sixty hours during a call on a measure.

38. Jerome Waldie, interview by the author, Placerville, Calif., Apr. 21, 2002.

39. Mills, *Disorderly House,* pp. 119–20.

40. Jesse Unruh, interview by Sherry Bebitch Jeffe, Jeffe collection.

41. Jerome Waldie, interview by the author.

42. Ibid.

43. George Zenovich, "Legislative-Governor Relations in the Reagan Years," oral history interviews, conducted 1983, by Steven D. Edgingon and Harvey P. Grody, Oral History Program, California State University, Fullerton, for the California State Archives State Government Oral History Program, p. 85.

44. Jesse Unruh, interview by Sherry Bebitch Jeffe, n.d.

45. Jerome Waldie, interview by the author.

46. Zenovich, interviews by Edgingon and Grody, 1982, p. 85.

47. Jerome Waldie, interview by the author.

48. Ibid.

49. Mills, *Disorderly House,* p. 129.

50. Ibid., p. 132.

51. Ibid., pp. 134–35.

52. *Sacramento Bee,* July 31, 1963.

53. Jesse Unruh, interview by Sherry Bebitch Jeffe, n.d.

54. Ibid.

55. Ibid.

56. Transcript of KNX editorial, Sept. 11, 1963, Unruh Papers, State Archives, box 10, file no. 7.

57. Houston Flournoy, interview by the author.

9. BACKSTABBING DEMOCRATS

1. Lou Cannon, *Ronnie and Jessie: A Political Odyssey* (Garden City, N.Y.: Doubleday, 1969), pp. 172–73.

2. Cheryl Peterson, letter to Larry Margolis, Aug. 29, 1964, Unruh Papers, box 29, file 3, Larry Margolis subject files, 1957–68, California State Archives.

3. Henry Lacayo, interview by the author, Thousand Oaks, Calif., Apr. 16, 2004.

4. Cannon, *Ronnie and Jesse,* pp. 121–22.

5. Ibid.

6. Larry Fisher, interview by the author, Lafayette, Calif., July 18, 2005.

7. Jo Freeman, *At Berkeley in the Sixties: The Education of an Activist, 1961–1965* (Bloomington: Indiana University Press, 2004), p. 98.

8. *Los Angeles Times,* Mar. 27, 1964.

9. *Sacramento Bee,* Mar. 7, 1964.

10. Freeman, *At Berkeley in the Sixties,* p. 131.

11. Reprinted from "The Free Speech Movement and the Negro Revolution," *News & Letters,* July 1965, www.fsma.org/stacks/covers/savio_studrebel.html (accessed Feb. 19, 2006). Copyright © 1965 by Mario Savio, © 1998 by Lynne Hollander.

12. Ethan Rarick, *California Rising: The Life and Times of Pat Brown* (Berkeley: University of California Press, 2005), p. 277.

13. Larry Fisher, interview by the author.

14. Frank Burns, interview by the author.

15. Harold Meyerson, untitled article in *American Prospect,* Feb. 12, 2001.

16. Tom LaMarre, "Southland Slices," *Golf Today Magazine,* June 2004.www.golftodaymagazine.com/0606/southland.htm (accessed June 30, 2006).

17. Tom MacDonald, interview by the author, Los Angeles, May 17, 2005.

18. Richard Mosk, interview by the author, Los Angeles, May 11, 2005.

19. Ibid.

20. *Memorial Book* (Department of Animal Science, University of California, Davis, n.d.).

21. Frank Burns, interview by the author.

22. Poll, Opinion Research of California, February 1964.

23. Unruh telegram, Feb. 21, 1964, "Political Campaigns, U.S. Senate," box 7, folder 20, Jesse Unruh Papers, California State Archives.

24. Tom MacDonald, interview by the author.

25. Frank Burns, interview by the author.

26. Richard Mosk, interview by the author.

27. Roy Greenaway, oral history interviews, conducted 1990 and 1991, by Amelia

Fry, Regional Oral History Office, University of California, Berkeley, for the California State Archives State Government Oral History Program, p. 204.

28. Tom MacDonald, interview by the author.

29. Rarick, *California Rising,* quotes conversation 2860/2861, Apr. 6, 1964, tape WH 6404.03, LBJ Library and Museum.

30. *Sacramento Bee,* Mar. 4, 1964.

31. Joseph Cerrell, interview by the author.

32. Frank Burns and Richard Mosk, interviews by the author.

33. Frank Burns, interview by the author.

34. *Los Angeles Times,* undated article, Madale Watson Papers.

35. Peter Kaye, *San Diego Union,* June 7, 1964.

36. Totten J. Anderson and Eugene C. Lee, "The 1964 Election in California," *Western Political Quarterly* 18, no. 2, pt. 2 (1965): 455. Reprinted by the Institute of Governmental Studies, University of California, Berkeley.

37. Kaye, *San Diego Union.*

38. Sacramento, Unruh Papers, Unruh political file, JMU campaigns, 1964, box 13, file 24.

39. Jesse Unruh, letter, Sacramento, June 1964, "Political Campaigns, U.S. Senate," box 7, folder 20, Jesse Unruh Papers, California State Archives.

40. Taylor Branch, *Pillar of Fire: America in the King Years, 1963–65* (New York: Simon & Schuster, 1998), pp. 417–18.

41. See *American Heritage Dictionary,* 4th ed., "George Wallace." And see also www.answers.com/topic/george-wallace (accessed Dec. 30, 2006).

42. "The clerk proceeded to call the roll. When he reached 'Mr. Engle,' there was no response. A brain tumor had robbed California's mortally ill Clair Engle of his ability to speak. Slowly lifting a crippled arm, he pointed to his eye, thereby signaling his affirmative vote. Few of those who witnessed this heroic gesture ever forgot it." "June 10, 1964, Civil Rights Filibuster Ended," www.senate.gov/artandhistory/history/minute/Civil_Rights_Filibuster_Ended.htm (accessed Dec. 30, 2006).

43. Frank Burns, interview by the author.

44. Gov. Pat Brown, letter, "1966 Gubernatorial Campaign," box 12, file 7, Jesse Unruh Papers, California State Archives

45. Don Bradley, an oral history conducted 1984 by Amelia Fry, Region Oral History Office, University of California, Berkeley. Courtesy, The Bancroft Library.

46. Kay Mills, *This Little Light of Mine: The Life of Fannie Lou Hamer* (New York: Plume, 1993), p. 105.

47. John Jacobs, *A Rage for Justice: The Passion and Politics of Phillip Burton* (Berkeley: University of California Press, 1995), pp. 141–42.

48. Robert Dallek, *Flawed Giant: Lyndon Johnson and His Times, 1961–73* (New York: Oxford University Press, 1998), p. 162.

49. Rarick, *California Rising,* p. 284.

50. Mills, *This Little Light of Mine,* pp. 120–21, 123.

51. Rarick, *California Rising,* pp. 284–86.

52. Mills, *This Little Light of Mine,* p. 129.

53. Roger Kent, "Building the Democratic Party in California 1954–1966," an oral history conducted 1976 and 1977 by Anne H. Brower and Amelia R. Fry, Regional Oral History Office, University of California, Berkeley, 1981, pp. 238–41. Courtesy, The Bancroft Library.

54. Anderson and Lee, "1964 Election in California," p. 455.

55. Jesse Unruh, speech to 64th Assembly District Democratic Volunteers Committee, Sept. 21, 1964.

56. Anderson and Lee, "1964 Election in California," p. 455.

10. DIRTY DEALINGS AND HIGH IDEALISM

1. Marvin Holen, interview by the author.

2. Allen Miller, oral history interview, conducted 1987, by Carlos Vasquez, UCLA Oral History Program, for the California State Archives State Government Oral History Program, pp. 173–75.

3. William Rintoul, *Drilling through Time: 75 years with the California Division of Oil and Gas* (Sacramento: California Department of Conservation, Division of Oil and Gas, 1990), p. 64.

4. Rintoul, *Drilling through Time,* pp. 89–90.

5. Ibid., p. 92.

6. Attorney George Hart Jr., letter to partners, Long Beach, July 2, 1992, Linda Unruh papers.

7. Harry Farrell, interview by the author, Dec. 22, 2003.

8. *San Jose News,* May 6, 1963.

9. Harry Farrell, *San Jose—and Other Famous Places* (San Jose: San Jose Historical Museum Association), p. 50, and interview.

10. Ibid.

11. Manning Post Papers, in the possession of Robert Hertzberg.

12. June-Adele Mallory, letter to Jesse Unruh, April 6, 1965, "Correspondence–Issues: Mental Health," box 14, file 6, Unruh Papers, California State Archives, Sacramento.

13. Eugene Bardach, *The Skill Factor in Politics: Repealing the Mental Commitment Laws in California* (Berkeley: University of California Press, 1972), p. 24.

14. Carolyn Fowle, "The Effect of the Severely Retarded Child on His Family" (Ph.D. diss., University of Pacific), quoted in *A Redefinition of State Responsibility for California's Mentally Retarded* (Sacramento: Assembly Ways and Means Committee Subcommittee on Mental Health Services, 1965).

15. See, e.g., the Columbia Electronic Encyclopedia, www.columbia.edu/cu/cup/cee/cee.html (accessed Feb. 23, 2006).

16. Jesse M. Unruh, "Unruh Looks at State Politics," *San Francisco Business,* December 1967, pp. 35–38.

17. Jerome Waldie, interview by the author, Placerville, Calif., Mar. 14, 2005.

18. Ibid.

19. Karsten Vieg, telephone interview by the author, Mar. 7, 2005.

20. Arthur Bolton, interview by the author, Sacramento, Mar. 28, 2004.

21. President John F. Kennedy, Feb. 5, 1963, quoted in report of the Frank D. Lanterman Regional Center, Los Angeles, 2001.

22. Arthur Bolton, interview by the author.

23. Jerome Waldie, interview by the author.

24. Jesse M. Unruh, speech to the California Council for Retarded Children, Los Angeles, May 15, 1965.

25. Arthur Bolton, interview by the author.

26. Ibid.

27. This summary of these issues is based on Bardach's book, interviews with Bolton and Waldie, and the author's experience in covering mental health issues in Sacramento and Los Angeles.

28. The committee's strategy and the political maneuvering to implement it were explained by the UC Berkeley scholar Bardach, who studied the work of legislators and aides for his doctoral dissertation. The work was later published in his book *The Skill Factor in Politics in Politics* (cited in n. 13 above).

29. Arthur Bolton quoted in Bardach, *Skill Factor in Politics,* p. 103.

30. Jerome Waldie cited in "The Dilemma of Mental Health Commitments in California" (California State Assembly Interim Committee on Ways and Means, Subcommittee on Mental Health, November 1966), quoted in Bardach, *Skill Factor in Politics,* p. 105.

31. California State Assembly Subcommittee on Mental Health, transcript of hearings, Los Angeles, Dec. 20, 1965, pp. 62–63. In the possession of Arthur Bolton.

32. Lou Cannon, *Governor Reagan: His Rise To Power* (New York: Public Affairs, 2003), p. 185.

33. Bardach, *Skill Factor in Politics,* p. 125.

34. Cannon, *Governor Reagan,* p. 193.

35. Bardach, *Skill Factor in Politics.*

36. Arthur Bolton, interview by the author.

37. Sherry Bebitch Jeffe, *Los Angeles Times,* Mar. 22, 1987.

38. National Association of State Mental Health Program Directors Research Institute, quoted in *Governing,* February 2004.

II. A FULL-TIME LEGISLATURE

1. Jesse Unruh, manuscript for a memoir, n.d., Sherry Bebitch Jeffe collection.

2. Manning Post, interview by the author, Los Angeles, Aug. 15, 1998.

3. Jesse Unruh, reminiscences dictated to Jay Kennedy, n.d. (1986), Sherry Bebitch Jeffe collection.

4. Ibid.

5. *Los Angeles Times,* Sept. 15, 1965.

6. Director, FBI, teletype to SACS [special agent] Los Angeles, San Francisco, July 27, 1963, Federal Bureau of Investigation File: Subject Jesse Marvin Unruh, file number 116–44924. Copy in the author's possession.

7. Undated communication to Atty. Gen. Robert Kennedy, FBI file, ibid.

8. Jesse Unruh, letter to Sam Cameron, Feb. 17, 1966, "Correspondence, Chron., Jan.–Dec. 1966," box 7, file 6, Jesse Unruh Papers, California Secretary of State Archives.

9. *Los Angeles Times,* Sept. 15, 1966.

10. Ray Lemon, letter to Jesse Unruh, Jan. 30, 1965, "Correspondence, Chron. Jan.–Dec. 1965," box 7, file 5, Jesse Unruh Papers, California Secretary of State Archives.

11. Jesse Unruh, reminiscences dictated to Jay Kennedy, n.d. (1986), Sherry Bebitch Jeffe collection.

12. Jesse M. Unruh, "Upgrading the California Legislature" (speech to the Kentucky-Tennessee Assembly on State Legislatures, Gatlinburg, Tenn., Apr. 15, 1967), Sherry Bebich Jeffe collection.

13. Jesse Unruh, reminiscences dictated to Jay Kennedy, n.d. (1986), Jeffe collection.

14. Ibid.

15. Ibid.

16. Ibid.

17. Gladwin Hill, *Dancing Bear: An Inside Look at California Politics* (Cleveland: World, 1968), p. 194.

18. Jesse Unruh, reminiscences dictated to Jay Kennedy, n.d. (1986), Jeffe collection.

19. Clem Whitaker Jr. and associates, report on the Proposition 1-A campaign to Unruh and other legislative leaders, Dec. 5, 1966, Sherry Bebitch Jeffe collection.

20. Jesse Unruh, reminiscences dictated to Jay Kennedy, n.d. (1986), Jeffe collection.

21. Jesse Unruh, recollections, n.d., Sherry Bebitch Jeffe collection.

22. Sherry Bebitch Jeffe, "For Legislative Staff, Policy Takes a Backseat to Politics," *California Journal,* Jan. 1987, pp. 42–45.

23. Jerry Gillam and Carl Ingram, "What Price Legislative Freedom," *Los Angeles Times,* Nov. 21, 1983.

24. Jeffe, "For Legislative Staff, Policy Takes a Backseat to Politics."

25. Unruh, n.d., Jeffe collection.

26. Gillam and Ingram, *Los Angeles Times.*

27. David R. Doerr, *California's Tax Machine: A History of Taxing and Spending in the Golden State* (Sacramento: California Taxpayers Association, 2000), pp. 69–148.

28. "Nolan, Hill Indicted in Capitol Sting, First Republicans Charged in Five-Year FBI Probe," *Sacramento Bee,* Apr. 28, 1993.

12. UNRUH, ROBERT KENNEDY, AND THE ANTI-WAR MOVEMENT

1. *The Free Speech Movement: Reflections on Berkeley in the 1960s,* ed. Robert Cohen and Reginald E. Zelnik (Berkeley: University of California Press, 2002), p. 23.

2. *What's Going On: California and the Vietnam Era,* ed. Marcia A. Eymann and Charles Wollenberg; Diane Curry, photograph editor (Berkeley: University of California Press, 2004), p. 4.

3. Frank Burns, interview by the author, Aug. 15, 2005.

4. Arthur M. Schlesinger Jr., *Robert Kennedy and His Times* (Boston: Houghton Mifflin, 1978), pp. 773–77.

5. Ibid., p. 773.

6. Frank Burns, oral history interview, conducted April 17, 1970, by Larry Hackman, Robert F. Kennedy Oral History Program of the Kennedy Library.

7. Frank Burns, interview by the author.

8. *Los Angeles Times,* June 24, 1967.

9. Frank Burns, interview by the author.

10. *Los Angeles Times,* June 30, 1967.

11. *New York Times,* Aug. 7, 1967.

12. Press release, "McCarthy for President," Nov. 30, 1967, Eugene J. McCarthy Papers, Elmer L. Anderson Library, University of Minnesota.

13. Jesse Unruh, transcript of comments on presidential candidacy of Robert F. Kennedy—recollections of Dec. 10, 1967–Jan. 11, 1968, box 24, folder 6, Jesse Unruh Papers, California State Archives.

14. Ibid.

15. Ibid.

16. Schlesinger, *Robert Kennedy and His Times,* p. 836.

17. Frank Burns, interview by the author.

18. Jesse Unruh transcript cited in n. 13 above.

19. Ibid.

20. Frank Burns interview by Hackman, pp. 15–16.

21. Jesse Unruh transcript cited in n. 13 above.

22. Ibid.

23. Frank Burns interview by Hackman, pp. 16–17.

24. Robert J. Donavan, *Nemesis: Truman and Johnson in the Coils of War in Asia* (New York: St. Martin's Press, 1984).

25. Doris Kearns, *Lyndon Johnson and the American Dream* (New York: Harper & Row, 1976), pp. 270–71.

26. Donovan, *Nemesis,* p. 139.

27. Lou Cannon, *Ronnie and Jessie: A Political Odyssey* (Garden City, N.Y.: Doubleday, 1969), p. 286.

28. Donovan, *Nemesis,* pp. 142, 161.

29. Frank Burns, interview by Hackman, pp. 20–22.

30. Ibid., p. 24.

31. Frank Burns, interview by Hackman, pp. 23–25.

32. Jules Witcover, *The Year the Dream Died: Revisiting 1968 in America* (New York: Warner Books, 1997), p. 96.

33. Peter Edelman, recorded interview by Jean Stein, Mar. 6, 1969, 20, Stein Papers quoted in Schlesinger, *Robert Kennedy and His Times,* p. 847.

34. Frank Burns, interview by Hackman, p. 25.

35. Ray King, letter, Apr. 13, 1968, Kennedy file, Unruh Papers, California State Archives.

36. Bill Thomas, letter, box 16, file 20, Jesse Unruh Papers, California State Archives.

37. Jeff Mullins, "'Human Tidal Wave' Greets RFK," *Spartan Daily,* Mar. 26, 1968, Madale Watson collection.

38. Witcover, *Year the Dream Died,* p. 245.

39. Frank Burns, interview by the FBI, June 11, 1968. Transcript given to the author by Burns.

40. Frank Burns, interview by the author.

41. Frank Burns, statement to the Federal Bureau of Investigation (see n. 39 above).

42. Jesse Unruh, statement to Los Angeles Police Department, July 21, 1968, Robert F. Kennedy Assassination Investigation Papers, California State Archives.

43. Virginia Unruh, statement to Los Angeles Police Department, September 1968, Robert F. Kennedy Assassination Investigation Papers, California State Archives.

44. Dr. Marvin Esher, statement to Los Angeles Police Department, July 12, 1968, Robert F. Kennedy Assassination Investigation Papers, California State Archives.

45. Sherry Bebitch Jeffe and Douglas Jeffe, interview by the author, Inglewood, Calif., Oct. 21, 2005.

46. Jaci DeFord, interview by the author.

13. UNRUH VERSUS REAGAN

1. Arthur Schlesinger Jr., speech at Democratic dinner, Chicago, Sept. 29, 1968, "Political Campaigns, 1962–69," box 21, folder 1, Jesse Unruh Papers, California State Archives.

2. *What's Going On: California and the Vietnam Era,* ed. Marcia A. Eymann and Charles Wollenberg; Diane Curry, photograph editor (Berkeley: University of California Press, 2004), p. 55.

3. Lou Cannon, *Governor Reagan: His Rise to Power* (New York: Public Affairs, 2003), p. 291.

4. W. J. Rorabaugh, *Berkeley at War: The 1960s* (New York: Oxford University Press, 1989), pp. 156–66; *New York Times,* May 20, 1969.

5. *Los Angeles Times,* Feb. 26, 1970, Apr. 21–22, 1970; *New York Times,* June 8, 1970.

6. *New York Times,* May 5, 1970.

7. Scott Sherman, *Columbia Journalism Review,* November–December 2001.

8. Sherry Bebitch Jeffe, interview by the author.

9. Vicki Gregerson, letter to Jesse Unruh, Aug. 15, 1968, "Correspondence, 1968," box 12, folder 6, Jesse Unruh Papers, California State Archives.

10. Jesse Unruh, letter in reply, ibid.

11. Ibid.

12. Cannon, *Governor Reagan,* p. 291.

13. ABC video from http://kronykronicle.com/1968/MayorDaley.html (accessed Dec. 10, 2006).

14. *Time* magazine, Sept. 6, 1968.

15. Sherry Bebitch Jeffe, interview by the author.

16. Jesse Unruh, statement to the Democratic National Platform Committee, Aug. 20, 1968, "1968 Presidential: Kennedy for President," box 26, folder F, Jesse Unruh Papers, California State Archives.

17. Cannon, *Governor Reagan,* p. 296.

18. Article (probably from the *Sacramento Bee*) dated Jan. 10, 1969, Madale Watson collection.

19. Jesse Unruh, "A Democrat Speaks to Question," *The Nation,* Feb. 17, 1969.

20. Jesse Unruh, speech to the Steelworkers Union, 1975, Madale Watson collection.

21. Robert T. Monagan, interview by the author, Feb. 5, 2004.

22. Jesse Unruh, interview with Sherry Bebitch Jeffe, Oct. 11, 1983, Jeffe collection.

23. Frederick G. Dutton, letter to Jesse Unruh, Jan. 7, 1970, "Correspondence, 1967–70," box 27, file 2f, Jesse Unruh Papers, California State Archives.

24. Frederick G. Dutton, letter and memo to Jesse M. Unruh, Jan. 7, 1970, box 27, file 4c, Jesse Unruh Papers, California State Archives.

25. John Van de Kamp, interview by the author, Mar. 3, 2005.

26. Ibid.

27. Philip Schott, interview by the author, Mar. 31, 2005.

28. *Los Angeles Times,* Jan. 13, 1970.

29. Chloe Pollock, memo to Phil Schott, n.d., "Unruh 1970 campaign plans," box 27, file 4c, Jesse Unruh Papers, California State Archives.

30. Unsigned memo, Madale Watson collection.

31. Unsigned memo, ibid.

32. *Los Angeles Times,* May 30, 1970.

33. Bob Levine, memo to John Van de Kamp, Feb. 1, 1970, box 27, file 9, Jesse Unruh Papers, California State Archives.

34. John Van de Kamp, interview by the author.

35. "Unruh, Salvatori Meet in Angry Confrontation," *Los Angeles Times,* Sept. 8, 1970.

36. John Van de Kamp, interview by the author.

37. Philip Schott, interview by the author.

38. "Country Music Vote: Is It Unruh's Tune?" *Los Angeles Times,* July 13, 1970.

39. "Stabilization Policies and Employment," Operations of the Federal Reserve Bank of St. Louis, 1970, research.stlouisfed.org/publications/review/71/02/Stabilization_Feb1971.pdf (accessed Feb. 19, 2006).

40. *Los Angeles Times,* Oct. 1, 1970.

41. Ibid., Oct. 29, 1970.

42. "Unruh Strikes Hard at Issues of Unemployment and Inflation," *Los Angeles Times,* Nov. 2, 1970.

43. Stuart Spencer, interview by the author, Apr. 1, 2001.

44. Cannon, *Governor Reagan,* pp. 344–46.

45. "Precinct Study Pinpoints '70 Voting Shifts," *Los Angeles Times,* Nov. 13, 1970.

46. Phillip Schott, interview by the author.

14. THE MAN WITH THE MONEY

1. Robert Fairbanks, "New Power for an 'Old Statesman': Unruh's $3 Billion Lending Machine," *California Journal,* February 1983, pp. 48–52.

2. Leo McElroy, telephone interview by the author, Feb. 28, 2006.

3. Stuart Spencer, interviews by the author, Orange County, Calif., Aug. 10, 2001, Dec. 14, 2005.

4. Douglas Ring, telephone interview by the author, Mar. 13, 2006.

5. Chris Unruh, interview by the author.

6. Grover McKean, interview by the author, Los Angeles, Dec. 5, 2005.

7. Stuart Spencer, interview by the author.

8. Grover McKean, interview by the author.

9. Bruce Van Houton, Dan Dowell, and Bill Sherwood, interview by the author, Sacramento, Feb. 5, 2004.

10. Ibid.

11. Ibid.

12. McKean, interview by the author.

13. Ibid.

14. Michael J. BeVier, *Politics Backstage: Inside the California Legislature* (Philadelphia: Temple University Press, 1979), p. 3.

15. Ibid., pp. 36, 38.

16. BeVier, telephone interview by the author, Feb. 10, 2006.

17. Ibid.

18. Jesse M. Unruh, transcript of interview with Paul Jacobs, May 20, 1986, provided by Grover McKean.

19. Jeff Raimundo, "King of the Street," *Golden State Report,* Fall 1985, pp. 27–29.

20. Fairbanks, "New Power for an 'Old Statesman,'" p. 49.

21. Raimundo, "King of the Street."

22. Fairbanks, "New Power for an 'Old Statesman.'"

23. Campaign contribution reports, California Secretary of State.

24. Ibid.

25. Michael Gagan, interview by the author, Los Angeles, Feb. 10, 2006.

26. Campaign contribution reports, California Secretary of State.

27. Michael Gagan, interview by the author.

28. Robert A. G. Monks and Nell Minow, *Power and Accountability* (New York: HarperBusiness, 1991), pp. 212–13.

29. Connie Bruck, *The Predator's Ball: The Junk Bond Raiders and the Man Who Staked Them* (New York: Simon & Schuster, 1988), p. 19.

30. Ibid., pp. 13, 164, and "Douglas K. Curley, Pension Power Player," *Executive Place* magazine (Sacramento), March 1986, pp. 22–27.

31. Monks and Minnow, *Power and Accountability,* pp. 213–14.

32. Ibid., pp. 216, 235.

33. "Douglas K. Curley, Pension Power Player," p. 25.

34. Paul Jacobs, "Treasurer Unruh: The Game Is Called Power and Firms Court Unruh for State Business," *Los Angeles Times,* July 13–14, 1986.

35. Transcript of interview of Unruh by Paul Jacobs, May 20, 1986, transcribed by the treasurer's office and given to the author by Grover McKean.

36. Bud Lembke, *Political Pulse* (Sacramento), Dec. 12, 1986.

37. Gerry Braun, "Ailing Unruh Returns, Talks of 5th Term in 1990," *San Diego Union,* Jan. 11, 1987.

EPILOGUE

1. "Leaders Pay Homage to Unruh," *San Francisco Chronicle,* Aug. 10, 1987.

2. James Richardson, *Willie Brown: A Biography* (Berkeley: University of California Press, 1996), p. 337.

3. "Jesse M. Unruh: Man of Power," editorial, *Los Angeles Times,* Aug. 6, 1987.

4. Fawn Brodie, *New York Times Magazine,* Apr. 21, 1968, pp. 30, 121–29.

Communists, Communist Party, 41, 47;
anticommunism, 5, 45, 46–48, 56, 222
community activism, civil rights movement roots in, 75
Congress of Racial Equality (CORE),
105, 142; state Capitol sit-in, 105–107
Connor, Bull, 90
Conrad, Charles J., 102, 120, 126
conservative politics: shift toward,
108–109, 118–119, 145, 196–197
constitution (California), 49, 53, 166–
167
Constitutional Revision Commission,
166–167
consumer protection legislation, 7
Contra Costa County, 123
CORE (Congress of Racial Equality),
105, 142; state Capitol sit-in, 105–107
corporate raiders, 216–217; federal legislation, 218; Unruh's shareholders' rights
advocacy, 216–218
Cory, Kenneth, 117–118
Council of Institutional Investors, 218
country music, 21, 22, 190, 203, 204
court cases: housing discrimination,
80–81, 135; Rumford Act repeal initiative, 109, 144. *See also* supreme court
(California)
Cowboy Church of the Air, 22
Cranston, Alan, 134–135; and Farrell exposé of Unruh fundraising operations,
149–150; and 1964 Senate primary, 134,
137–138, 139
Criswell, John, 181, 182
Cronkite, Walter, 182
Crose, Jack, 178–179, 183
cross-filing, 49, 54
Crown, Robert W., 130
Curry, Edsel, 34–35

Daley, Richard J., 194–195
Dallek, Robert, 143
Dawkins, Maurice, 91–92
Dean Witter Reynolds, 215
Decision Making Information, 200
defense industry, 203, 204
DeFord, Jaci, 14, 114, 189–190
DeKruif, Robert M., 72–73
Democratic clubs, 54–55, 77. *See also* Cal-

ifornia Democratic Council; Demo-
cratic Guild
Democratic Guild, 46, 47–48
Democratic Leadership Council, 192
Democratic Legislative Dinner Committees, 152
Democratic Party, 7, 16, 42, 43–44, 57;
California Central Committee, 131;
gains in state senate, 86, 104–105; internal divisions, 16, 98, 173, 190, 192;
Robert Kennedy campaign and, 191;
Los Angeles County Democratic
Committee, 45, 46–47; minorities in,
77; in 1950s assembly, 60; and 1952
cross-filing ban initiative, 54; 1964
election losses, 144–145; 1964 National
Convention, 142–144; 1968 losses,
196–197; 1968 National Convention,
193–195; 1970 election gains, 206;
1970s-80s shift to center, 192, 206; in
postwar Los Angeles, 45, 48–49; postwar revival of, 20, 46, 61; traditional
blue-collar base, 20, 98–99, 145, 173,
191, 197, 203; and Unruh's gubernatorial campaign, 205–206
Democratic voters, civil rights issues and,
100–101
Dempsey, Van, 104
Derby Club, 96, 106
desegregation: white opposition/resent-
ment, 80–83, 92, 98, 103, 108–109, 140.
See also specific civil rights entries
Desmond, Earl, 70–71
Despol, John, 47–48
Dewey, Thomas E., 44
Dills, Ralph, 63–64
disability discrimination, 87
discrimination: government-sanctioned,
82–83; housing, 32, 40, 41, 74–75,
79–82; Progressivism and, 50. *See also*
racism; segregation; *specific civil rights
entries*
Disney. *See* Walt Disney Productions
A Disorderly House (Mills), 121
Doda, Carol, 115
Doerr, David, 171
Donovan, John, 48
Donovan, Robert, 181
Douglas: Unruh's job at, 20, 29

1967 Century Plaza antiwar demonstration, 175, 176

Los Angeles Times, 50, 51, 61, 63, 77, 91, 169–170; author's coverage of 1973 Los Angeles mayoral campaign, 209; author's story on Reagan gubernatorial campaign, 200; reporting on Reagan's 1970 reelection, 205–206; reporting on Unruh investments, 165; on Unruh's death, 222

Lynch, Thomas, 167, 177, 180

MacArthur, Charles, 35
MacArthur, Douglas, 35
MacDonald, Tom, 137, 138
Mankiewicz, Frank, 43, 47, 178, 221
March on Washington (1963), 90
Margolis, Larry, 11, 14–15, 130, 157–158
McCarthy, Eugene, 176–177, 183, 184, 186, 193, 194
McCauley, Jim, 150
McCullough, Frank, 77
McDaniel, Hattie, 80
McElroy, Leo, 207–208
McGovern, George, 194
McKean, Grover, 209, 210, 211, 215, 220
McLain, George H., 51–54, 56
McWilliams, Carey, 50, 51
media: anti-Vietnam war sentiment in, 182; campaign publicity consultants, 168; civil rights movement coverage, 76–77, 90–91, 105; lockup episode and, 126, 127, 146; McLain radio broadcasts, 52–53; 1960s reporters at the Capitol, 2–3; and politicians' private conduct, 3, 111, 146; in postwar Los Angeles, 32; Proposition 1-A support, 167–168; Sleepy Lagoon murder case and, 75; Unruh and, 3, 39–40, 103, 122, 220, 221–222; World War I veterans' benefits crusade, 35–36. *See also* journalism; newspapers; television; *specific newspapers*
Mennonites, 23–24
mental health policies/programs, 153–162; Lanterman Petris Short Act, 160–162; Reagan governorship, 160–161; treatment of the mentally ill and retarded,

8, 58, 153, 154–155, 158–159; Unruh's reform efforts, 155–162; Waldie subcommittee, 156, 157–160
Merrill Lynch, 215
Mexican Americans, 74–75, 83
Meyerson, Harold, 134–135
Milken, Michael, 217
Miller, Allen, 66, 97, 147–148
Miller, George, Jr., 104
Miller, Loren, 99
Mills, James, 111, 120, 121, 122, 126
Mills, Kay, 142
minority representation, 8, 77, 78, 143
minority underemployment, 196
Minow, Nell, 218
Mississippi Freedom Democratic Party, 142
Mississippi Summer, 133, 142
Mitchell, Jim, 39, 40
moderate politics/voters, 4, 5, 61,192; Unruh's centrism, 4–5, 6, 42, 46–47, 55, 135, 145, 173, 191–192
Monagan, Robert T., 118, 119–120, 121, 167, 196
Moniz, Egas, 155
Monks, Robert A. G., 217–218
Moore, Robert, 28
Moore Drydock Co., 22–23
Morton, Harold, 66–67
Mosk, Edna, 138
Mosk, Richard, 136, 137
Mosk, Stanley, 81, 101, 135–136, 137–138, 139
Moss, John, 64
Muchmore, Don, 100, 101
Mulford, Don, 122, 125
Mullins, Jeff, 185
Munnell, William, 56, 59, 68
Murphy, George, 140, 145
Murray, Esther, 47
Murray, J. Edward, 77
music, country-and-western, 21, 22, 204; Unruh's love of, 190, 203

NAACP, 84, 85, 99, 101, 143–144
The Nation, Unruh article in, 196
National Association of Manufacturers, 196

Priest, Ivy Baker, 209
Professional Golfers Association (PGA), 135–136
Progressives, Progressivism, 45, 48–50, 168
property taxes, 171
Proposition 13, 162, 171
Proposition 14 (Rumford Act repeal initiative), 108–109, 140, 144, 145
Proposition 63 (2003), 162
prostitution: at the Capitol, 113–114
protests: Birmingham civil rights demonstrations, 90, 95; CORE sit-in at state Capitol, 105–107; Sheraton Palace sit-in, 131, 132–133; Vietnam war protests, 5, 109, 173, 174–176, 192, 193, 194–195
Prudential Bache, 215
public campaign financing, 170
public education. *See* education
Public Health Committee (assembly), 96
publicity firms, 168
public opinion polls. *See* polls
Public Utilities and Corporations Committee (assembly), 68
public works projects, 1, 7, 15–16
Putnam, Jackson K., 49

Quimby, John, 14, 102, 105, 113–114, 122

racial tensions and riots, 77, 109, 140, 145, 185, 192, 203
racism, race discrimination: housing discrimination, 32, 40, 41, 74, 79–82; postwar Los Angeles, 58, 74–75; Progressivism and, 50; race discrimination in the Navy, 32; Southwestern immigration and, 22–23, 75, 118; Unruh's views on racial injustice/inequality, 93–94, 94–95, 116, 143; Vietnam war and, 185. *See also* segregation; *specific civil rights entries; specific minority entries*
radio: McLain broadcasts, 52–53; Unruh's reporting stint, 207–208
Rafferty, Max, 181
Ralph, Leon, 8
Rattigan, Joseph A., 117, 120, 126; school finance bill stalemate, 116, 117–118, 120–127

Reader's Digest: 1960 article on payola, 67–68, 69
Reagan, Ronald, 68, 113, 171, 198, 201, 203; CalHFA bill and, 212, 213, 214; and mental health policy reform efforts, 160–161, 162; 1966 election to governorship, 118, 163, 173, 191, 206; 1970 campaign and reelection, 200, 205–206; Proposition 1-A endorsement, 168
Reagan presidential administration, Council of Institutional Investors founding and, 217–218
reapportionment, 8, 78, 88, 143
Rees, Tom, 55, 67, 71, 123
Regan, Edwin J., 108
Reingold, Beth, 112
religion, religious values, 21–22
Republican Party, 46, 49, 50; assembly opposition to Unruh, 118–122, 127; in the 1950s, 50, 60, 61; and 1952 cross-filing ban initiative, 54; 1964 gains, 145; 1968 gains, 196–197. *See also* conservative politics
restrictive covenants, 40, 41, 79, 80–81
Rhodes, Roy V., 80
Richfield, 72
Ridder, Hank, 137, 151, 165
Ridder, Herman, 149
Ridder, Joe, 149, 151
Ridder newspapers: *Long Beach Independent and Press Telegram,* 149, 150–151, 152, 165; *San Jose Mercury News* exposé of Unruh fundraising operations, 147, 149–152
Riesman, David, 44
Ring, Doug, 209
Ring, Selden, 209
Ringer, Vivian, 32
riots. *See* social unrest
road construction, 58–59, 60
Roberts, Bill, 200, 208
Robie, Ronald, 110
Roosevelt, Franklin
Roosevelt, Franklin D., 18, 28, 36, 118, 148, 191. *See also* New Deal
Roosevelt, Jimmy, 47
Rosen, Ruth, 112
Rules Committee (assembly), 125, 127

Text: 11/14 Adobe Garamond
Display: Knockout
Compositor: Binghamton Valley Composition, LLC
Indexer: Thérèse Shere
Printer and binder: Maple-Vail Manufacturing Group